W9-AEH-096

Praise for *Northern Waters:*

"*Northern Waters* is one of those magical books that pretends to be about something perfectly ordinary, like fishing, and then turns out to be about everything under the sun that matters. It is wise and exhilarating, and it makes you care about things you never knew you cared about."

Paul Gruchow, author of *Boundary Waters*

"A voice like Jan Zita Grover's has never before been heard from Minnesota's trout water. . . . or, quite possibly, from anyplace else in the natural world. It is articulate, feisty, erudite and in the literary tradition of fly fishers Roderick Haig-Brown and Robert Traver. Fly fishing is a solitary, contemplative craft and Grover writes about its mystical insights with passion, reverence and an exquisite knowledge of trout and their habitat."

John Henricksson, author of *Rachel Carson*

"*Northern Waters* is a sparkling-fresh, new approach to trout streams, fish and other water-inhabiting animals, and fishing. Grover's exposition of what she loves in the streams of the North Woods is at once no-nonsense and lyrical. She explores tiny, alder-choked creeks for tiny brook trout, braves the woods as a woman alone and the spookiness of a river at night, and gleans fly-tying materials from her immediate environment (such as sheets of anti-static Bounce for mayfly wings). Grover's book will help us all to understand the fascinating 'streamwebs' that sustain our fellow river creatures, and thus to effectively protect them for the future."

Thomas F. Waters,
Professor emeritus of Fisheries,
University of Minnesota

Also by Jan Zita Grover

North Enough: AIDS and Other Clear-Cuts

Northern Waters

JAN ZITA GROVER

Graywolf Press
Saint Paul, Minnesota

Publication of this volume is made possible in part by a grant provided by the Minnesota State Arts Board through an appropriation by the Minnesota State Legislature, and by a grant from the National Endowment for the Arts. Significant support has also been provided by Dayton's, Mervyn's, and Target stores through the Dayton Hudson Foundation, the Bush Foundation, the McKnight Foundation, the General Mills Foundation, the St. Paul Companies, and other generous contributions from foundations, corporations, and individuals. To these organizations and individuals we offer our heartfelt thanks.

Excerpt from Beston, Henry, *The Outermost House: A Year of Life on the Great Beach of Cape Cod*, Copyright © 1992. Henry Holt & Company, Inc. Best efforts were made on the author's behalf to secure permission.

Excerpt from Haig-Smith, Roderick, *A River Never Sleeps*, Copyright © 1991. Reprinted by special arrangement with The Lyons Press.

Excerpt from Harkin, Duncan A., "The Significance of the Menominee Experience in the Forest History of the Great Lakes Region," from Susan L. Flader, ed., *The Great Lakes Forest: An Environmental and Social History,* Copyright © 1983. Reprinted with the permission of the Unversity of Minnesota Press.

Excerpt from Hubbell, Sue, *Broadsides from the Other Orders: A Book of Bugs*, Copyright ©1993. Reprinted with the permission of Random House, Inc.

Excerpt from Lyons, Nick, "Bad Pool" from *Confessions of a Fly Fishing Addict*, Copyright © 1999. Atlantic Monthly Press. Reprinted with the permission of Nick Lyons.

Excerpt from Pyle, Robert Michael, *The Thunder Tree: Lessons from an Urban Wildlife,* Copyright © 1993. Reprinted by permission of Houghton Mifflin Co. All rights reserved.

Excerpt from Traver, Robert (pseudonym), *Trout Magic.* Gibbs Smith Publisher. Best efforts were made on the author's behalf to secure permission.

Excerpt from Williams, Ted, "The Ugly Trade in Gorgeous Feathers," from *Atlantic Salmon Journal* (Winter 1995), reprinted in *The Insightful Sportsman: Thoughts on Fish, Wildlife and What Ails the Earth*, Copyright © 1996. Down East Books. Reprinted here with the kind permission of Ted Williams.

Excerpt from Wright, Leonard M., Jr., *Neversink: One Angler's Intense Exploration of a Trout River.* Copyright © 1991. Atlantic Monthly Press. Best efforts were made on the author's behalf to secure permission.

Published by Graywolf Press
2402 University Avenue, Suite 203
Saint Paul, Minnesota 55114
All rights reserved.

www.graywolfpress.org

Published in the United States of America

ISBN 1-55597- 294-2

2 4 6 8 9 7 5 3 1

First Graywolf Printing, 1999

Library of Congress Catalog Card Number: 99-60735

Cover design: Julie Metz
Cover fly tied by Jan Zita Grover

To Judith, Jean, and Miranda,
who stop with me by waters

Northern Waters

We need another and a wiser and perhaps a more mystical
conception of animals. Remote from universal nature, and
living by complicated artifice, man in civilization surveys
the creature through the glass of his knowledge
and sees thereby a feather magnified and the whole image
in distortion. We patronize them for their incompleteness,
for their tragic fate of having taken form so far below ourselves. And
therein we err, and greatly err.
For the animal shall not be measured by man.
In a world older and more complete than ours
they move finished and complete,
gifted with extensions of the senses we have lost or never attained, living by voices we shall never hear.
They are not brethren, they are not underlings;
they are other nations,
caught with ourselves in the net of life and time,
fellow prisoners of the splendour and travail of the earth.

—Henry Beston, *The Outermost House*

Northern Waters

1 Introduction

PEOPLE COME TO FISH AND FISHING in a variety of ways. I grew up in a family whose only outdoor activities were playing golf and splashing white gas on a charcoal broiler. So when I recount the pleasures and lessons I've discovered on northern streams, I am describing strictly personal discoveries, ones unaided—and unhindered—by family history and custom. I mention this in the hope that my experience may encourage others unfamiliar with the watery world: with love and patience, both angling and stream life can be decoded.

Why fish at all? I credit an incredibly tedious and happily former job with pushing me toward running water. Stuffed into an "office" that made Dilbert's cubicle look roomy—it also served as the janitor's storage room for brooms, mops, and toilet supplies— I dreamed almost continually of the North Woods' bright streams and resinous forests. They were my imaginary antidotes to the sweating concrete block walls, concrete floor, and tiny, slitlike windows that surrounded me.

One day, I realized that learning to fish might teach me a deeper way of understanding places I already loved but hadn't explored with any particular purpose. Besides: hadn't angling, and fly fishing in particular, inspired an entire, very satisfying literature? For this writer, that aspect of angling all but conferred an imprimatur. I would take up fly fishing and approach streams with new intent. This sudden revelation all but figuratively toppled the concrete walls of my nine-to-five prison. On my lunch break that day, I checked out books on fly fishing from the library. I was off on a quest that hasn't slowed down or softened after six years, though it has spread so that today I also pursue fish with cane pole, spinning, and baitcasting gear, but mostly with nothing but unarmed curiosity.

Why certain folks become possessed by fish and moving or still waters is no clearer to me now than it was when I began my headlong pursuit, but it's a common enough phenomenon. Yet of the many who feel called, few, it seems are chosen; as John Randolph, editor of the magazine *Fly Fisherman*, explained to me, "The percentage of people who stick with fly fishing once they realize that fine gear can't catch fish for them is really small. You can't buy your way into angling skills—you've got to put in time, lots of time."

The briefest acquaintance with fishing taught me that I was more interested in learning about the worlds that fish inhabit than in hooking them. Notice that I don't say *merely* hooking them: to catch fish consistently, you need to know a fair amount about their lives. But I discovered I could learn this not only through the feedback loops of catch-and-release and catch-and-kill but also through watching individual fish patiently, hour after hour, from streamside, winter as well as summer; through watching the instream and terrestrial life on which they de-pended; and through learning about the hydrodynamics and chemistry of the northern waters I live by.

But because I am also interested in my own tribe's relations to fish, I have pursued the angler's offstream knowledge, too, and this has less to do with fish than with human culture: the roles of rods, reels, lines, flies, fly tying, lures, baits, topographic maps, and other bits of fishing's material culture that move us down-stream toward the deepest pools of fishing's mysteries.

Angling regularly brings me up square against my own limi-tations, my own ignorance. In my first couple of years of fishing, I discovered, and it was a very quelling discovery, that I probably didn't like myself very much. I was impatient and almost unimaginably cruel to myself while learning the basics of stream-craft. Do I like me better now, or have I merely reached a level of fishing competence that lets me off the hook? Only a modest time into this discipline, and self-taught at that, I certainly can't claim competence as the explanation. Learning to fish well takes a lifetime. I have to believe instead that time midstream, spent on something approximating the fluid rhythms of a fish's day, has forced my awareness onto the beautiful watery world and away from myself, gently drowning self-consciousness.

Hooking fish is the paradoxical method by which anglers rap on the watery door of the animals we seek. The late Roderick Haig-Brown, a British Columbian angler and judge, and the pre-eminent lyricist of North American angling, explained the lure of fishing this way in *A Fisherman's Summer* (1959):

> What did I want of [the fish]? Not to kill them certainly, nor to eat them, though I would probably do both these things. Not even to match my skill against their instincts, because I cheerfully assumed they would be rising frequently, as Arctic grayling so frequently are, and present no problems. Nor for the excitement of setting light tackle against their strength and watermanship, for I had long ago learned to handle faster and stronger fish on lighter gear than they would make me use. Really, it was only to see them and through them somehow to become more intimate with the land about the streams their presence graced.

I wish hooking fish occasionally weren't necessary to me, but it is: I need—or have I merely transmuted desire into necessity?—to touch fish with wet and, I hope, reverent hands, to feel their bodies torquing away from me, leaving a fresh and acrid scent on my fingers that lingers as potently, as alluringly, as the smell of sex.

———

THIS BOOK IS ALSO ABOUT ONE WAY of coming to know a place by kenning its waters and its fish. I started pondering the challenge of learning how to become at home in a new place shortly after I arrived in Minnesota, fresh from San Francisco and years spent there in furious, often despairing reaction to the AIDS crisis. I wrote a book out of what I discovered after moving here, and doing so reconciled me to living with the destruction I saw around me—the human ones caused by AIDS, the environmental ones caused by overpopulation and carelessness. *North*

Enough was a retrospective book written to understand past experiences. *Northern Waters,* in epidemiologists' terms (you see, I can't entirely let go of the past), is instead prospective: a description of my current and, I trust, continuing obsession with fish, moving waters, and the North Woods. From a condition of sorrow and solitude, I've moved on to one of peace and sociability in the polite, highly ritualized company of other fishermen. We know many of the same things, we anglers, and these turn out to be things that are both deeply felt and largely subverbal. I can spend a day on the stream with fishing friends and never speak with them for six hours—for that matter, not *see* them after the first fifteen minutes. But by the time we climb wearily out of the river in the dark, we are of one mind and heart, communicating chiefly through heartfelt silence, a companionable thrumming of fingers on the side panel of the truck, our shared pleasure in the dry air punching through the open windows at our sweaty hair and shirts, a "May I?" before searching for a different radio station or ramming a new tape into the player. That may be the only thing said for the forty-minute ride back into town.

It's enough.

My way of making sense of what I've found in the waters of the North Woods has led inevitably outward, to matters and places well beyond the banks of northern streams, because any seemingly narrow quest, pursued passionately enough, opens out into realms of unexpected immensity. And so it's been with my quest to learn the North Woods' streams and their inhabitants. My pursuit has taken me to the strange fall rites of fishing for transplanted Pacific salmon below a hydroelectric dam on the Lower Peninsula's Manistee River and to the spring sucker runs in arctic drainages along the Minnesota-Canadian border. It's also taken me into the files of the Federal Energy Regulatory Commission (FERC), which licenses the dams that have so altered fishes' lives throughout North America. It has taken me up North Shore streams, looking for remnants of a once-healthy population of immense coaster brook trout who dwelled in Lake

Superior and came inland only in fall to spawn in feeder streams, but it's also taken me into nineteenth-century anglers' accounts of (over)fishing for these char, taking one hundred pounds of them apiece each day for the sheer hell of it.

In short, pursuing experiences and knowledge of northwoods streams has taught me, as any such quest will, not only *what* I've learned, but also *how* I've learned. It has taught me about myself just as it's taught me about a part of the world I deeply care for and want to protect.

———

I HAVE ANOTHER REASON to write about fish and their waters besides wanting to learn and to honor them, and that is to celebrate local victories in human attempts to right the wrongs we've committed against our earthly home. Though it seems horribly clear that collectively we humans are destroying the bases of all life with our poisoning of air and water, our destruction of fellow creatures' habitats, I cannot live only within the despair such evidence prompts. Here in North America, at least, some of the waters that by the 1960s had become so polluted, warm, and deoxygenate that they no longer supported fish life have been returned to a semblance of health.

The Mississippi near where I lived in Minneapolis for six years is a case in point. As late as the 1920s, anglers lined its banks on Sundays, fishing for pleasure and Sunday supper. By the mid-1960s, that same stretch of the Mississippi had become a watery wrecking yard of junker cars, old refrigerators, moldering mattresses, rusty bedsprings, discarded oil drums. Streamers of toilet paper and human shit floated over the gelid surface of this running sewer. The river was posted against swimming; it was almost redundant to post it against fishing, so devoid of life had the waters become.

The significant cleanup started in the 1970s, when so many of our nation's waters began their return to health under the provisions of the 1972 federal Clean Water Act. Today fish in the

Mississippi along Minneapolis's shoreline lead pretty healthy lives. Creatures who thrive only in clean, cool water swim there again: smallmouth bass, sauger, walleye. Those who live in the river's bottom reaches—the channel cats and bullheads—are again deemed safe to eat, their flesh no longer dangerously charged with heavy metals.[1]

I don't intend to suggest that the upper Mississippi, designated year after year by the watchdog environmental organization American Rivers as one of the U.S.'s most polluted rivers, has been saved. Even at Minneapolis, which lies above the intensive Minnesota-Iowa-Illinois agriculture that annually pours hundreds of thousands of tons of fertilizers and pesticides into the river, processed human wastes in the water are being transmuting into estrogenic compounds that alter the reproductive organs of male fishes. All is not yet well in this revived and improved stretch of the Father of Waters.

But it is better. And on some of the northland's waters, it is better than it has been since Europeans first arrived to log, mine, and fish commercially. Some of these local victories have introduced exotic species of fish into waters changed so profoundly from their historic selves that they are no longer capable of supporting their original inhabitants. The trout, for example, that thrive now in the Menominee tribe's swift-flowing miles of Wisconsin's Wolf River are not native brook trout but a strain of Pacific Coast rainbows who can tolerate higher water temperatures than the smaller natives. But in other rivers, such as the headwaters of the Brule in northwestern Wisconsin, brookies have begun reclaiming their own, displacing the introduced brown and rainbow trout as stream conditions improve.

---

[1] The *Minnesota Fish Consumption Advisory* (Minnesota Department of Health, May 1998) recommends that children and women of child-bearing age consume some species of Mississippi River fish in reduced quantities on some stretches of the river. Significantly, most of these advisories apply downstream of Minneapolis and St. Paul on stretches of the river that are fed by agricultural runoff. Most of these advisories are designed to restrict consumption of PCBs rather than of mercury.

Streams are not places of escape for me. They speak in their own terms to the ongoing history of their place, and on most of the streams I know, that history has not been very pretty. I observe and participate in their life not only because they are places of quiet and relative tranquility but also because they are living repositories of political and cultural choices, registers of decisions made hundreds, sometimes thousands of miles upwind of their watersheds, and these interest and move me. They are palimpsests on which seven generations of European-American settlers' industry have left their marks.

In his book *The Thunder Tree: Lessons from an Urban Wildland* (1993), Robert Michael Pyle writes of such places, "It is through close and intimate contact with a particular patch of ground that we learn to respond to the earth, to see that it really matters. We need to recognize the humble places where this alchemy occurs, and treat them as well as we treat our parks and preserves—or better, with less interference."

There is no "pure" stream in my part of the world, nor do I particularly wish for one, though I would love to see, just once, what a wholly intact watershed looks like. But humans are colonizing, environment-changing animals, and the streams and forests I live near reflect that fact. I love and study them not for their approximation to the "pristine"—a word I detest for all that it suggests about an abstract, unattainable, and wholly human standard—but for their individuality, an individuality no less valuable for being shopworn.

THIS IS NOT A BOOK ABOUT FISHING, not exactly. I fish pretty often—never less than twice a week, sometimes every day—but I don't catch many fish, and I don't much mind that, either. I love fishing for the beauty of (some of) the places it has taken me to: the tannic black waters of Michigan's Upper Peninsula (locally called *the U.P.*) and Wisconsin's Bayfield Peninsula; the alder-crowded inland creeks, narrow as ceccae, of Minnesota's Superior National Forest; the first-order bedrock streams of

Minnesota's North Shore, way above the falls where they tumble down to the big lake. But I also savor the industrial sublime of Duluth's urban fisheries, from the Lester River with its planted Kamloops rainbows to the heated, nutrient-rich waters of the city's harbor, where smallmouth bass feed along the outflow current from the regional sewage treatment plant. Just above the usx Superfund cleanup site, walleyes crowd the St. Louis River in spring to spawn up against the dam. In the shadows of grain elevators alongside the ship slips at Superior, Wisconsin, bass, walleye, and perch hang in the depths amid downed concrete cribs and discarded rebar. Off Port Wing on Wisconsin's Bayfield Peninsula, pike wallow and spawn in the spring shallows. And below dams on Wisconsin's Wolf River and the U.P.'s Sturgeon River, lake sturgeon the size of golden retrievers pile atop one other each March and April, spawning as close to their homewaters as FERC and its licensees will let them. I want to celebrate these animals' toughness and flexibility, the beauty of their adaptability.

———

WRITING ABOUT FISH AND FISHING presents problems to anyone wanting, as I do, to woo nonanglers into reading about these topics. Arnold Gingrich, *Esquire's* founding editor and publisher, saw a paradox in fishing literature's simultaneous richness and narrowness:

> Now fly-fishing for trout and salmon . . . is blessed with the greatest body of literature ever devoted to one branch of a single sport, but it is cursed with the circumstance that almost all of it is classifiable under the heading of preachments to the converted.

I hope to avoid that conflict here. I don't intend this to be a book chiefly for anglers but for readers curious about one writer's exploration of her obsession. If you are not an angler, I guarantee that I won't bombard you with the arcana of fishing. In fact, the finer points of angling technique probably don't interest me any more than they do you. (*But give me a few more years . . .*) Fishing was and remains simply one means to the end of getting to know this place better than I otherwise might. But along the way, fish watching became an end in itself, and one that you can enjoy without ever firing a line out over water. If you are an angler, I promise that there's nothing I know about fishing that will come as a surprise to you: I know of no subtle presentations, no killer flies or secret lures. I'd probably embarrass you on the stream. But as I see it, angling literature's chief pleasure lies in its evocation of places we've all been, sights we've all seen, experiences we've all had, and those I can offer, and this time they're coming from streams not much noted in America's fishing literature outside the fine work of Judge John Voelker (Robert Traver) and Jerry Dennis.

———

FINDING A DISCIPLINE that teaches you what you want to know is as much a matter of pure dumb luck as it is of curiosity, intelligence, and persistence. In midlife, I was lucky enough to stumble upon a mode of inquiry that taught me just about everything I wanted to know through the North Woods' moving waters. Learning to see streams as ripe with history, complexity, and yes, with promise molded me in the way all disciplines shape their disciples: it taught me to view the world differently, more fully. Now, whenever I cross a little black stream meandering between thick-grown banks, I wonder who swims beneath its lacquered surface. Sometimes my timing is lucky enough to treat me to the fine sight of a fish nosing through the surface, sending a thrilling telegraphy of concentric rings across the shivering face of a pool. Sometimes, like today, I witness fish launching themselves clear out of the water. This is not a case of luck: I deliberately seek out such sightings, and these quests have changed who I am. Are the fish as thrilled by their seconds in my medium as I am by the sight of them? Do our joys overlap, intersect, in the long light of this afternoon?

— JAN ZITA GROVER
Duluth, Minnesota

2 Small Northern Places

I SPENT AN EARLY AFTERNOON late in October, although the stream trout season up here in the North Woods was already over, lingering alongside the Brule River, like a lover reluctant to leave her bed. If I couldn't fish, at least I could watch. Besides: snow was already in the air, so this short afternoon would not only be my good-bye to the stream before winter but also a farewell to the warm and easy days of rambling around in uninsulated Bean boots, Supplex canoeing pants, and light flannel shirts. Soon I'd have to crack out mukluks and mackinaw, and soon the riverbanks below me would be shrouded in deep snow, for northwestern Wisconsin's lake-effect snowstorms are notorious. The water would narrow and slow to a flow like Jell-O. Along its banks, deer would soon crop the alders and dogwoods down to snow level, and the stream would look even more naked than it did this day. And empty, too. In January fish don't leap from the water as they did this afternoon, and the skies wouldn't be blue and cloudless but low and cottony, cut open only every now and then by the dark spread of Raven oaring overhead.

I'd driven down to the Brule to check out some new trout accommodations, but at first I saw nothing to break the superficial monotony of the dun riverbanks and the dark water running between them. Small northern places like this stretch of the Brule above Douglas County Road P look featurelessness and anonymous in fall and winter; only time spent there can change that. Even knowing how reluctantly such streams yield up their secret charms, I am usually as guilty of overlooking last season's tawny grasses and leafless alders as the short-cutters hellbent to reach the reservation casino at Red Cliff.

A few minutes of standing on the Highway P bridge, though,

revealed something I would have missed from the car, even if I'd been driving in first gear. About ninety feet upstream, tiny brook trout, most of them no longer than my middle finger, the biggest of them maybe as long as my hand, arced out of the Brule, pursuing something I couldn't see, and re-entered the river in quicksilver saults. The rings that spread across the stream to mark their passage were so small and shallow that they were almost undetectable from where I stood. But now that I had spotted them, I knew that they would look more impressive, more complex, from closer up, so I struggled down the steep bank and thrashed as quietly as possible through the willows and alders, the dried water hemlock and wild carrot of last summer, through the compressed grasses where deer and otter made their beds, until I arrived at a little peninsula that jutted out into the river.

The peninsula was actually a wobbly pedestal of peat about the size of a footstool and surmounted by a cap of living sphagnum moss, the only bright green in that steadily dulling landscape. I teetered on the peat mound, scanning the water for the fishes' rises. Of course these were random, from a human point of view, so seeing them meant entertaining a Heisenbergian dualism: focus *here,* focus *not at all,* since it wasn't possible to anticipate where exactly one of the little fish would appear. Such watching takes intense concentration, the same kind that fishing itself can take. Both are utterly exhausting and satisfying.

Just downstream of where I stood, brook and brown trout had been spawning recently atop the gravel that Wisconsin's Department of Natural Resources and volunteers from the Brule River Sportsmen's Club had placed in the streambed the previous summer. Some 167 cubic yards of pea-sized gravel had been hauled to the teeny headwaters of this famous stream by wheelbarrow and handbucket as well as dropped elsewhere on the river by helicopter to gussy up the area. *Improve their quarters, redecorate, and they'll move in,* the thinking went: "New gravel, cooler water—I *like* it! Let's spawn!" A few hundred yards below the bridge, the fish had inspected their new digs, apparently found them attractive, and got down to business. Now I could see the redds they had built with sweeps of their tails—white swaths of clean gravel along the silty streambed.

Time raced by and the light dropped toward the southwest, leaving the stream deeply fretted by alder shadows. How long had I been standing there, watching fish? I no longer wear a watch, but the length of the shadows told me I had been there for over an hour, although subjectively it felt like only a few minutes. In that time, these headwaters had shapeshifted on me from a narrow creek occupied by minute fish to a Missouri-broad river. Those fish rising into air and plummeting back microseconds later were brookies, but earlier in the year—late May, say—they might have been voracious little cohos fueling up to smolt and then drift down to the big lake. In either case, seen against this tiny headwater, the tiny fish seemed salmon sized—animals to match the roaring Snake or Clearwater of Idaho. I felt as if I, too, had shapeshifted and was flying high above some remote northern place in a DeHavilland Twin Otter, looking down at a mighty river system and its immense feeding salmon.

Waters shapeshift like this for me almost every time I go out on them, which is partly why I seek them out. Learning to see miniaturized landscapes and finding them full, seeing the effects of human wastefulness and discovering the plenitudes existing alongside them is a discipline, a form of grace, that I regularly court. And the North Woods give me plenty of places to practice: I live in northern Minnesota, where most of the streams I explore and fish are small, rocky places, watery kingdoms of scanty food and cover for their occupants. These waters run through forests ranging from recent clear-cuts to hundred-year-old trees.

This region, the old Northwest of a nation that 150 years ago barely extended west to the Mississippi, is what is now called the North Woods. It extends west from the sandy jack pine woods of the Lower Peninsula of Michigan across the Upper Peninsula's boreal forests and pine barrens to Wisconsin's and Minnesota's mixture of the same. The North Woods swing north across

Minnesota into Ontario, Manitoba, and northeastern Saskatchewan, petering out to tundra in the lowlands near Hudson and James bays.

Despite their immensity, the North Woods figure very little in most Americans' awareness of forested country. Perhaps it's the ignominious history of the North Woods that makes them so unremarkable to the majority of my countrypeople. Most of the national and state forests and parks here were established not as they were in the Far West—to preserve wilderness, to keep ecosystems intact—but to administer lands so ruined that their legal owners had abandoned them. The North Woods are for the most part tax-default public lands that fell under county, state, and federal control after timber and mining companies had finished exploiting them. Today much of this region is covered in early-succession aspen and jack pine, and it may remain populated by these pioneering species indefinitely, because these are trees that grow quickly and can be cut for pulp on forty- to sixty-year rotations, so they're managed that way.

The Brule's headwaters wind through such forest, which accounts for the place's skinned look in winter, its perpetual instability. This makes it fascinating to me, if in a different way from lush old forest, for here there are few old trees to anchor the soil against the floods of spring runoff, few kinds of tree, shrub, forb to attract a variety of animals. A scanty place, you could justifiably say. Nonetheless, there are more places like it than not—places hard-used by humans, treated chiefly as repositories of "natural resources" to be forcibly extracted (fish, fur bearers, timber, copper, iron). It's easy enough to learn to value wild places, but any honest look around North America tells us that there are precious few wildlands still intact. There are many more semi-wild places, some of them recovering from America's first industrial age. The North Woods are some of those places, and fish are some of their most visible inhabitants.

FISH ARE SO MUCH EASIER to move around in breeding-sized populations than other vertebrates that they have been introduced into watersheds thousands of miles from their native waters, both casually and as a matter of policy. All it takes, after all, is a vessel of water containing eggs or fry and some hospitable nursery waters in which to establish them. It is likely that some of the North Woods' brook trout were planted in streams above Lake Superior's barrier falls by the region's native peoples before Europeans arrived; it is certain that brook, lake, brown, and rainbow trout, as well as smallmouth bass and walleye, were introduced into streams and lakes to which they were not native by European settlers and anglers. (Don't let me even get started here on the aquarium of exotics that Lake Superior has become.) Even before the U.S. Fish Commission started sending railway cars of fish across the U.S. by train in 1872 to repopulate streams too warmed by logging to support trout any longer, the animals were being packed from watershed to watershed on horseback and on foot by timber cruisers, hunters, backcountry anglers, and loggers.

These involuntary migrations are part of the fishes' ongoing story as well as of the story of human efforts to repair the damage we have done. That we can now see some of these attempts as naive, self-serving, and unwittingly destructive does not alter the fact that they were well intended, just as current ones are. The Iowa cartoonist and conservationist J. N. "Ding" Darling wrote in 1931,

> We cannot bring the old conditions back, and we must not resent or despair of a situation which is now history and cannot be rewritten. But we are unworthy of our intelligence . . . if we do not immediately act to preserve what there is left of our outdoor natural endowment and bring back gradually, where practical, the waste areas which never should have been cleared, purge our rivers of pollution and repopulate them with their native game and fish, not only for our enjoyment and well-being but as a heritage for those who shall follow after us.

I would add that we need to do these things because they are *just:* our obligation is not merely to human enjoyment, well-being, and future generations but also to the water animals we have already displaced and killed. I mean here to record local efforts to restore these lost worlds, without, I hope, ignoring the costs.

———

WHEN I FIRST DECIDED to acquaint myself with streams and fish, I started with the limestone creeks that lay closest to my then-home in Minneapolis. In the mostly slow-moving, spring-fed waters of southeastern Minnesota, I could turn over almost any rock and find there colonies of writhing, crawling, or encased creatures—the larvae and pupae of caddisflies and midges, the larvae of stoneflies and mayflies, the worms, leeches, and crayfishes that trout and bass feed upon. Skimming the surface of those streams were waterboatmen and beetles, along with shoals of dead or dying adult mayflies, caddisflies, and stoneflies. Whether they fed beneath the clear waters or sucked in food from the surface, the predacious fishes in those parts were wonderfully well fed.

Three years ago I moved to Duluth, on the southwest shore of Lake Superior. The distance between Duluth and Minneapolis is about 150 miles, give or take a light-year or so. Minneapolis turns its figurative back on the Mississippi, which flows uncelebrated through the city's mostly industrial landscape; Duluth instead turns its face toward the great cold lake and the many bedrock streams that course down the city's hills to feed it.

Nothing about my move north made the difference between these two places more vivid than their nearby streams and rivers. In the North Woods of Minnesota, Wisconsin, and Michigan's U.P., the likely inhabitants of most streams are few in number—string trios or quartets, say, to more southerly streams' symphonic orchestras. In fact, so few and far between are many northern streams' fish, and so small are they, that fishing for these animals often seems like a Zen koan:

What is the sound of one hand clapping?
What is the nature of fishing where there are no fish?

On most northwoods trout creeks, average-sized brook trout are smaller than most spinning lures, smaller than the minnows used by bait fishermen hunting the big Pacific salmon who now inhabit Lake Superior. One spring morning last season I stood amid the thick-coming growth of sweet fern and watched tiny, four-to-six-inch brook trout race like computer-controlled toys from the brushy shelter of a downed tree to the creek's midstream miniature pools and runs, and then back, zigging and zagging at warp speed, nervously dodging and weaving through the clear tannic waters in anticipatory dread of Death from Above: a kingfisher, a heron, a gull. Watching them taught me, as nothing else had done, how small their race needed to remain in order to survive amid such thrifty, shallow waters. Only full-grown animals smaller than the average frozen fish stick were fitted to those lushly green but nonetheless impoverished places. Introduced fishes—the Pacific rainbow and coho salmon, even the European brown trout—would either starve or succumb to predators in the miniature world of the brook trout.

The stream on which I observed those bonzai brookies was Miller Creek, which arises out of fens just above Miller Hill Mall, Duluth's own contribution to the malling of North America. The stretch of stream inhabited by brook trout lies downstream of the mall, a seemingly counterintuitive fact that has led mall spokesmen to boast of the shopping center's enviro-friendly presence.

But that would be to mistake proximity for cause. Quite the opposite is true, in fact. That there is viable trout habitat below a large mall is a good illustration of why fish watching and fish catching are appealing: they have introduced me to the complexity that is the world and have taught me the cautionary accuracy in all things fishy of the qualifier, *it depends.*

Below Miller Hill Mall, the creek picks up speed as it begins its fall toward the lake. No longer lazing through and over peaty soils, it now rushes over bedrock, becoming more oxygenated (good: trout and the insects they depend on need water with lots of oxygen in it), its watercourse now shaded and deeper. Trout live within the waters of this dim-lit little gorge because of these factors, not because the mall above them exerts any benign influence.

In fact, the mall does just the opposite, for it increases surface runoff to the creek, thanks to its acres of parking spaces, its flat-topped emporia, and the roads connecting it to the Iron Range and nearby towns. Meltwater from winter's snows and rainwater from the rest of the year flow across those impervious surfaces too quickly to cool down or to settle out sand, salt, and rubble, so the waters from the vicinity of the mall enter Miller Creek warm and thick with creature-choking debris.

Fortunately, the steep grade of the stream as it tumbles toward the lake helps to aerate and cool down these waters and to settle out sediments, but during and after midsummer rains, stream temperatures in even the darkest reaches of the watercourse become too high for anything but mere survival of the tiny trout.

The fate of Miller Creek and Duluth's other nine trout streams is uncertain. One after another, they have fallen to mall parking lots, streamside housing developments, and vaguer forms of neglect or abuse. Such streams occupy a peculiar no person's land, administratively: because they were not navigable, they were not statutorily protected by the state Department of Natural Resources until designated as such by the legislature in the 1970s. Given their marginality as coldwater streams, they have little capacity for surviving the continued insults of development. Happily for some of them, champions have come forward to clean up their banks each spring, plant trees to shade their waters, and to watchdog further attempts to develop them.

Some people, including many anglers, would say that the fate of Miller and Tischer creeks' tiny brook trout do not much matter—what matter are the trout as long as your arm out in Montana, the eighteen-pound chinook taken three miles offshore of Duluth. I flinch when I hear such opinions, not because of people's obvious fascination with large fish, but because of what an exclusive pre-occupation with large fish says about them: they lack under-standing of their home streams.

A six-inch brook trout in a creek less than two yards across is a big fish. As my angling friend Mike Tidmus, recently trans-planted from Los Angeles to Bainbridge Island, Washington, says about headwaters fish in his new home, "It's a question of scale." The North Woods' diminutive brookies are every bit as *big*—I'd say every bit as well-proportioned—to their homewaters as a twenty-inch rainbow is to the Bighorn. When someone dismisses the plight of local fish because those fish are tiny in absolute terms, I learn something about him that I'd rather not know: he lacks perspective. He's superficial. He measures worth in crudely quantitative terms. He is not in touch with where he lives and the creatures with whom he shares the place.

———

MOST OF THE FISH I CELEBRATE HERE are small because most of Minnesota's northern waters are small. Where northwoods fish are very large, it's chiefly because they have been imported from places that could better support their usual size. In Lake Superior and its tributaries, they do not remain very big for very long. The anadromous steelhead that find their way home to the North Shore's Knife River each year have evolved into a genetically distinctive strain that is lighter, smaller, and more streamlined than the steelhead returning to South Shore streams, never mind than those behemoths who call Lake Michigan or the north Pacific home. Superior's chilly waters don't offer locally adapted steelhead the same rich menu they enjoy in their native Pacific Northwest or in warmer Lake Michigan. Are North Shore steelies worth less because they—too few of them, it seems, to remain a viable popu-lation much longer—have adapted to straitened circumstances? Why celebrate only what has succeeded spectacularly?

My haunts are mostly quiet backwaters occupied by unspectacular but nonetheless highly successful fish who wrest their livings from streams still recovering from logging and mining. Like other immigrants, most of these fish didn't start out in these scanty places; they were imported, then overfished, then left to manage as best they could. Their triumph is that they're still here. Every one of them is a miracle independent of her physical size. No water seems too small to hold a population of these survivors, too small to hold human imagination.

3 The Creatures in Question

FOR MOST NORTH AMERICANS, fish occupy a peculiarly invisible niche. Few of us dive or snorkel in lakes or streams, so we see little of underwater life. Except during insect hatches, few fish spend much time at the surface, and then only those species who include hatching or dying insects in their diets. A child may capture a creek or pond minnow in a glass jar, bring it home, watch it die, but the fish is then flushed down the toilet with little regret. In short, fish remain all but invisible, too unlike ourselves for us to feel very implicated in their fates.

For some of us, however, fish are emblematic of natural systems that we want to protect and enjoy. Many anglers are happy just knowing wild fish are *there,* occasionally signaling their presence by rises, by their spring or fall spawning migrations. We also like the feel of fish: their extraordinarily supple musculature, their light skeleton, their sheathed grace.

But besides anglers, who even concedes the fish his status as animal? People for the Ethical Treatment of Animals (PETA) would have you believe that its members are concerned with water creatures' status as sentient animals, but the organization offers no evidence that it understands fish as members of complex aquatic ecosystems—it appears that only their status *as animals* concerns PETA. That fish can suffer as much as people or cattle from overcrowding, pollution, and inadequate shelter is not part of their concern: *Save the animals,* even if it's only to return them to degraded habitats. In that respect, PETA is similar to human "pro-life" forces: intensely concerned with saving individual lives without much demonstrable regard for how and where they will live out the remainder of their existence.

Before I became interested in fishing, the only living fish I was familiar with were neon tetras, angelfish, and guppies, staples of casual aquarists who swam in my father's aquarium, and the koi who lurked in my mother's backyard pond. As for fish who were already dead, each fall my mother and I drove down to the Greyhound bus station to pick up an oily cardboard box of smoked Rogue River chinook mailed to us by my uncle in Oregon. In an abstract way, I understood that those pungent orange slabs had once sheathed living fish, but I wouldn't have known the difference between a chinook and one of the introduced white catfish who swam in the nearby Sacramento River. The only fish most people I knew ever saw were dead—either cooked, or on their way to being cooked. This has to affect how we view the animals: suppose the only dogs we ever saw were dead ones being prepared or served as food?

The essence of living fish is their buoyancy and movement, qualities long gone by the time most of us get our first look at them. Out of water, fish acquire the same gravity-bound gracelessness that we land animals possess when still. Lying dead there on the cutting board, their skin slackens, their eyes cloud over and sink, their stomachs sag. Nothing could be further from the living creatures in their own weightless medium.

Fish differ almost as much from each other as they do from other vertebrates. Some fish can breathe air, like members of the catfish family, but most filter oxygen only from water through the plush surfaces of their gill filaments. Most fish have scales, though some, like sturgeon or gar, have more ancient forms of armored protection. Sturgeon wear bony plates called *scutes,* while gar are sheathed in diamond-shaped ganoid scales. Others, like catfish, have no scales at all, relying instead on spiny dorsal fins for protection. Most North American freshwater fish have bony skeletons, but the sturgeon, bowfin, and lampreys of the North Woods have softer, cartilaginous notocords, the same support structures that sharks and rays possess. These are evolutionarily earlier structures, but ones that clearly still work, because they've been doing so for 100 million years.

Anglers know that fish possess uncanny abilities to hear and see us even when we approach waters stealthily. The very medium fish live in aids their hearing each other and us. Because water is much denser than air, sound waves travel farther in it before dissipating, as anyone who has overhead far-off conversations rolling across a lake can attest. Fish have "ears" that hear sound as frequency-differentiated tones, much as ours do, though in their case sound rolls as watery waves against their otoliths, solid, stonelike structures that serve the same function as our liquid-filled eardrums.

Fish possess an additional hearing source which we mammals lack that enables them to detect even silent movement around them. This is the lateral line, and it is probably this mechanism that accounts for their spookiness when we move through water with even the greatest caution. The lateral line runs the length of the fish's body, in most cases about halfway up each side. It consists of a series of tiny pores, each one containing hairlike cilia. When the water surrounding a fish moves even slightly, it causes the cilia within each pore to wave, transmitting signals to the fish's brain via one of two neural pathways. Imagine being covered with hairs so fine that the passage of a cat or a beverage cart causes these hairs to stand on end, and you'll have some sense of the lateral line's power and function. The lateral lines of fish who feed at the surface are closer to their topsides so they can detect food immediately above them. In bottom feeders like catfish and sturgeon, the lateral line is supplemented by barbels—whiskery organs that depend from the fishes' upper jaws and that bristle with sensing organs, including tastebuds. These trail beneath the bottom-hugging fish, signaling the presence of food.

I may be making too much here of the anatomical and physiological differences between fish and ourselves. Their adaptations to a medium so unlike our own (although it is subject to many of the same laws) can make them sound so otherworldly that we fail to recognize and empathize with them. They are another nation, and we do not know enough about them to do more than build our own theories about what they feel and why they do what they do. Even the ways we categorize them are mere human hunches: we assign greater significance to certain of their anatomical features and activities than to others and then call those *defining differences.* Sue Hubbell, that graceful writer, observes in *Broadsides from the Other Orders: A Book of Bugs* (1993):

> The Algonquin Indians classed some insects by their desire to bite us, lumping together the bugs we would separate and name mosquito, black fly, biting midge. They called them *sawgimay,* which means, roughly, small-person-who-flies-and-bites-so-fiercely.

Who among us knows how fish view each other? Like and unlike, ally and enemy, surely—but are such discriminations made on the basis of appearance, behavior, sound, pheromones? Does a pike strike terror in a walleye because of the way she lurks motionlessly, the way she lunges suddenly, the way she stinks of her previous victims' distress hormones? We humans have theories about all this, but in the end we don't know very much.

In the hierarchy most of us assign to living creatures, fish suffer doubly for not being mammals and for occupying a medium so foreign to our own. It's no coincidence that prideful anglers lift their catches from the watery world and grasp them, suffocating, in midair for victory photographs. Even when their intention is to return fish to their own world, most fishermen symbolize victory by launching their captives into ours. Our prey, our air.

If, as some psychoanalysts suggest, the engine of desire is absence, then perhaps this explains my almost painful attraction to fish: I shall never experience fish within their own medium, or they me in mine. I cannot strain oxygen from water, nor they from air. I cannot know what it is like to be supported, not by spine and extremities, but by the very medium I live in, any more than they can know what it is to stand upright on land. Our media, our very bodies, are mutually unknowable. I can only sit on a bank or in a canoe, stand or wade among them, watch, and admire.

———

MOST OF THE FISH who make appearances in these essays are members of a coldwater clan called the salmonids. In the northern hemisphere, these are probably the most valued and coveted of fishes—fish biologist Peter Moyle, with admirable clinical detachment, characterizes their "significance to European and North American anglers [as] almost mystical" and as having "led to such arcane activities as catch-and-release fly fishing and the planting of domesticated trout in suitable waters all over the world." In northern Minnesota, salmonids are arguably eclipsed by the walleye, a coolwater animal so popular with inland lake anglers that it has been designated our official State Fish. But among stream and Lake Superior fishermen, salmonids are incontestably at the top of the heap. In 1997, Minnesota spent an average of $600 on each chinook salmon who was raised and subsequently caught by a Minnesota angler. There's a lot of reverence, a lot of political clout behind producing such costly playthings.

The farther north you go, the more likely that the fish you encounter will be salmonids, native and otherwise, or that other circumpolar denizen, the pike. That is why salmonids make up the bulk of the water animals I discuss here. Personally I find all fish fascinating, and the peculiar hierarchies that humans have created—for example, trout as noble, pike as Queen of the Waters, bass and pike as redneck opportunists, walleyes as canny strategists of inland waters—are interesting to me only as the odd shadow play of our human character. But it is chiefly trout, char, and salmon who account for the peculiar human institution of the hatchery, so it is they whom you will mostly meet here.

Here is most of the cast of characters you'll meet:

The coldwater cast—

Salmonids

    Char

        brook trout*

        lake trout*

    Trout

        brown trout**

    Salmon

        rainbow trout (Kamloops, steelhead)***

        chinook***

        coho***

        pink***

    Other Salmonids

        whitefish*

        lake herring*

    Lampreys

        sea lamprey§

        chestnut lamprey*

        northern brook lamprey*

The coolwater cast—

    Walleye*

    Northern pike¶

    Smallmouth bass∞

---

*native to the North Woods and Great Lakes

**native to Europe; introduced into the North Woods

***native to the Pacific Northwest; introduced into the North Woods

§native to the Atlantic drainages and Atlantic Ocean

¶circumpolar; native to the North Woods and Great Lakes

∞ native to Mississippi drainage; introduced into the North Woods

———

IMAGINE FOR A MOMENT that a state agency undertakes the fertilization and rearing of white-tailed deer, moose, and waterfowl.

Vast factories arise in the fields to raise these "wild" animals so that citizens can shoot them. Up to 80 percent of state wildlife budgets are spent on building these animal surpluses, which are then released each fall just before hunting season. This is the story of contemporary gamefish in most North American states and provinces. Fish are the only large vertebrate that is commonly raised under hatchery/factory conditions and then released to be killed.

To clarify my own position: I am not opposed to catching and killing fish. I am only too happy to catch a hatchery fish and eat it; it is unlikely to live through one of our winters, anyway—it has about a 20 percent chance of living that long, and if anything, my removing a few each season from the stream increases the chances of survival for the rest. I am worried about the diluting genetic effects of hatchery fish on wild, streambred fish. We humans still know so little about fishes' lives, fishes' constitutions, that presuming to engineer them seems to me the height of arrogance and folly. But what I chiefly want to draw attention to here is the indifference with which most of us greet the factory production of these animals, who are then introduced into semiwild conditions and told, "Here you go—hope you make it." If we released weaned puppies and calves into the national forests to survive on their own, I suspect many citizens would be outraged. For that matter, when most people hear about conditions in a puppy mill, they are outraged. But little such outrage greets fish hatcheries. They are, in fact, tourist attractions in states with big salmonid programs, as are those Golgothas of migratory fish, the fish ladders on so many North American dams.

What do we see when we look into a fish's eyes? Do we see a consciousness looking back at us? Do we see a mystery sheathed in scales, a rival, an enemy, a prey?

4 Why Fish?

Fish (fly-replete, in depth of June,
Dawdling away their wat'ry noon)
Ponder deep wisdom, dark or clear,
Each secret fishy hope or fear.
Fish say, they have their Stream and Pond;
But is there anything Beyond?
. . . somewhere, beyond Space and Time,
Is wetter water, slimier slime!
And there (they trust) there swimmeth One
Who swam ere rivers were begun,
Immense, of fishy form and mind,
squamous, omnipotent, and kind;
And under that Almighty Fin,
The littlest fish may enter in.
Oh! never fly conceals a hook,
Fish say, in the Eternal Brook,
But more than mundane weeds are there,
And mud, celestially fair;
Fat caterpillars drift around,
And Paradisal grubs are found;
Unfading moths, immortal flies,
And the worm that never dies.
And in that Heaven of all their wish,
There shall be no more land, say fish.

—Rupert Brooke, "Heaven" (1915)

WHEN I DECIDED TO TAKE UP FLY FISHING, I discovered that things would not be so simple as I had imagined. For one thing, this discipline involved my entire body; I was going to have to learn to coordinate my legs and feet, my arms and hands to keep twenty, then thirty, then thirty-five feet of weighted line moving with adequate speed to place a fly onto moving water and then drift or dart it in plausible imitation (or evocation?) of an insect or small fish. I was going to have to learn to see the faintest trace of movement or shadow within the glitter of moving water. Tall orders for a pale feral scholar. Most difficult of all, I would need to learn how to be patient and kind to myself while acquiring these other skills. And this, perhaps predictably, proved to be the greatest challenge. Because intellect had nothing and everything to do with it.

I cringe at the memories I can summon up of my first two seasons on the water: a crabby, excruciatingly agitated Old Girl standing in midstream, reproaching myself fiercely for such unforgivable sins as hanging up my fly in an overhanging tree, wrapping my leader around the tip of the rod, and introducing wind knots into my leader, as if these weren't leitmotifs of everybody's earliest stream fishing. I can see and hear me still, and the memory makes me burn with shame:

YOU STUPID FUCKING IDIOT—

WHAT WERE YOU DOING?

WHAT WERE YOU DOING?

IDIOT. *IDIOT!*

CAN'T DO ANYTHING RIGHT.

YOU'RE NEVER GOING TO GET IT. NEVER. GET. IT. . . .

This was the voice of my father. The first time I realized it, I stopped still as a heron in the current, appalled. As far as I believed I had come from him, as successfully as I believed I had put him behind me, my father nonetheless crouched within, a piece now of myself. That his impatience with me had surfaced now, more than thirty years later, in a discipline I had chosen for myself and had already come to love—such was the terrain of my mortification. I may have chosen angling for myself, wanting only (I thought) to learn about life in moving water in a stressless, noncompetitive, reposeful, and keenly attentive way, but I seemed instead to have slipped into a thalweg rushing directly downstream toward my father.

Well, I'd say sensibly each time I heard myself channeling his censure, *as soon as you're not enjoying yourself,* QUIT. Such advice, however, ran counter to my father's do-or-die approach to chosen challenges: KEEP AT IT UNTIL YOU GET IT RIGHT. DO IT PERFECTLY OR DON'T DO IT AT ALL.

Poor unhappy man, I'd think, or try to. *Maybe,* I'd think, *he was only trying to toughen me up.* Life, after all, had been no picnic for my father, the youngest child in a prosperous family impoverished by my grandfather's slow death from cancer. Perhaps my father had only wanted to prepare me for how rigorous, how unhelpful, the waiting world could be. Perhaps his laughter at my discomfort was part of some larger plan.

Surely, I'd tell myself, slapping the water with yet another ineffectual cast, *it's possible to enjoy yourself without doing this well.* But even as I bluffed my way through such hearty reassurances, I could feel their falseness. The truth was, I *wanted* to cast/drift/read water/play a fish better than I already could because I believed I would enjoy angling more. And to the extent that enjoying it more might mean beating myself up less for my incompetencies, I was right: I would probably become a more stressless, reposeful, attentive angler once I could no longer find such abundant reasons to berate myself.

———

I OWN A ROD THAT HAS LEANED in its ivory tube at the back of my study closet for close to five years now. I've probably used it only a dozen times. Sometimes when I wonder how I am going to survive until I get my next freelancer's check, I take out that rod. It's short and light, sheathed in a shiny, deep burgundy coat, spun in burgundy wraps and fine white tipping, with a burnished rosewood reel seat and fancy nickel-silver hardware. I sit there, fondling it, and I think about selling it. But I doubt I ever will: it was the first rod I cast successfully, and that alone gives it tremendous symbolic value.

If you grew up playing tennis or baseball or soccer or paddling a canoe, perhaps mastering—or, to be more precise, acquiring a minimal competency in—a new sport may not seem like a very big deal. But like so many women of my generation, I grew up with little sense of myself as embodied. My father had built his life around the conviction that intelligence leveled all playing fields, that it was superior to kindliness and animal knowledge. He raised me to be like him, and like his, my body did not extend itself much into the world. I walked and bicycled—I had to, to get around our sprawling fifties suburb—but mostly I spent my childhood and adolescence indoors, wrapped/rapt in books and music. I lacked conviction that I could learn, never mind enjoy, physical play. To avoid girls' softball and basketball in high school, I took a second language. Latin and Spanish I could handle easily. Softball, never. Besides: mind was what mattered—it would take me places. As an adolescent, I barely masked my contempt for jocks and peacemakers. The body—what was that for? *Sex.* Social graces: what were they for? *People too stupid to win arguments.*

I wasn't developing into a very pleasing animal. But then what did I need to be pleasant for? I was going to polish my mind until it dazzled. The body could tag along if it wanted; I wasn't going to give it any encouragement, though. When I thought about my body at all, it struck me as a poor, unwanted thing. Mind, only mind, mattered—mind, and what it could do. I would succeed without the body, without phony social graces. After all, hadn't my father?

———

LATER I WOULD SPEND a great deal of time out of doors, but I spent it passively, for the most part, propped up first against lodgepole pines in the West and then later against white pines in Wisconsin and Minnesota. I watched deer, eagles, and harriers on the edges of fens at dawn, stationed myself, still as Lot's wife, near the watery entrances of beaver lodges, waiting for their residents to return home; I snowshoed across icy February lakes under thin chill moons. But these activities did not call for new physical skills, for entering more fully into my body; they demanded mere patience, attentiveness, a high tolerance for stillness.

Learning to cast was different: it involved not only unfamiliar movements and timing but also overcoming my lifelong conviction that I was not a very physical person. And I needed to test out this tentative new rapprochement with my body in fairly public places, because you cannot practice unfurling thirty feet of line in the privacy of your bathroom.

The day I first cast a rod successfully, I was exploring tiny Brown's Creek, a meandering, mostly warmwater stream whose last mile plunges over bedrock to the St. Croix River along the Minnesota-Wisconsin border. In my ignorance, I first splashed upstream from County Road 95 to see what lay in that direction. The sandy bottom and palpably warm water, even on that early spring day, didn't augur well for finding trout, but the little stream seemed otherwise picture perfect: overhung with willow, alder, and ash, its banks mounded with water hemlock and wild carrot and marsh marigold. Warblers warbled and watergrasses trailed lazily in the slow current.

I followed the creek's meanders upstream until I could see the pale rooftops of a new townhouse development rising like a bad dream above the willows. Beyond them, I reckoned, I would not go. A small pool below the townhouses looked as if it offered enough room for backcasting without hanging up my flies in the trees, so I stood on the inside bend's warm compacted sand and practiced casting for a while.

In the Upper Midwest, a day like that one is called a *bluebird day,* the kind on which you expect to see those small spring migrants flitting about the business of feeding their families—bright and sunny, the northern sky deep blue and piled high with laundry-white clouds, the air windless and almost warm. Through my polarized sunglasses, the bankside green shone with deep, almost pulsing energy, positively pumping out sugars and oxygen, and the moving water slid transparently over scalloped sand.

Here I cast for—I don't know how long; even back then I didn't consult my watch while fishing, a most unfatherly touch. Despite the open space around me, I still managed to hang up my flies in a nearby tree with wearisome frequency, and my brief calm began to unravel. I started to curse my incompetence. CAN'T DO ANYTHING RIGHT, I spit, and after I had sacrificed all the flies I'd brought along to the river gods, I banished myself back to the shadows downstream.

As I slouched back in defeat, I stopped to cast again every twenty feet or so. I knew, or thought I knew, what I was trying to do. Certainly I knew how a beautiful cast *should* look: its long, gradually accelerating uptake from water; the volute forming as line gains speed overhead, then straightens out behind; the straight, singing recurve as the backcast shoots forward, then dips slightly, unfurling its tip like a party favor; the leader's final, almost weightless collapse to the water's surface.

But I could not do it. And this frustrated me so much that I took little notice of what I *could* do, which was to get the line onto the water, however gracelessly, and then drift a fly downstream. But we choose what will satisfy us, don't we?—and at that point, the cast mattered to me far more than the drift.

What exactly was I doing wrong? I couldn't tell. Somehow my line failed to become a living thing dancing through air, then alighting insectlike on the water. Instead, it jerked sluggishly backward, then lunged forward, slapping the water as a beaver's tail beats out a warning. *Slap slap.* I tried everything I could think of, or so I thought, as I waded downstream through the bright spring corridor of trees, the shifting spectrum of light. *Slap slap.* Clouds of tiny, almost transparent insects rose and plummeted waveringly above the water.

I saw all this, I even appreciated it—the creek, after all, was a place I wanted to be—but I was not *of* it. Somehow I had convinced myself that full participation in this mazy little world depended on my being able to cast well, but my clueless body had not yet figured out how to pull this off.

A successful cast moves the line backward at a speed fast enough to maintain its momentum even after it has stopped, fully extended, in the backcast. Halted abruptly, the line is then impelled forward by a short forward cast, moving fastest at its tip, losing momentum only gradually, continuously turning over upon itself. When the forward cast unfurls fully, its loop opens and you drop your casting arm a bit. The line falls, silent and straight, to the water. But so far this was only head/book knowledge to me.

Farther downstream, the water sheeted steeply toward the St. Croix, its channel narrowing. The sandy upstream bottom gave way to bedrock, the stands of streamside willows and alders thinned out. Here taller trees grew thickly up the walls of the steep gorge, forming a shadowy network high above the water. Soon the creek lay entirely in shadow, only the silvery crests of the riffles ahead brightly visible. The current made its way now around increasingly larger rocks, as if long ago some force had sorted out the sand first, then pushed the truly big stuff downstream toward the St. Croix. This is the opposite of how creek materials usually get sorted, and noticing this made the stream seem even more wonderful, a (familiar) intellectual challenge: I could call around to geologists, DNR hydrologists, Trout Unlimited streamkeepers, thumb through books to find out how and why the usual hydrologic order seemed to have reversed itself here.

I continued to cast absentmindedly as I waded, no longer stopping to position myself, instead simply raising and lowering my arm like a child with a willow switch. Ahead and far above hung the railroad bridge. Splines of light pierced its ironwork and splashed across the boulders receding down the gorge. Salvator da Rosa would have loved this narrow valley's picturesque gloom, charged as it was with the theatricality of *chiaroscuro,* like an alpine scene in miniature, the haunt (here the ghost of John Muir could make an effective appearance) of development-doomed trout. Everything—running water, boulders, bedrock, iron bridge, trees arching overhead—gradually became compressed to

Whistleresque monotones: black, dark gray, lighter gray, more black. At the downstream end of the watercourse, a few trees shimmered greenly, illumined by a small aperture of sunlight.

That's where it happened, there beneath the bridge. My line, cast carelessly as I stumbled through a field of boulders, hurtled forward now like a living creature, incandescent with the light that pierced the ironwork. Its narrow loop opened smoothly into a half ellipse, then a half circle, and fell, limp and silent, to the rushing creek.

I stared stupidly after it, wondering if I had seen what I thought I'd seen—my own cast flicking out and then drifting delicately to the surface of the water. A second later, I knew that I had, because my arm remembered the feeling and knew how to repeat it. So I tried again. And again, and again. And each time, the line danced its dance, and each time I lengthened the cast a bit, until eventually the line unfurled somewhere far enough downstream of the bridge that I could no longer see its surrender to water.

I stood there close to tears. Understand: casting was the first physical skill I had set out to acquire since learning to roller skate. My first successful casts were as momentous as discovering that I loved mathematics, that I actually *got* graphing and differential equations. Perhaps more so, because they did not reinforce the family way of knowledge, did not merely confirm that I could jump through whatever new set of intellectual hoops I chose. Casting taught me instead that my body and mind were inseparable, that whatever I thought I knew when I tried to experience or understand them separately was an impoverished thing, lacking the body's blind knowledge or the mind's ceaseless winnowing. Casting on Brown's Creek taught me that intellect had very little to do with learning how to make a line dance; in fact, apparently I learned better when my mind was compressed to a very fine tolerance, plastered by sensory data, drowned by the body.

I didn't want to leave the water: experience simply couldn't get any better than this near-swoon, this wordless conversation between my eyes, muscles, skin, and brain. Oh, and ears: those early spring warblers. I wanted nothing but more of the same. I had passed over some invisible bar, and now I could not disremember the casting stroke. I knew I could improve on it almost endlessly—there was certainly nothing lyrical or precise about it—but already new neural pathways wound through me, new memories that I would not forget until all became forgotten. I was a miser savoring a big new addition to her hoard: *New skills! Me! Newly embodied, born of waters, age forty-nine!*

And that is why I'm unlikely to sell my little Sage bush rod. Several Februarys ago, I took it out again and rotated its smooth, slender length in my hands the way I sometimes do when winter binds local streams in its icy lattice, stilling them. I could see broken light on black water, hear the rising pitch of a stream running faster as it picked up speed over a steepening grade. I could feel the sense of completion that came with those first successful casts, the pleasure that came with that first truce—no: that first embrace—between my body and mind. Like old lovers, they've since learned to rely on each other to complete their mutual business. I looked down at my hands, which held the rod, and I saw in them the same now-familiar amalgam of mind and spirit. They were brown now with liver spots, scoured like glaciated rock, dry and leathery with age, but knowing; they were pretty adept at their pleasures, these hands. I liked them—they were strong, no nonsense, like the rod they held. Reasons enough to give closet space to a small tool and welcome to a body.

And then, that summer, I passed on the little creek rod, like a torch and a blessing, to a dear friend who also cherishes small waters.

WE UP THE ANTE ON OURSELVES constantly, so my frustrations with angling were hardly at an end after I devised a serviceable cast. If anything, they multiplied more quickly, because angling's knottiest complexities only begin once you can cast a line where you want it to go. What was I going to tie to the end of that line? At what depth was I going to fish that fly? What was I seeking with that fly and line? What would be the stakes, the rules I imposed on myself while pursuing fish?

As I learned to read water, mend line, and fish streamers and wets during my second fishing season, I still managed to put myself regularly in the path of my father's rebuke. Evidently I couldn't simply cozy my way into new experiences. His voice continued to frame my every act, snapping out sarcasms at my poor performance:

FOR CHRISSAKE LOOK BEHIND YOU BEFORE YOU CAST!
OH GREAT — SO NOW YOU'VE HUNG THE FLY UP IN A TREE.
TOO STUPID TO LIVE. DON'T YOU KNOW
WHAT THOSE THINGS COST?

Did I *need* this voice?

And then, during my third year of angling, I began to hear my father less frequently, more faintly, like a radio barely picking up a station at the edge of its range. I was still hanging up flies in trees, still missing current seams that probably held fish, still picking the wrong sections of water to fish at the wrong times of day. But increasingly I didn't care. Sometimes I went to the stream without a rod at all; I simply wanted to figure out where fish were likely to be and to watch them. I could have dropped stones into likely lies instead to see if fish flushed from them, like celebrity angler Jim Teeny, but I wouldn't stone your house to see if you were at home, and I wouldn't stone a fish's, either. Instead, I called on the fish at different times of day, watching for them from behind streamside alders. Sooner or later, they usually appeared, and I learned something about their preferences for times of day and qualities of light.

By then I had also given myself the supreme gift of time by moving north, where I could work less and fish more on a smaller income, so now I had to answer to no one but myself and the fish for the hours I spent watching them. I grew more comfortable and speculative in my fishing. Angling was not, I realized, a quest to score trophies or to rack up quantity. It was not about my father at all. It was about experience that lay beyond judgment, mostly beyond words, certainly beyond conventional concepts of time. I had come to a mile marker my father had never reached or I had failed to noticed him reaching. Simple, kindly attentiveness had come to matter more to me than intellectual prowess; I was drawn now to other humans who were demonstrably kind of heart and physically at ease with themselves, women and men who were able to pleasure themselves in a stream's sensory flood and to steward such places and their creatures. Most of them would not have made my father's A list, but his tragedy, it now seemed to me, had been in judging people—himself included— solely on intellect. He had believed that keen trained intelligence superseded kindness and attentiveness to this beautiful world. He was an almost wholly disembodied person, living anoxically through mind.

I now saw that his would not become my fate, as I had so long feared, yet striven to assure. In slipping irrevocably from his standards, I had plunged brain and skin and breasts and eyes and memory and toes into moving water. Duck bumps rose on my skin and my nipples puckered and my teeth chattered. *All* of me had entered the stream, and I was never going back.

And so I relaxed. I began experimenting with my own ways to cast, and while they weren't elegant, they worked. I began tying flies from my dogs' fur and my freezerful of roadkill. These, too, worked as often as not, and when they didn't, so what?—the point was to be out there on the water, honoring creation. I recovered my earliest childhood's delight—immersion in the almost wholly sensory world that comes at you in images rather than words in places you know you're in, fully in, because you feel the water hitting the back of your knees and shins, the minnows nibbling at your bare toes, the soft air dibbling at your shoulders. I smelled the faint fetor of slow-moving stream water, saw the motes of cottonwood and dust and sedges dancing above the current. *Let*

the rest of my life be lived like this, I prayed, *floating through creaturely knowledge, adrift finally from abstraction.*

Then I began to prowl smaller and smaller streams—some of
them, to my delight, still unnamed on USGS 7.5° topo maps.
Alone in the black water, surrounded by alders and clouds of
mosquitoes and deer flies, I plied bathtub-sized pools with my
Pass Lakes and Owl & Oranges, and watched for the flicker of
white-tipped fins as slithy little brook trout surged from their
hidey holes to inspect the streamers or to flee my too-heavy foot-
steps. Each time they revealed themselves, I knew I was witnessing a miracle. I could not seem to stare at them long enough.

Fish are, quite literally, otherworldly creatures, having their
being in a medium that would drown us as surely as ours would
suffocate them. This gives them an aura of improbability, of ex-
oticism that puts them right up there with unicorns for me.
Here, not more than a foot below my bent face, outsized by my
hand, fins a tiny lithe creature marked by lightning forks of yel-
lowish green. His sides pale toward his belly, and they are sprinkled with small dots of red, yellow, blue. When I unhook such a
writhing, six-inch char beneath the dark transparence of his
home stream, the small, tender fish, likely as not, wears both
spawning colors and parr marks, like a fourteen-year-old boy in
an adult's come-hither clothes. The fins beating against my hand
are striped, white-red-black. Though he possesses scales, they are
deeply embedded beneath a mucosal layer that makes him look
vitreous, like a Fabergé enamel. Lying lightly on his side, he opens
and closes his minute mouth, and with each gulp, his gills flare
open and red, pumping water across tiny arches of bone whose
filaments sieve oxygen from the water for him to breathe. His
clear round eyes, lidless and watchful, are gold-irised, their pupils
immense and black.

I want him to swim back freely into his own medium, but I
also badly want to know what he knows. In my hopelessly human
terms, I come closest to doing so only like this, by holding him
lightly beneath the water's surface, feeling the supple flex of his

muscles, the near-weightlessness of his hollow bones, the mucous sheath that surrounds him like an aura. I spread my hands, and he is gone with a single shiver of his pelvis. I can see him for a few seconds as he flickers away, and then the stream, clear and brown as Darjeeling tea, seems to absorb him, and he disappears.

Fish on a larger scale I am less likely to handle but no less likely to observe. Spring and fall on the North Shore of Lake Superior bring the great transplanted sea-going fish from the North Pacific into the mouths of our local rivers. These anadromous rainbows, cohos, and chinooks run up inland streams during spawning season to mate and then to die, or, in the case of the steelhead, perhaps to head out into the great lake again. Compared to brook trout, these are barge-sized fish, and they hang in the pools below the barrier waterfalls like so many soaked logs. The Kamloops come in pale from the lake, darkening almost immediately, then slowly swithe through the pools—over, under, around each other, undulant and powerful. They mass in the shallowest of waters, and if I remain still, I can watch them from a mere foot or two away. In their native British Columbia, Kamloops (a lake strain of rainbow trout) grow fat on the rich stew of inland lakes; here, they apparently thrive in the thriftier waters of Lake Superior. Instead of becoming plump B.C. footballs, they become long, lean L.S. torpedoes—survivors of an increasingly more populous and competitive environment.

After a morning of watching such fish, great and small, I crawl onto the bank in my soaked neoprene pelt and scud broadly on my butt to make a sitting hole amid the muscular alders. Then I pull a Ziploc bag from my pocket and eat my lunch beside the bright brown water, the backs of my legs resting atop cushions of marsh marigold, my feet refracted to tiny rubbery things in the glowing stream. High above, contrails dissipate to nothingness against the curve of blue. Watching the waters, I contemplate the enormity of what I do not know about fish and the places they live. Somehow, in the course of these past six years, that burden has become transmuted from a monumental rebuke into a treasure hoard. I've enough still to explore and learn to last for several human lifetimes. Wordless, bone-deep content.

This business of losing myself in running waters, like learning to cast, did not start in my head but in my body, and it flung me into streamtime, which is liquid and meandering and sometimes flows backwards, as eddies do. You can harbor safely there, alongside swifter waters.

5 Minnehaha Creek

MY HOME STREAM FOR FOUR YEARS was a Zen fishing paradise: a mazy, meandering tailwater that ran twenty-eight miles from dam to mouth, most of it beneath a pleached archway of elms, ashes, cottonwoods, and poplars. Kingfishers, green-backed herons, great blue herons, white-breasted nuthatches, tree and barn swallows, swifts, hooded mergansers, goldeneyes, and Canada geese rode its waters and dived from its streamside trees. A few warm days in winter opened up channels broad enough for casting, and in summer the water was usually high enough to provide two to three feet midstream, and often more along the grass-lined outer bank.

But a *Zen* stream? Well, yes. This creek offered fishing, but no fish—a daily ritual of casting, feeling the water eddy 'round my legs, noting the changes in water level and temperature, the progress of seasons marked by vegetation, insects, and birds. But as for fish, those were few and far between—according to the DNR's metro manager, a few sunfish, bluegills, the vagrant bass or pike who washed over the dam far upstream.

In any case, the creek's few finned beings were wholly safe from me. I not only didn't seek them, I didn't even cast a fly. But I was nonetheless gratified when I ran into fish—or rather, when one of them ran into me. One late spring morning, for example, I was standing midstream, casting against the current, when something with the resilience of an inflated inner tube bumped hard into my left calf and briefly wrapped itself around my leg. A dark shape glimpsed, then gone beneath the hard-running water. My first and only thought was a pike—several years ago, a child angler had caught a respectable eighteen-inch snake, as small pike are sometimes called locally, in a pool just upstream of where I now stood. But before I could further puzzle out the fish's identity, rain began dimpling the water, and the crowns of the creekside trees fanned open beneath a heavy northwest wind. A late May storm was coming on, thunder predicted, so I reluctantly reeled in and left the water for the morning. Five minutes later, when the storm broke, I was already at home in southwest Minneapolis.

My homewater was Minnehaha Creek, which is fed by Lake Minnetonka and regulated at Gray's Bay Dam by the Minnehaha Creek Watershed District (mcwd). The creek may have been fishless for all intents and purposes by the time it reached Fifty-second Street and Xerxes, where I faithfully haunted its waters each day, but it was in every other way an interesting stream.

Before it was dammed for lumber, furniture, and grist mills in the 1850 to 1870s, Minnehaha Creek swam with pike, bass, sun-fish, and suckers. In 1852, Colonel John Owens, publisher of the weekly *Minnesotan* (St. Paul), wrote about an expedition he and his party had made to Lake Minnetonka, during which they "caught fish enough to feed all twelve hungry men" from Minnehaha Creek. "Fishing for about twenty minutes more, they brought in more than a total of about forty pounds." Even the first generation of dams on the creek apparently didn't destroy its fish populations; Coates P. Bull, whose family farmed along-side one of the creek's tributaries around 1900, recalled pickerel, bass, sunfish, and other fish in great numbers: "Suckers and Redhorse each spring swam from Lake Harriet through the out-let into Minnehaha . . . . They 'paid toll' aplenty; for settlers, even from Eden Prairie and miles to the west, brought their spears to harvest bushels of these fish to eat and to feed pigs."[1]

---

[1]The pickerel whom Bull refers to would have been snake or hammerhandle pike; pickerel are not native to the Upper Mississippi drainage. Redhorse are a variety of sucker.

Bull's, Owens's, and Schussler's reminiscences were collected by Jane King Hallberg and published in her *Minnehaha Creek, Laughing Waters* (Minneapolis: Cityscape Publishing Co., 1995).

But as the wetlands adjoining Lake Minnetonka and the creek were drained for farms, roads, and homes, the creek's water level began to drop and to fluctuate dramatically. There were years when the creek almost dried up. By 1928, when Otto Schussler published his *Riverside Reveries,* Minnehaha Creek had "almost ceased, for a great part of each year at any rate, to be a stream." Finally, in 1963, the MCWD was formed to regulate water levels and water quality in the creek's 169-square-mile watershed. At the Gray's Bay Dam on Lake Minnetonka, waters above a set minimum level are released into the creek. Creek levels are also increased during peak canoeing/tubing season (July to August) unless there's a drought. In 1979, the Creekside chapter of the Izaak Walton League cleaned up the creek from Gray's Bay down to Minneapolis; the garbage they collected filled two dump trucks.

Living about twenty-one miles downstream from Gray's Bay Dam, I witnessed the creek's almost daily and seemingly fickle fluctuations. In early May, despite snowmelt and ice going out on Lake Minnetonka, the creek was usually starved for water throughout its Minneapolis course. Even the old mill pond below East Minnehaha Parkway at Thirty-fourth Avenue receded from its usually brimming banks. Farther upstream, every storm drain leading into the creek hung suspended three or four feet above the usual water level. Ducks waiting for open water crowded into discontinuous puddles like so many commuters pressing onto rush-hour trains.

And then, just as inexplicably, sometime during the night near the end of the month, the water would begin spilling over the dam again. The next morning, the creek was a good three feet higher, its muddy flats vanished. Buffleheads and mallards floated contentedly on winter-cold pools beneath the naked trees.

Most of the Minneapolis miles of Minnehaha Creek provided great opportunities for everything that makes fly fishing gratifying *except* the likelihood of hooking fish. The creek's width varied roughly between ten and twenty-five feet when the water was running 150 cubic feet per second or faster. Its structure was classic: runs, riffles, pocket waters, pools filled with many of the same aquatic invertebrates I had learned to expect to find in trout waters: stonefly, mayfly, and caddisfly nymphs colonized the rocks that dotted its sand bottom; black-fly larvae clung there, too, swaying by silk threads in the current. Winter and summer, fine blooms of midges lifted suddenly into the air at twilight, followed in summer by great cartwheeling hoards of swallows and swifts, who picked them off as quickly as they arose from the water. In late June and July, iridescent blue damselflies courted and mated in midair, on the surface of the water, on the yellow flag and cattails at the water's edge.

By foregoing the opportunity to cast for fish, I was able to sample other pleasures in a focused, relaxed way. No two and a half-hour drive, no burning of hydrocarbons to get my conservation-minded self farther and farther out of town; no night driving. In exchange for an absence of fish, I got everything else that made small-stream fishing worthwhile. Need I add that the creek was uncrowded? The only time I found anyone else casting there, it was because I had told Sam and Kim about it. But I did not see them on the creek again.

Plenty of people stopped their cars alongside my stretch to ask if there were really fish in Minnehaha Creek or to comment on my casting. After I told them that the creek was practically fishless and pulled my line from the water to show them the yarn at the end of my tippet, most of them just stared at me, bemused or disgusted, shook their heads, and climbed back into their cars. I, in turn, was bemused by sidewalk anglers whose view of fishing was so instrumental that they were flummoxed by my admission that I wasn't even rigged to catch anything. But I savored the company of others who stopped to reminisce about their favorite streams, try a few casts with my rod, or comment that midcity, midstream casting looked like a great way to unwind after a day's work.

The last year I haunted Minnehaha Creek, I was occasionally

tempted to tie on a fly, *just in case.* Like the boy in Dr. Seuss's *McElligott's Pool,* how did I *know* what I might find swimming in those clear rushing waters below the roadway? But I didn't really want to connect with any of the creek's few fish via a hook. Life in that creek of wildly fluctuating temperature and depth was hard enough for them; why add to their stresses? I had come to value the creek for itself and for the complex community of creatures who populated its banks and streambed.

Occasionally, as if stringing me along, the creek presented me with fishly surprises. I found the little pike floating head down in the shallow water of the creek one late July evening, his V-shaped lower jaw pointed toward the sand, his tubular body stiff with muscle—or was it with death? I filled a plastic bucket from the car with the water he had died in and took him home.

Over the sink, I took the pike out and turned him over and over. Sheathed in a transparent film like human snot, he slid through my fingers speedily, as if even dead he still wanted to get away. His scales were so embedded that he seemed scaleless, suited instead in a shiny green lamé cape that paled where it descended his sides to an opal white belly. Pale yellow-green jottings fretted his back as if he had been stippled with a Magic Marker. His eyes were still clear, a large luminous yellow, and flat. He would have seen well to the sides but perhaps not immediately ahead.

I admired his head: long-billed, like a fishing duck's. His gill covers were bright green, and behind them bristled rows of short, thick gill rakers, waxy-white prison bars of bone. I pried open his mouth and ran my fingers lightly over the dog teeth in his lower jaw, the volmer teeth crowding the roof of his mouth like stalactites, and those that heaved upward from his tongue, the teeth of a predator who clamps down on his prey and shakes or crunches it to death. (It is not uncommon for anglers to catch pike with the tails of their most recent prey still protruding from their bills.) On his belly I found the tiny anal opening—an inny like a child's umbilicus—and dorsal and anal fins riding his body far to the rear, faintly red, just like in pictures. I held him up to my nose and sniffed: *Fresh*. He smelled of fertile water and the creatures living in it.

Next I laid the pike on his back on my cutting board and sliced him open from throat to peduncle. This was not an easy task; his skin was a sturdy tegument, for all its slithy suppleness. In the end, I used my kitchen shears below the first inch of incision, cutting rather than slicing my way toward his tail. It was like cutting through particularly thick felt or leather. His skin and muscle lifted away from the bones beneath and parted like an open shirt beneath my blades. The bones were transparent and delicate, almost weightless: they had none of the gravity and opacity of mammal bones, having no need to support the animal's weight in his weightless medium of water. Instead, they merely wrapped and secured his organs, provided anchors for the muscles that attached his fins.

Within him the scent of creek was stronger and more distinct than without. I smelled water, dust, decay, mold, green bottom grasses, elodea, and algae, as if the incision I made had torn open the creek itself. They were pleasing, pungent smells, ones I knew I could not easily erase. They bloomed into my kitchen, which became odorous and charged with the smell of water and dying. The dogs gathered at my ankles and cocked their heads, beating their tails softly against the linoleum, questioning, hoping.

The pike's liver was long and pale. Over it hung his swim bladder, a deflated balloon. Behind and below the liver I found his heart and kidney, dark glowing stones, and farther down, his testicles, creamy and elongated. I took these out and returned them to the bucket of water.

His stomach and intestine were what I was after. Like his predator cousin, the human, the pike has a sizable stomach capable of expanding or contracting dramatically with the fortunes of feeding, and a simple intestine—a straight-shot tube for absorbing flesh. I removed the stomach and intestine and opened them. They were pale, glassy organs, almost vitreous in appearance, shining and clean. Both were empty, untenanted. They hardly seemed to be doing the job of absorptive organs: they had no apparent work.

Had the small pike starved, then, or had he simply died after absorbing his final meal? He was about sixteen inches long from the tip of his snout to mid-peduncle, and in girth no more than five inches. He would have found few creatures other than bottom-dwelling nymphs of mayfly, stonefly, damselfly, and caddisfly in the creek's low waters, and few of them at this time of year. I had found him twenty-one miles downstream from the dam where he would have entered the creek. Only the first four miles below the dam are rich with crustaceans in the muddy bottoms; only those first four miles and the mill pond farther below are deep enough to provide a coolwater fish with the temperature range his kind prefers.

He had appeared, already dead or dying, in less than three inches of warm downstream water, the dam at Gray's Bay having been mysteriously closed for over a week, sending others, I am sure, to a similar fate.

But had he starved to death? Pike feed at the top of the food chain they are links of. They are versatile predators who eat insects, crustaceans, other fish, birds, and small mammals, including, if popular lore is to be credited, pet toy poodles. Larry Finnell's 1982 to 1986 study of fish in Elevenmile Reservoir, Colorado, found that the stomach contents of pike consisted of about 7 percent kokanee salmon; 9 percent other fish (suckers, bullhead, dace, etc.); 18 percent crayfish; 25 percent rainbow trout; 36 percent miscellaneous invertebrates (scuds, damselfly and mayfly nymphs). Thirty-seven percent had empty stomachs. No one knows what to make of the high incidence of pike with empty stomachs. They are opportunistic feeders, more sluggish in warm weather than in cool, so perhaps they simply weren't feeding heavily when caught. In a reservoir whose level was less manipulated by humans than Minnehaha Creek, the pike would either have been eaten or have found adequate prey of his own, not this death in what amounted to a watery desert after the floodgates had closed.

Warm, shallow water: little of the dissolved oxygen a fast-moving, ambushing predator relies on. Even to my 37° C human toes, the water had felt ripe with rot, and sun-warm. Perhaps, then, he had suffocated? Suffocated, or starved?

The underside of his jaw was waxy white, the skin over his submaxilla pierced by ten sensory pores, five to a side. The gill covers flared. His throat skin was crêpey and fine as pongée silk. I sunk my index and middle fingers beneath the archway of his lower jaw, using what is known as the Leech Lake lip lock, a method for handling living pike without being bitten by them. I hefted him for weight: perhaps two pounds. Then I cut off his head and opened his gills, whose rakers promptly sliced open the palm of my hand.

YOU CANNOT LOOK AT A FISH'S BONES and think of them as you do a dog's or human's. In fact, as I discovered when I foolishly set the pike's head in simmering water to remove the fat and skin, the skull I so coveted melted away as promptly as its casings. I have boiled frogs' and small mammals' bones for hours in brine and they only grew harder, more marmoreal; this pike instead dissolved back into the medium that had grown him.

I took him back to the stream the next morning to release his jellified bones and skin into the water so he could feed the other creatures who lived there. I stood and watched as his graying remains floated down the current, then almost imperceptibly sank beneath it, like rotten ice. In a day or so, I reflected, whatever of him hadn't been eaten might reach the Mississippi below Minnehaha Falls. The current might take that pike all the way downstream to gar country and beyond that to the Gulf of Mexico. These were fine thoughts with which to pick up my rod and cast in the direction of the Mississippi, as if I could lash the water into compliance: *Take him, take him,* the line seemed to urge.

————

THE SUMMER I FOUND THE SMALL PIKE, after two years of faithful attendance on the mostly fishless waters of Minnehaha Creek, I woke one day and decided I wanted to fish not so much *for* fish as *in the presence of* them. I wanted to stand in waters that the DNR had designated as trout waters. This had less to do with my growing appetite for blood or hookups than with my curiosity about how fishy waters differed from what I knew about Minnehaha Creek. My curiosity had grown, as had my confidence: I thought I knew now what to look for when exploring new waters for fish. So I began driving to the nearest certified trout streams: Eagle Creek, Hay Creek, the Kinnickinnic and Rush rivers, the Brule. And I found that what I had learned on Minnehaha Creek served me well: sometimes I found fish where I expected to, and occasionally I even caught them.

But those streams, beautiful and "productive" (as fisheries biologists call them) though they were, lacked the heart-tugging familiarity of Minnehaha Creek. I missed knowing what occurred on those distant streams during the many days when I couldn't visit them; I missed the dailiness of time spent on a nearby stream. What those fine waters offered in terms of fish per mile couldn't compensate me for what they couldn't give: the knowledge earned through daily intimacy. Was the creek up or down today? How close to hatching were the caddisflies in the riffle downstream of the big cottonwood? Had the chubs and shiners built their nests yet?

Today I am lucky enough to live close to not only two neighborhood streams but to ones with resident trout and lake-run fish. Like Minnehaha Creek, stretches of them are cool, leafy, seemingly untouched. In spring I can lie on warm streamside boulders and stare down into their transparent miniature pools at shiners and nervous little brook trout, just as I used to watch chubs on Minnehaha. These are streams I not only savor, but work to protect; I have come to see the need to fight for such precious urban waters. I doubt that I shall ever be more fond of them, though, than I was—still am—of Minnehaha Creek.

It is the place I first fell under the spell of moving waters and came to see them as animate, storied, and plastic enough to accommodate and challenge me, no matter how little or much I knew. It is the place where I first kept faith with a part of myself I hadn't known before: the creature capable of a great, unexpected patience, a faith that I could crack the code of waters, the skills of casting and fishing. It is the place that taught me that faithful attendance on a single place—in this case, a stretch of stream no more than 500 yards long—could yield unimagined complexity, a microcosm so rich that I am still its beginner, its postulant.

Minnehaha Creek taught me a way of seeing that enriches my life and my writing. Just now, on a visit to Minneapolis, as I sat alongside the creek's edge once again, admiring it from my truck on a mid-June morning, a great blue heron drifted weightlessly across the opaque white sky. A leaf green inchworm bobbed from his silk line beneath a drooping elm branch, and I saw both of them. Because my eyes had been opened in and by this place, I knew how succulent a surface-feeding fish would find the inchworm, and how such fish would gather eagerly beneath the branch, waiting for him to drop.

The rains had finally come after an exceptionally hot, dry spring, and now the creek flowed wide and shallow. Watergrasses that wouldn't have been there most years until mid-July streamed in the current, and the heavy thickets of grasses anchoring the north bank crowded out over the water, their pale heads already seeding up.

This was a place that humans nearly destroyed and then helped to rebuild. That handsome curve on the inside of the creek just below me covered with mosses and grasses wasn't even there three years ago when I moved north to Duluth. It was a human-made structure concocted of sandbags, mesh, and soil designed to narrow the creek where it was throwing up sand and cutting back into the bank.

I felt enormous satisfaction in these evidences that people could partially heal what we have damaged, that a place like Minnehaha Creek has restorative powers of its own. I learned these lessons on an urban stream, and I believe they made me a different and a better person. The prospect of revisiting the creek whenever I travel to Minneapolis remains exquisitely exciting. Each time, I strain forward over the steering wheel, peering eagerly through the windshield, waiting for my first sight of it.

"Jeez, *Mom*," my daughter protests. "It's not like you ever caught anything there."

But I did. Fishing in that nearly fishless place taught me what I most wanted to learn: the patience, attentiveness, and submission needed to love a place well.

6 Old Fish

TWO DAYS AFTER THE NORTH SHORE'S 1997 record spring low—24° on May 12—I set out for the Big Sucker below Highway 61 in a light rain. A scrim of fog hung over the tops of the spruces and cedars. It all seemed very wet and atmospheric and north-woodsy. A DNR creel surveyor sat sucking on a Big Slurp in her state station wagon, heater roaring. A sort of complicity seems to exist between me and other women involved with fish, one in ex-cess of the (usually) easy camaraderie that exists among anglers, so when she got out of her car and flashed me a big smile, I re-turned it. She began exclaiming over the number of trucks and 4WDS in the muddy parking lot.

"I didn't expect so many people out on a rainy day," she said.

I found nothing remarkable in that: many of the guys fishing Lake Superior tributaries in spring are steelheaders, and this mild drizzly day in the thirties was almost tropical by their standards—they often fish in cold so deep that their lines freeze in the guides.

"Fish like to run when it's gray," I said gnomically, idiotically—what did I know about these fishes' preferences, after all? I had never fished up here before, only watched.

I headed down the trail.

This proved not to be a fun journey—the muddy clay path was festooned with sodden napkins, discarded minnows, a plas-tic bag filled with tangles of monofilament, a plastic water bot-tle, just about everything except the obligatory spent condom, and that I could probably have found, too, if I had bothered to look for it. Discouraged, I stopped to stuff the barbarians' dis-cards into my jacket pockets, wondering for the nth time why I didn't just keep a stash of small garbage sacks in my vest, since they invariably were needed. Hope, I suppose: my evidently un-realistic but persistent will to believe that people, particularly

those fond of remote and semiwild places, will regulate themselves well enough to leave beautiful streams as clean as they
found them, or more so.

A vain hope, that day. Still, there was something to be said for
being the angler who cleaned up after those who had preceded
me: if I hadn't the pleasure of stopping at the head of a trail and
gazing down on an unsullied streamside, I could still enjoy the
purr of virtue that came from cleaning up for whoever would
follow.

At the mouth of the trail, I saw an angler standing out in the
stream, casting into the froth below the first falls. By the time I
had strung up my rod, he was climbing back up the slick bank,
empty-handed. "How'd you do?" I asked, willing into my voice
the neutrality that would leave room for him to admit without
shame that he'd been skunked.

"Two."

"Kamloops?"

He nodded.

"Release them?"

"One's up in the trunk. I let the other go." He faced back toward the shallow pool below the falls. "I been chasing a big old
half-dead 'looper around that pool for the past hour." He started
up the trail, then turned back again. "Good luck."

The water was so fast that initially I had a hard time figur-
ing out its depth. Gradually I realized that the streambed below
consisted of overlapping plates of bedrock interspersed by algae-
slick boulders. The water running over them was no more than
two to three feet deep.

I cast into the falls and let my line wash down into the pool.
Then I cast into the head of the pool. I cast into a seam at the far
side of the current, where the dark clear water eddied like stirred
varnish beneath the overhanging cedars. With wonder I watched
my Mickey Finn dart through the pool toward me, so plausibly
transmuted into a minute shiner that I had to remind myself that
it was only something I had concocted at my tying desk, pinch-

ing, winding, and gluing it to a hook. Separated from me by yards of soft damp air and two feet of amber water, the streamer became a tiny golem I had created to do my bidding, finning and respiring within its own medium.

No fish rushed to inspect or mouth my Mickey Finn, but I didn't care: I intended this first day of fishing on a North Shore stream mostly as a rite of passage into my new life, a celebration of having pulled off the move from Minneapolis to Duluth. I had sold my house in Minneapolis, found another at less than half its cost up here, close to the tributaries of Lake Superior and the glacial lakes of the Canadian Shield, and I had done this unpartnered, unassisted, even unemployed. In one fell swoop, I had halved my monthly expenses and made full-time writing and close to full-time fish watching possible.

So on this Wednesday morning, standing shin-deep in the Sucker, I was celebrating the successful fulfillment of my own dream. What did I need with a fish? It seemed almost overkill, certainly ungrateful or greedy, to expect anything more than inhabiting this moody northerliness: the mist rising picturesquely off the macadam on the bridge just above me, the rain-beaded trees, the stream braiding its complicated way lakeward.

IN THIS, MY FOURTH YEAR OF FISHING, the most satisfying part of the game was learning to read water. Where were the pools deepest? the current swiftest? the cover—whether trees, broken water, or shade—the best? I stood balancing on a boulder in midstream for upward of twenty minutes, trying to see these things, knowing that water had an architecture of its own, that each stream was composed of the twined variables of streambed structure, grade, water sources, volume, and fluctuations, streamside vegetation, the vagaries worked on all these by weather and other factors I'd probably never learn to identify.

The Big Sucker is a narrow river repeatedly scoured in the late nineteenth and early twentieth centuries by spring log drives.

Wherever such drives occurred, streambeds were altered almost beyond recognition: banks gouged and eroded, midstream boulders and cobble sent tumbling down to the big lake, streambed scoured to bedrock, and the stream's inhabitants, large and small, rammed and mangled and washed downstream. Add to those destructions the annual fluctuations of spring runoff, midsummer drought, fall rains, and it became clear that for all the vernal calm I was wallowing in that day, the Sucker's waters were, at the best of times, scanty and dangerous ones for large aquatic animals to inhabit. In fact, the Sucker probably had not been home to any large trout before this century's "plantings" by settlers.

What native fish remain here tend to be small: farther upstream, you can find six- to eight-inch brookies holding in tiny pockets and undercuts beneath the slow-moving waters. But far downstream, where I stood that day on a teetering rock, the Sucker picked up grade and became a frothed, tumbling torrent in spring, and here the Kamloops ascended from the lake into the rocky river mouth to spawn.

I realized suddenly that I was looking at one now—a fish so still and dark that he seemed a part of the streambed rather than a living creature. He rested directly below me, his massive shoulders atop a flat submerged rock, his pectoral fins moving almost imperceptibly. Over his back and sides he wore a mantle of saprolegnia, a fungus that often coats the scales of worn or aged or failing fish. Against his dark olive back and its cloud of dense black spots, the saprolegnia glowed a shocking white. He was a big Kamloops, perhaps thirty inches long, though the stream's distortions made it difficult to know exactly. He wasn't as deep and stocky as the younger fish I had watched at their prespawning games on a stream a few miles to the west. Instead, he was lean and torpedo shaped, more like a steelhead. Unlike the bright pink on stream rainbows' sides, the streak down his sides was a deep, smoldering red, almost woundlike. Through the wavering current, I could see that his hide was tattered, seemingly dissolving—returning to undifferentiated river matter. This, I supposed, was the old "half-dead" Kamloops the other angler had described. The fish had swum up from the lake to this pool below the first falls. Was his presence here in response to the spawning rites of spring? to an imperative to die in his native stream? Was he eating at all?

The longer you watch stream fish, the more individual they become. They have their own crochets, rituals, preferences. This old fellow—Kamloops usually live for three to five years—didn't seem interested in what drove his fellows into the mouth of the French just west of here, where great dark fish swithed and splashed in preparation for mating, often heaving themselves half out of the water in their exuberance, cleaving the surface and scattering it with their strong speckled tails. Earlier that morning, the pool below the DNR fish trap on the French had seethed with a dozen or more strong Kamloops, shimmying and coiling around each other, crowding companionably together in their annual ritual of sex, although before and after spawning, they roam the great lake alone, too big and voracious to feed in company.

But here on the Sucker at 10 A.M. that wet spring day, the pool below the falls held only one immense, dying fish, and he was resting against a rock, his pointed, white-lipped snout facing upstream.

I cast to him in a variety of ways, sending my Mickey Finn bumping over his nose, but I had little hope or desire that he would rise to it. In fact, had he done so, it would have posed a dilemma for me, for I had no wish to make the old fellow use his waning energy to throw my hook, and I could not imagine being able to power such a large fish out of the water in order to unhook him. Even my imaginary best-case scenario—he would wait quietly in his pool, and I would wade out to unhook him, *fat chance*—seemed vastly overdrawn and unnecessary. So I cast, really, to study the different routes my leader took through the complex currents. The red-and-yellow Mickey Finn stood out with a bright particularity in the tea-colored water, and as it glided downstream through a maze of rocks toward the old fish's snout, I taught myself the invisible underwater paths that led into the calm pool where he lay.

The old fish grew restless, if you could call his barely visible movements away from his rock and around the pool restless: they were mostly a drift, I think, a letting go from the slight finning that had kept him positioned over the rock. Now he swayed like water grass wherever the current moved him, prey to the dynamics of rushing water. But always, in the hours I spent casting over and observing him, he returned to his rock rest.

Soon the light was almost overhead and I had fallen into the stream twice, filling my hip boots with 52° water and soaking my pants, shirt, and socks. Rain continued to fall from the felted sky. The wet felt glorious—chill northern spring to the core. I considered staying on, wondered if I might be lucky enough to witness the great fish's death, see him swept sightlessly down to the lake, food now for scavenging gulls and lake trout. I imagined myself setting up a vigil, as I have for so many human creatures nearing death, this time provisioned with tent, binoculars, sketch pad, perhaps a camera. How long might his death take? Or would he slip back to the lake to die, drift downstream with the current, still facing the falls, that final barrier to his kind? I imagined finding his picked bones, his impressive skull, some weeks hence, knowing that his substance had gone out into the foxes, gulls, ravens, crows, flies. This thought pleased me, like the end I enjoy imagining for myself: I've told my daughter, only half-jestingly, that I'd like to be strapped into a shower chair and left midstream in my favorite North Shore river. The end result would be the same for me and the old fish: a return of our individual waters, proteins, and fats to the earth and its creatures, as equitable a return on the biological principal we have used, interest free, all our lives, as most of us human animals can make. Generations of creatures dependent upon the space and resources I am using crowd the wings, waiting for an opening. I hope to have the courage to yield myself willingly to them when I falter; I hope my wish to be returned to the waters can be honored.

In the meantime, though, I was still shivering amid the severe architecture of the narrow Sucker, watching an old Kamloops trout approach his death. If human ethicists are correct, such an animal has no consciousness of impending death, cannot imagine ceasing to exist. But I've watched enough nonhuman animals die to know that most dying creatures possess some awareness, if only of acute dis-ease. The old fish left his rock, circled the pool slowly, circled, rested again. His was a rhythm of rest and preparation, but for what? He was not reposeful, but neither was he anxious. I could not shake the feeling, anthropomorphic as it inevitably was, that he was looking over this amazing place, his watery world, and seeing it as if for the first time, now that it was his last.

The stream would seem beautiful, with comforting, slow-water holds beneath and between boulders, with wavering, watery light, changeable and transformative, with familiar bottom and deep, sheltering pools. The waters themselves were soft and sweet, bearing the aroma of spruce and fir, of the North Shore's thin young soils and upstream peat bogs, and whiffs of bottom-dwelling sculpins and minnows. Dappled light would form almost physical walls to the old trout's world, casting here a gleam on the bottom sand, over there highlighting a boulder and its tender single-celled skin of green algae. The water was plastic with sound: the muted clatter of unsteady rocks, the nearby thunder of the little falls, the high notes of current washing downstream to its meeting with the lake.

My Mickey Finn, darting and stalling amid this vivid atmosphere, sang an inaudible song that the old trout may have felt as a skin-tingling sensation along his lateral line, alerting him to its presence. But now that he was no longer eating, he would sense the streamer not so much as prey as simple presence. His world was animate beyond human imagining, a place of such liquid dynamism that its light, contours, sounds, and creaturely presences shifted constantly, creating a plastic geometry. It was probably deeply familiar to the old fish, a home he had returned to annually for most or all of his life, as known a resting place as a creature awaiting an unimaginable journey could occupy. He cruised the pool, stopped, rested, cruised it again.

As I've said, I wanted to witness the moment in which he ceased being an individual part of that wavering flow. But now my own needs asserted themselves: my cold, puckered skin began to shiver, and my belly, unfed for sixteen hours, wanted food. So I picked my way over the slippery rocks to the east bank of the stream and heaved myself out, dripping forth in my neoprene hide like the Creature from the Black Lagoon. Once up the trail, I looked back down at the pool. I could still see the old trout resting over his rock, seeming, from this distance, more like a shadow on the streambed than ever.

I slogged through the mud to the truck, stripped off my waders and emptied them of water, pulled on clean dry clothes, then backed the truck onto the vapory pavement. The roadway had heated up, and steam now rose mazily from the macadam like stage fog. By noon I had followed its strange white luminescence back to the peopled world of the Scenic Café and a plunge pot of coffee.

7 Lo, the Gentle Sturgeon

THE FIRST LAKE STURGEON I EVER SAW was swimming in a lethal-looking tank at the Fond du Lac Band's Black Bear Casino near Carlton, Minnesota. It was a young fish who had been taken from the nearby St. Louis River and plopped into this aquarium as an example of a local species. It floated near the bottom of a four-foot-high tank no wider than my hand is long. The water was colorless and clear, completely free of algae and other plants. The floor of the tank was covered with red-and-pink gravel instead of the rich brown silt-and-muck stew beloved by bottom-feeding sturgeon. In this minimalist waterscape, the young sturgeon floated like a designerly bath toy. Scaleless but sharply ridged by seven rows of bony scutes running the length of its body, the animal bore an uncanny resemblance to Disney's Dumbo: teacup-sized gill covers; outsized, fan-shaped pectoral fins; and winsome, upturned nose. It had a weakling chin and four pendulous barbels that hung (mournfully, I thought) from the underside of its upper jaw. Its small eyes were yellow-irised, and they shifted lidlessly about, as if hurt by the powerful light above the tank. It reminded me of what's often been said about the moose: an animal that seems to have been designed by a committee. Badly.

Though I had never seen a live one before, I recognized the creature as a small lake sturgeon. And though I thought I cared nothing about fish at the time, I felt stung by the sturgeon's plight. It looked doomed.

I remembered the great white sturgeon who had appeared occasionally on the front page of the *Sacramento Bee* during my childhood—big females who weighed upward of 400 pounds, flaunted by sports who had winched them out of the Sacramento River. Those white sturgeon had looked prehistoric and monstrous, right up there with the occasional gray whale who made its way up the river delta from San Francisco Bay and hung out for a while before chugging back to the Pacific. Like the Sacramento's immense naturalized channel catfish, white sturgeon thrived on what the river fed them year-round from California's famously fertile tributaries: crustaceans, clams, crabs, estuary fish, the occasional domestic cat.

But this doughy pink animal in the casino's fish tank would have had a much harder life in the St. Louis River or Lake Superior than the white sturgeon on perpetual R&R in the Sacramento. Intrigued to find out more, I questioned the casino's security guard about the fish. He called over a manager, who told me the fish had been caught from the river and that it was fed fish flakes. They'd had it since the casino opened several months earlier.

I left Black Bear after a fine meal that took the chill off my foggy mid-March camping trip down the road. Before the doors closed behind me in the cold, I looked back at the tank, which glowed like a jeweler's window in the casino's atmospheric gloom. The knobby pink fish finned slowly at the bottom, surrounded by invisible gallons of purified water. A showpiece, not a part of a living system.

I date my passion for fish from that evening, although it took me a long time to realize the seed was planted then and not on a trout stream years later. The little sturgeon didn't last long. Before I moved from Minneapolis to Duluth, I used to stop at Black Bear on my drives north just to visit it, and within months it had disappeared from the tank.

"What happened to the sturgeon?" I asked the same guard later that summer.

He shrugged. "Died, I guess."

I left sad. Was this one creature's sympathy for a fellow animal, or was it mere projection on my part—sorrow for my own eventual death prefigured in this small animal's? I didn't want to dismiss my reaction to the sturgeon's death as mere anthropomorphism, but neither did I want to sentimentalize or trivialize the fish by valuing it only for its likeness—or dissimilarity—to myself.

Sturgeon did not stir much cross-species compassion among recently settled North Americans until the last decade. Among northwoods Ojibwe, the lake sturgeon figured as *Na-me* (pronounced "nah-me"), one of the most powerful of spirits, the water dweller who orchestrated the movements of other water beings and who determined humans' success on the water roads. Kitche Manitou, the creator, endowed Na-me with strength and depth of character; members of Na-me's totem clan are teachers. Sturgeon were revered even when they were hunted on their spawning runs, at which time they become spectacularly vulnerable to shallow-water spearing.

When European explorers and settlers arrived in the North Woods, they were awed by the size and number of lake sturgeon. In 1660, Pierre Esprit Radisson saw over one thousand sturgeon drying on racks at a native village on Superior's South Shore. Two centuries later, U. S. Army Lieutenant J. Allen wrote about an Ojibwe weir for catching lake-run sturgeon on the U.P.'s Ontonagon River seven miles upstream from Superior. The natives relied "so exclusively upon this fishery that they hunt but little and make no effort to cultivate the soil beyond the raising of a few potatoes." Both the Hudson's Bay Company and the North West Company urged the Ojibwe to harvest sturgeon for isinglass, a gelatinous protein from the lining of the sturgeon's swim bladder that was used in fining wines and beers and in making a superior furniture glue. But the Ojibwe resisted such impious suggestions, and eventually a white commercial fishery grew up to satisfy the trade.

Commercial sturgeon fishing ended a way of life for Ojibwe hands that had depended on the fish as a major source of food. Between 1823 and 1884, the Hudson's Bay Company shipped anywhere from 100 to 1,500 pounds of isinglass annually from its Lake of the Woods trading posts. It took about ten forty-pound sturgeons to yield a pound of isinglass; Canadian geographers Tim E. Holzkamm, Victor P. Lytwyn, and Leo G. Waisbey estimate that 275,415 pounds of sturgeon were taken annually between 1823 and 1884—enough fish to have supported at least 207 people in each of those years.[1]

After railroads made shipping of fresh sturgeon flesh and roe (caviar) from the Great Lakes possible, the market value of sturgeon rose even higher, extinguishing all other claims that might be made for the fish. Ebenezer McColl, a provincial Indian inspector for the Province of Manitoba, reported to his governors in 1888,

> The destruction of their fisheries by the white men was the burden of [the Ojibwe's] speeches and the eternal nightmare of their apprehensions. They frequently pointed out to me at their councils how the buffalo, the principal source of subsistence of their kindred in the plains[,] was destroyed by the effective weapons of destruction furnished hunters by white men, and implored me to use my influence with the Government to have their fisheries protected from being irretrievably ruined before it was too late.

Noting the increase in commercial fishing on the U.S. side of Lake of the Woods, McColl predicted, "Unless the fisheries, upon which [the Ojibwe] mainly depend now for support, are rigidly protected, not many years will elapse before they will become wholly dependent on the Government for subsistence." Canadian Indian agent Robert Pither visited the bands along the Rainy River in 1891 and found that they "were almost starving, as very few sturgeon went up the river to spawn and they hardly caught enough for personal use."

Despite the pleas of the Rainy Lake Band and the devastating falloff in the sturgeon fishery on the U.S. side of Lake of the

---

[1]Quoted in "Rainy River Sturgeon: An Ojibway Resource in the Fur Trade Economy," *The Canadian Geographer* 32:3 (1988), pp. 194–205.

Woods, the Canadian government opened its waters to commercial fishing in 1892. Between 1895 and 1899, over one million pounds per year of dressed sturgeon were pulled from Lake of the Woods. By 1909, sturgeon had almost disappeared from Lake of the Woods. The Ojibwe's treaty rights had been overridden and one of their chief cultural and material resources had been destroyed. All told, between 1888 and 1914, commercial fishermen scooped almost fourteen million pounds of lake sturgeon and 700 thousand pounds of caviar from Lake of the Woods.

Not surprisingly, sturgeon are now relatively uncommon throughout Na-me's northern kingdom. But Ojibwe bands on both sides of the U.S.-Canadian border—for example, the Manitou Band of Rainy Lake First Nations, the Fond du Lac Band of Minnesota, and the Bad River Band of Wisconsin—are now rearing and restoring sturgeon as heritage fish to waters where they once "swarmed . . . in almost incredible numbers."

The best-known and probably most resilient population of lake sturgeon dwells in the Lake Winnebago system of Wisconsin. Winnebago provides a luscious home for sturgeon: it's big, fertile, and offers over one hundred miles of its tributary Wolf and Fox rivers for spawning. Much of the Wolf has been riprapped for flood control, and the sturgeon, deprived by Shawano Dam of their upstream spawning sites, now drift through the humanmade shallows each spring, dropping eggs and milt over the Corps of Engineers' handiwork. In winter, most of the system's sturgeon stay in the lake, roaming sluggishly beneath the ice or stacked up like cordwood in deep holes. The State of Wisconsin holds a brief winter spearing season each year, but by the time the season opens in February, most of the year's spawning females have long since moved up from the lake into the river, where they crowd companionably into holes, awaiting the arrival of warmer (50°) water suitable for mating.

THE IMMENSE FISH APPEARED in the dark water at Koepke's Landing like dreams only gradually taking form. Most of them were males thirty to forty-five inches long. Their heads swelled like the blades of shovels from snout to a point slightly behind their deep maroon gills and from there their bodies harrowed sharply to sleek, streamlined tails. Those tails were heterocercal, like sharks', larger and more pointed on the upper fins. Along their spines and sides ran rows of scutes rubbed smooth and round. Their pectoral fins were broad, short, and paddlelike.

Sturgeon are members of an ancient tribe of fish that preceded the more modern ones like bass and perch. Instead of the bony skeletons of later-evolving fish, sturgeon are cartilaginous; instead of spinal columns, they have smooth, continuous notocords. This doesn't make them obsolete holdovers, however; the twenty-five remaining sturgeon species are highly successful at adapting to the curveballs continually thrown at them by human technologies. Sturgeon, like all animals, are individuals as well as members of a species, and each one I watched that day at Koepke's Landing was a different color, ranging from pallid cream through rich chocolate through reddish green to deep army drab. Some bore white scars from collisions with wing dams, riprap, human predators; others were evenly colored except for the white on their snouts, scutes, and throats.

It was late April, an unexpectedly warm day, the air temperature 71°. Along the shallow riprapped shoreline, the water was a balmy 61°, higher than sturgeon supposedly prefer for spawning. Despite human theory, the sturgeon were spawning actively along the outside bend at Koepke's Landing. Most of the males hovered just above the bottom, switching their powerful tails into action only when one of the big females swam in from the deeper midstream water and released her eggs. Dark, hugely magnified shadows of the eggs drifted downstream like elongated clouds in the clear water. Farther downstream, the pale lips of opportunistic males popped out from beneath their chins like short white vacuum hoses, sucking in the eggs before they could adhere to rock or gravel.

The wind came up, pleating the surface of the brown water and sending corded patterns rushing across it. Willows on the near banks sprouted chartreuse catkins; the grass had already greened up. A yellow-headed blackbird fluttered across the Wolf River, headed for the marsh on the far side of the parking lot. With the exception of the deciduous swamp forest on the far bank, under whose still-naked branches walleyes had splashed and spawned the previous week, this stretch of river had the look of full spring.

Certainly the fish seemed to think so. I had already seen dozens of them that afternoon, floating tranquilly in pods or roiling violently alongside one of the females. So oblivious were they to the humans watching them from the bank that it was easy for me to dip my hand into the water and touch their sides, run my palm down the row of scutes along their spines. The scutes felt like polished bone and were neither deep nor sharp. The animals' sides were scaleless and had the plushy, resilient texture of wet chamois or a stiff foam mattress. They were not cold to the touch. They finned tranquilly in place while I ran my hand along their sides. Spawning and consuming the spawn were their only apparent concerns.

Some of the males had short, perky faces, some, long ones. Their eyes were far apart, on either side of their broad, flat heads; whatever binocular vision they had must have been for things far in front of them. Sturgeon depend more on their scenting ability and sense of touch than on sight for locating mates, fellows, and food. Their upturned noses twitched and their bodies followed with quick, decisive moves in the direction of whatever interested them. Their gills: immense, crescent chambers lined with bowed rows of gill filaments plush with oxygenated blood. On a thirty-five-inch fish, the opening behind the gill cover was wide and deep enough for my entire balled fist to fit inside. The gill cover itself resembled an elephant ear set laterally. When it flared open, it was outsized, fleshy.

These particular fish had traveled some seventy miles upstream from Lake Winnebago to spawn. The big females, sixty to one hundred pounds, floated like logs just beneath the surface in water so shallow that their tails and backs frequently broke into bright air. The smaller males, sometimes nine or ten of them to a single female, swam up alongside and waggled their heads, setting off shivers that shimmied down their streamlined backs to their deeply split tails, where they ended in a series of jolts. Afterward they bumped or slid along the length of the female's body, releasing clouds of milt, dense and opaque, which trailed away to a milky translucence. Upstream a few feet, the tails of another waiting pod of males breached the surface like dark nunataks.

———

I WAS STATIONED at Koepke's Landing in a semiofficial capacity. My duty: to prevent spawning, oblivious sturgeon from being poached. Nothing would have been simpler—any human could wade among them, touch them, spear or shoot them. For that matter, you could probably have staved in their heads with a good-sized rock. So I was sitting there, not four feet away from the swarming fish, wearing a green seed cap that read—

PATROL
STURGEON
FOR TOMORROW
1997

—and armed with a flashlight, polarized fishing glasses, and a walkie-talkie. The big ripe females were worth somewhere in the neighborhood of $10,000 on the black market, ample reason for the State of Wisconsin to protect them. With the help of volunteers—the group Sturgeon for Tomorrow, a retired DNR field officer nicknamed the Sturgeon General, and anglers from all over the Upper Midwest who came to stand watch in twelve-hour shifts for three weeks each spring—the WDNR managed to protect the Winnebago system's spawners from being served up elsewhere as steaks and caviar. I was pleased to help out. I was getting what I can't get enough of: an upclose look at fish going about their own business rather than responding to whatever we choose to impose on them.

Spawned-out sturgeon return to the big lake by floating downstream, still facing into the current. It takes them about two days to swim seventy miles upstream to spawn, but they can float back, using their tails and fins to stay in midchannel, in a single day. I saw how easy such backward travel might be: whenever one of the males stopped using his scythelike tail to stay in place, he began floating gently backward and sideways into the main current, like a small truck slipstreaming into the wake of a speeding semi.

There was something enormously pleasing about sitting on the riverbank that unexpectedly mild, 71° afternoon, watching the caudal fins of busy, engaged fish dance above the surface while they flicked water and sound downstream, creating splashy rise rings. A few sported aluminum tags on their dorsal fins from previous taggings; 1997-tagged fish wore Day-Glo orange plastic ones. One by one, the humped dark backs surfaced in front of me, glittering like seals.

A big female swam so far up on the riprap that her entire body was out of the water; only the tip of her snout remained beneath. Another big female appeared out of the murk nearby and seemed to be crawling more than swimming, inching forward over the riprap. Smaller males flanked her, shimmying and bumping up against her sides to release her eggs. They could smell each other during sex, just as other animals can. *What does fish sex smell like?* I wondered. The odor of fish, to the extent that I can detect it with my poor human nose, is one of my favorites: I relish smelling it on my hands, clearly alive, clean, slightly acrid, somehow green. It persists even after a shower—a faint reminder that I have touched another, and quite different, life.

———

WATER POURED OVER THE TAILRACE, plunged down, and rebounded into air, picking up oxygen and spilling back into the river as a head of faintly colored cream. There in the torrent at the base of the dam, sturgeon were stacked atop one another—immense dark females swithing their long tails over the cobble in water two- and three-inches deep, smaller males launched atop the females, like loons heaving themselves onto land: Island Female.

Before the two dams were built in 1913 and 1927, the Wolf River above Shawano Dam was these animals' spawning grounds. I found something immensely moving in the spectacle of the sturgeons' urgency to return to it, piled as they now were at the base of the dam, holding steady in water that moved at a white-water pace of 1,120 cubic feet per second. The back eddies along the shoreline bristled with raised caudal and dorsal fins and humped backs, a sea of them. The fish were so large and the water so shallow that I could reach out and stroke the big females' backs. They lay quietly for a bit, then surged back into the foam below the dam's face.

A high-school biology teacher arrived with a group of gum-snapping ninth graders to watch the spawning fish. I stood among them, wondering how different my life might have been if I'd had the door to mysteries like these animals opened to me as a young girl. Mine had been an urban-suburban education—catching tadpoles and boiling scavenged bird and frog bones, then reassembling them—the extent of my childhood contact with the nonhuman natural world.

As if to show me what might have been, a troop of fisheries students from Ohio State University arrived just then, armed with vials and fish boards and equipment to take scale and blood samples for genotyping the sturgeon of the Winnebago system. They and WDNR staffers waded into the foam armed with salmon nets, which they used to unceremoniously scoop out the biggest females in the water. Exposed to the air, the sturgeon became unnervingly defenseless. A broad young man in a white lab jacket stretched a dripping forty-five-inch female onto her back and stroked her white belly until a few unripe eggs pearled out of a small, tender pucker near her anal fin.

"Green," he said shortly.

Someone wrote that down.

Laid out on the measuring board like an immense slab of white meat, the sturgeon panted steadily through her tubular lips like a swimmer short of breath. Seeing her exposed thus, eggs dribbling out onto the board, belly heaving in fright or labored respiration, I wanted nothing so much as to see her returned to the water, even to see her heave herself fecklessly against the face of the dam, seeking those home waters her tribe somehow knew still lay upstream. How did fish communicate such a fact to each other? All across the base of Shawano Dam, sturgeons' tails cut the white water, holding in seemingly impossible positions amid the maelstrom below the tailrace. Did they sense, did they believe that the dam's face would melt away, the waters run free, so they could crowd upstream again as their kind had before the dam was built?

The long drive back to Duluth from Shawano gave me plenty of time to think about the sturgeons' persistence in trying to get back upstream. I drove by way of the Menominee Reservation, which lies above the dam and surrounds the upper Wolf River. The Menominees wanted to see the dam come out in order to restore sturgeon to their historic spawning grounds, but the political reality was that nothing like that would probably happen soon.

The Menominees' land holds more uncut, old-growth northwoods forest than any other stretch in Wisconsin—three times the board-foot volume of Wisconsin's average woodlands—so it was a privilege and a pleasure to drive through it. Hemlock flourishes there as it does nowhere else in Wisconsin because deer get hunted all year and the herds stay small enough that they don't destroy seedlings as they do everywhere else in northeastern Wisconsin. The first time I saw the Menominees' forest, it came as a shock: the understory was old and rich and varied—the closest word is probably *luxuriant*—in a region whose conifer woods usually look scant. I realized then that I had made the foolish if understandable error of assuming that the semi-healed North Woods I knew—Michigan's Upper Peninsula, northwestern Wisconsin, and northeastern Minnesota—had recovered enough to resemble prelogging-era forests. Even allowing for subregional differences, I now saw plainly that the Menominees' woods had a depth and intricacy those recovering places did not.

The Menominees had maintained their ancient forest at considerable cost to themselves. The tribe had resisted most of the pressures brought by white lumbermen as well as by some of its own members to clear-cut its trees. Until 1910, the federal government, acting as the tribe's agent, managed the Menominees' forest for sustainable-yield logging. But after a thick stand of pine and hemlock burned and was then clear-cut for salvage, the clear-cutting continued, as if that single exigent cut had been unstoppable. By the time the government's loggers stopped in 1926, 20,326 acres had come down. In 1937, the tribe sued the federal government for mismanaging its forest during the clear-cutting era. After lengthy hearings, the U.S. Court of Claims in 1951 awarded the Menominees $8.5 million in damages. The decision said witheringly:

> The management of the forest was left in the hands of men whose main experience had been in commercial lumbering operations and who had little knowledge of, and no sympathy with, forestry as a science or conservation as a principle in the management of the forests. . . . We conclude that the United States has not

fulfilled the required standards applicable to an ordinary fiduciary in its management of the timber operations on the Reservation, either as a commercial or industrial enterprise or in preserving the Indians' only capital, the forest.[2]

The Menominees regained control of their forest, but they were soon presented with an unpleasant political *quid pro quo*: in order to get their award monies, the Menominees would have to accept termination of their tribal status.[3]

The Menominees reluctantly accepted Congress's offer of termination so that they could receive and distribute some of the monies awarded them by the court—$1,500 per tribal member. The Menominee Termination Act was passed by Congress in 1954, and the reservation dissolved to become Menominee County. Thereafter, the temptation to log off more old-growth timber than sustainable-yield forestry called for must have become particularly great, for the tribe lost its federal payments and began to incur the expenses of operating a county government. But still the tribe refused to petition for an increase in the cutting of its forest. Then, in the 1970s, federal termination acts were reversed. The Menominees returned to tribal and reservation status in 1973. For 140 years, their forest has been managed through cutting so selective and careful that they harvested more than twice the current stands of trees. "Start with the rising sun," a Menominee chief reportedly counseled the tribe,

> and work toward the setting sun, but take only the mature trees, the sick trees, and the trees that have fallen. When you reach the

---

[2]"U.S. Court of Claims (Case 44304), 10 July 1950," quoted in Duncan A. Harkin, "The Significance of the Menominee Experience in the Forest History of the Great Lakes Region," in Susan L. Flader, ed., *The Great Lakes Forest: An Environmental and Social History* (Minneapolis: University of Minnesota Press, 1983), pp. 102–103.

[3] The Menominees had been identified by a 1947 Bureau of Indian Affairs study as one of ten tribes whose cultural, political, and economic resources made them suitable for "release" from federal supervision.

end of the reservation, turn and cut from the setting sun to the rising sun, and the trees will last forever.

So far, with the exception of the era of rogue logging in the early twentieth century, this is how the Menominees' forest has been managed. You can imagine, with good reason, that this is what all of Wisconsin's north-central woods once looked like.

WISCONSIN 47 SHOT OUT OF the Menominees' forest into Langlade County as if headed for another planet. From the old forest's darkness, lit only by the pale ghosts of the previous year's vine maple and the compact candles of arbor vitae, I drove into a landscape of plowed fields, eroded banks, dead bearing trees standing alone at the section edges, and whippy young saplings alongside trailer homes. The earth in Langlade looked as if it had been skinned.

What was it in my ancestors that so loved a scalped land? Forests figured as grim and expendable to them—cash crops, totems of primitivism, signs of sloppy stewardship. Instead of trees and wild creatures and flowing streams, settlers produced mined, exhausted land, the ditched and dammed waters I now saw ahead of my truck. If I had not just passed through Menominee County, I might have believed that this relentlessly vanquished landscape was more or less how Langlade County had always looked, that it had never nourished 150-foot white pines and thickets of hemlock, sugar maple, and 100-foot-tall yellow birches, had never been threaded by rivers running with brook trout and pike and immense lake sturgeon. Yet what was now Langlade County supported those beings for millennia after the Wisconsin glaciers melted back toward Hudson Bay.

I drove home to Duluth stunned by the contrast between Langlade and Menominee counties, between the concrete dam at Shawano and the wild waters the sturgeon sought so passionately in the country above.

8 Vampires of the Inland Sea

"MEET *LIVE* LAMPREYS, the vampires of the inland sea," read the invitation to the Great Lakes Aquarium's member-appreciation event. *Hey—sounds like a fun Friday night,* I thought. *Count me in.*

I had already met a native northern brook lamprey, one of the Vampires' nonpredacious cousins, down in the Whitewater Valley and had found her a charming animal: a slender little fish about the length of a garter snake, one of three exclusively freshwater species found in Minnesota, and the only one not parasitic as an adult.

The sea lamprey *(Petromyzon marinus),* on the other hand, is such a culturally loaded animal here in the Great Lakes region that a lot of fishermen won't even touch one. So the opportunity to meet some of these nemeses of the Great Lakes fishery excited me no end. At the conference center where the Vampires were on display, I threaded my way through the crowd to a fifty-gallon fish tank attached to an elaborate pumping system. Inside were a couple inches of white sand and three sea lampreys plastered to the glass walls. This gave me a good opportunity to observe their celebrated mouths, which are unique among fish and which inspired their taxonomic name, *Petromyzon,* from the Greek *petro* [stone], and *myzon* [to suck], about which more later.

You could call lampreys mouths with fish depending from them. Once plastered into vacuum-producing grips on prey or on the walls of a fish tank, their mouths are so much wider and so much more vivid than their scaleless bodies that the latter look almost like afterthoughts. Each round mouth contains radiating whorls of bright yellow "teeth"—not real teeth like a salmon's, but horny little nubs that the lamprey uses to attach itself to its victims. These teeth produce "ride marks"—suctionlike scars that bear witness to lampreys who have either attacked or merely hitched rides on finned fish, like the *placas* made by urban graffitists. These whorls radiate toward a central cavity containing a pinkish tongue. This, too, is armed with teeth, and it is these fang-y numbers that rasp into the sides and heads of other fish, auguring holes through which the lamprey can lap out blood and tissue.

The three lampreys in the tank were young adults probably no more than a foot in length (in Lake Superior, they usually grow to about eighteen inches). Their mouths were .75 to an inch in diameter but eventually could become as wide as 1.5 inches. With these mouths, free-swimming adults attach themselves to other fish. After a lamprey has fed enough by steady gorging, it drops away from its victim and swims off.

Fish who die from such attacks do so from loss of fluids[1] or from secondary infections. The Great Lakes Fisheries Commission, founded in 1955 to develop cooperative U.S.-Canadian programs for controlling sea lampreys and restoring the lakes' native fisheries, estimates that each adult lamprey is responsible for killing about forty pounds of trout during its free-swimming twelve to twenty months in the big lakes. Even now, while lampreys are at only 10 percent of their historic 1960s high, lampreys appear to kill as many fish each year as sport and commercial fishermen combined.

The agents of this impressive destruction are not nearly so harrowing-looking as such statistics would lead you to expect. Other than the toothy rosettes of their mouths, sea lampreys are exceptionally handsome creatures. The three I met had sinuous

---

[1]The fact that fish can die from loss of fluids while in water may seem counter-intuitive, but consider this: the ionic composition and osmotic strength (concentration) of a fish's blood and tissues differ from those of lake water. When a fish's interior tissues become exposed to surrounding water through a wound, movements of water and ions between the water and the fish's fluids increase to the detriment of the fish. For example, necessary ions in the fish's blood flow out into the water to equalize the osmotic strength on both internal and external surfaces. To put it another way, the same sort of thing happens when a balloon is pricked: highly concentrated molecules flow out of the balloon through the hole to equalize the concentrations within and outside the balloon.

black bodies mottled gray on their backs and flanks, and pale, almost white, bellies. Their heads, viewed from a less prejudicial angle than dead on, were deep and tapered smoothly to their snouts. They had but a single nostril, and seven round ports behind their eyes on each side, like old Buick Roadmasters. Behind these pores lay their gills. Their eyes were large, huge-pupiled, with golden irises. A long, divided dorsal fin drifted like a bolt of dark chiffon the length of their backs.

A dozen Duluth children crowded with me around the perimeter of the tank.

"Who wants to touch one?" asked museum director David Lonsdale.

"I do!" I shouted in unseemly haste. I would have shoved the kids aside if necessary.

The kids drew back. *"Ewwwwwwwwwwwwwh . . ."*

Lonsdale, an amiable man in blazer and striped shirt, donned a cotton-knit tailing glove, the kind used to lift large fish by their caudal peduncles, and began poking around in the tank with a green aquarium net. Hugely magnified human eyes pressed against the far side of the glass tank, watching the lampreys undulate away from their would-be captor.

Lampreys aren't particularly fast or strong swimmers—the farthest one is known to have swum in Lake Superior is six miles in a single day—and soon Lonsdale had snared the largest. Out of the water, the creature looked very snakelike, if scaleless. It writhed about in Lonsdale's grasp until I offered it my right index finger. Then its mouth spread like naval jelly, engulfing the second joint of my finger. Its grip was firm, like a tight ring or a doubled rubber band. I couldn't feel its teeth.

"Would it rasp a hole in me eventually?" I asked.

Lonsdale shook his head. Apparently not: sea lampreys prefer cold-blooded creatures. In the North Atlantic, their ancestral home, lampreys sometimes attack whales, but it's thought that they do so because those warm-blooded animals are so well-insulated by blubber that lampreys cannot distinguish them from fish. The only human beings attacked by sea lampreys have been long-distance swimmers whose skin became so chilled that the fish initially mistook them for cold-blooded animals. "But they drop away eventually," Lonsdale told me. "Once they detect that you're warm blooded, they lose interest."

The demonstration lamprey had not yet reached that point with my finger, so I gently squeezed its gel-like head to break the suction. The mouth came away reluctantly, with a long sucking sound, like a cork being pulled from the neck of a bottle. Impressive.

I wandered off to ponder the lamprey's performance after the Sturgeon General, the aquarium's costumed mascot, arrived and upstaged the Vampires of the Inland Sea. The S.G. spread his immense lamé pectoral fins for the crowd and began chanting, "JUST SAY NO TO ROE!"

Between lampreys and sturgeon, the soon-to-be-built Great Lakes Aquarium has almost cornered the U.S. market on relict fish. (*"Big gray fish,"* the museum's detractors have dismissively termed the lakes' remarkably muted denizens.) Lampreys and their distant relative, marine hagfish, are the oldest surviving members of earth's first vertebrate tribe. Fossil remains of lampreys have been found in late Cambrian and middle Ordovician sediments laid down 500 million years ago. Evolutionary biologists believe that lampreys were at their most diverse and powerful 420 to 350 million years ago. Jawless, scaleless, supported by cartilage rather than bone, lampreys swim out of a history deeper than that of any other large creature on the planet. Remarkably, the eighty species alive today differ little from their fossil ancestors. At one time, like all animals, they were sea beings, but most lampreys are now freshwater fish like the brook, silver, and chestnut lampreys of the North Woods.

Unlike them, the sea lamprey is anadromous—that is, it hatches and grows to maturity in freshwater streams, then drifts downstream to salt water for its adulthood, returning to fresh water only to spawn and die. Somehow, though, in the space of only 150 years, Atlantic sea lampreys managed to make the transition from sea dwellers to freshwater lake dwellers after migrating inland from their homes along the Atlantic coast to the Great Lakes. Nobody knows exactly how sea lampreys got to Lake Superior. They are native to streams of the Atlantic provinces and states, where they spawn and die following twelve to twenty months in the North Atlantic. Chances are they did not migrate above Lake Ontario before the 1830s. They are incapable of surmounting high falls and of swimming against strong currents, so they must have hitched rides on ships or on the bodies of more powerful westering fish whom they parasitized. The construction of the Erie Canal and the Welland Canal provided them with routes into waters no sea lampreys had lived in before, and introduced a new predator to the upper Great Lakes' resident fish against whom they had no resistance. Breeding populations of sea lampreys were first spotted in Lake Ontario in 1835, in Erie in 1921, in Michigan in 1935, in Huron in 1937, and in Superior in 1946. As their numbers grew in lake after lake, the population of their prey plummeted: lake trout, lake whitefish, lake herring, burbot.

When sea lampreys living in Great Lakes tributary streams metamorphize from their larval form (ammocoetes) into adults, they drift downstream to the big lakes and swim out to deep water, where lake trout, burbot, and big chubs are found. There they feed avidly for twelve to twenty months. Toward the end of that period, they move closer to shore, where they continue to feed on fish found in the shallows: whitefish, lake herring, walleye, yellow perch, sucker, carp. At the end of their second winter as free swimmers, lampreys gather outside the mouths of streams, sometimes hundreds of miles from their birth streams (hitching your buccal cavity to a strong swimmer isn't likely to keep you near home) and wait to ascend them after the first spring runoff. Humans think lampreys detect suitable streams through the presence of pheromones or other molecules produced by their dying comrades or by ammocoetes in the stream. Once they begin staging for their runs upstream, lampreys eat less or stop eating. Their digestive tracts degenerate and their livers stop functioning. The resulting buildup of waste materials turns their bodies jaundice-yellow, the hue they wear while swimming upstream. Their sexual organs develop and swell, fueled by energy released through degeneration of muscles, skin, and eyes. They lose weight, length, and girth.

Once upstream, males construct nests by picking up stones in their prehensile mouths and piling them into crescent-shaped mounds on gravel or sand streambeds beneath fairly strong currents. When the nests are completed, females attach themselves by their mouths to stones in the nests, while males attached themselves to the back of the females' heads. The males then press their bodies against the females' and wind their tails about them. The females shiver, showering eggs. Each mating lasts two to three seconds and sends twenty to forty sticky eggs down through the sand and gravel. The fish mate repeatedly, every one to five minutes for one to three days, until they have deposited 24,000 to 107,000 fertilized eggs in their nest. And then the adults die.

Their offspring, the ammocoetes, hatch ten to fifteen days later but remain within the nest's protective lattice until they are twenty days old, at which point they drift upward through the gravel to quiet eddies and back pools downstream, where they burrow into the sand or silt. There they live for three to twenty years as small (three- to four-inch) filter feeders, poking their heads from their tunnels to sieve drifting diatoms and other microscopic food from the passing water. And then, in a truly sci-fi-like transformation, one summer the small ammocoetes explode in growth, expanding exponentially, swelling to twelve- to sixteen-inch, free-swimming adult lampreys. In autumn, they drift downstream to the big lakes.

IF YOU CAN DIVORCE YOURSELF from whatever queasiness the term *lamprey* induces and think instead about its life cycle, the lamprey will remind you of another fish: the Pacific salmon. Salmon, too, are conceived in streams by parents who spawn and promptly die; some of them, too, spent a year or more in their natal stream before transforming into smolts and drifting downstream to live relatively brief lives (two to four years) in ocean or big lake, then return to the stream, their bulging reproductive organs crowding out the rest of them. They, too, no longer feed after entering their spawning streams, and disintegrate as they swim upstream, build their nests, lay their eggs, and die.

Part of what humans love about salmon, of course, is the resonant symbolism of the faith they reputedly keep with their native streams. We are creatures hugely invested in myths of origin—think about how many creation stories our species has devised!—so much so that strong men are reduced to tears while witnessing the salmon's constancy to its natal stream. We tend to overlook the fact that plenty of salmon don't succeed in locating their birthplaces, in which case any stream with the right water temperature, current flow, and substrate (streambed) will do. I sometimes wonder if part of the ignobility we attribute to sea lampreys may not be related to the fact that, unlike salmon, they readily ascend *any* stream of suitable temperature to spawn and die. Such pragmatism is a great deal less poetic than the salmon's supposed insistence upon *my river, right or wrong*. But the lamprey's sturdy practicality is certainly no more ignoble than the choice made by, say, a salmon who lacks infant memory of a particular stream because she was hatched and raised in an egg incubator and a concrete run, like the glamorous replicant in *Blade Runner* with her *faux* childhood snapshots.

The poetics of homing is not, of course, the chief cause of human indifference to the majesty of the sea lamprey's life cycle, so close in detail to the salmon's. The real problem is that sea lampreys prey on the same fish that human anglers want to catch. Think about it: do we cast aspersions on salmon because they eat herring, rainbow smelt, and alewives? We do not. Their prey are small beans to human anglers, so we generously interpret the salmon's predaciousness as a sign of his lordliness, his fine aggression. This makes us look better when we catch him, too, as if his predatory nature somehow made fishing for him a battle between equals. Sea lampreys, on the other hand, are small, weak swimmers who attach themselves to animals many times their size and strength, yet often best them. This is not something we see as admirable; lampreys get no points from humans for their David *vs.* Goliath, tortoise *vs.* hare victories. If we characterize their method of living at all, it's to condemn it as parasitic, as passive-aggressive.

Charter-boat captains, commercial trawlers, and trolling boats make their living from attacking and killing the Great Lakes' top predators, too. In the baldest terms, we humans consider that what's right for us isn't equally right for other animals. Lampreys must be controlled at any cost.[2] The discourse in which such odd transactions occur is curiously disembodied: the fish are said to have *invaded* the Great Lakes ecosystem, as if our having built the means by which they got here were incidental to their arrival rather than its direct cause. This is about as crackpotted as believing we can build highways and have them used only by law-abiding motorists. *Huh?* "Build it, and they will come" is a more realistic way to look at the effects wrought by canals, ocean-going grain and ore boats, and the bilge water they regularly discharge into the Great Lakes (thought to also be the source for such recent arrivals as Eurasian ruffes, zebra mussels, and round-eyed gobies). It is unbecoming for us, the engineers of dispersion, to cast ourselves as the victims of other creatures

---

[2] In 1997, the Great Lakes Fisheries Commission's lamprey-control program cost $12.4 million. In 1997, the cost per caught chinook salmon in Minnesota's waters of Lake Superior was over $600 per fish, based on the expenses of the chinook program administered by the Minnesota DNR through its French River hatchery. See "Status Report on Chinook Salmon in the Minnesota Waters of Lake Superior, Staff Report" (February 1998), p. 17. In other words, we subsidize the expense of killing lampreys and we subsidize the expense of producing fish for commercial and sports fishermen to kill.

who have taken advantage of the means we have provided. Besides: who *are* the lamprey's victims, anyway? Not us. Only the fish we ourselves want to catch and kill.

In other aquatic systems—the North Atlantic and Lake Champlain—the sea lamprey and its prey seem to have come to a wary evolutionary truce that enables the lamprey to eat without killing too many of its hosts so that both can flourish. These are accommodations that took millennia to develop. Here on the Great Lakes, the stone eater hitched a ride through human-built canals less than two hundred years ago and tumbled a system already a-tremble from the perturbations of logging and commercial fishing. No wonder, then, that the Vampires of the Inland Sea are hated by our kind. But they are only predatory fish, doing what predatory fish do, part of which is adapting to new circumstances faster than we, who would kill them off.

9 Bloodmeal

*Ah! this pest, this inevitable pest of the sportsman and detractor
from his happiness! We hear all about the poetry of trout-fishing,
but very little of its stern actualities. We read of pleasant pools,
refreshing shade, and tumbling foam, but who has courage to tell us
all the truth of these blood-thirsty little fiends, the flies and mosquitoes?
Who has ever dared to paint the picture in its true colors?*

—Charles Hallock, *The Fishing Tourist* (1873)

IN ARCTIC SUMMERS, thick-coated caribou sometimes stampede to get away from biting insects. Even here, 18° farther south, European explorers, voyageurs, timber cruisers, and mapmakers wrote about men reduced to madness by the North Woods' swarms of black flies, mosquitoes, and no-see-'ems. Sportsman Robert Barnwell Roosevelt (uncle of TDR), who fished the North Shore in 1864 and wrote about his experiences in *Superior Fishing: Or, The Striped Bass, Trout, and Black Bass of the Northern States* (1865), described the problem succinctly:

> The great drawback to this section of country . . . is the immense number of mosquitoes, black-flies, and sand-flies. These pests are found numerously everywhere in our woods, but nowhere are they so plenty [*sic*] or combined so equally as along the shores of Lake Superior. All day long the black-flies watch their chance to find a bare spot of human flesh to sting and tear; immediately on the falling of the shades of evening the almost invisible sand-flies, the "no see 'ems" . . . make their appearance in countless millions of infinitesimal torture, and all night long the ceaseless hum of the hungry mosquito drives sleep from the wearied sportsman's eyelids. . . . even with the best protections, the warm days that give these insects unaccustomed activity are scarcely tolerable.

I recalled that dismal history as the hoards settled avidly upon me. It was midspring and midafternoon, sunny and almost warm, and I had wound my way down to the shaded banks of the upper Sucker, a poetic-looking place when viewed from the fishermen's path: marsh marigolds in cheerful bloom, rue anemones, wood violets. The trees and shrubs hadn't leafed out yet but were covered with tight chartreuse pom-poms. Here the river was about twenty feet wide, a deep, tannic chestnut brown. This was to be my first day fishing the brookie portion of the stream as a resident of the North Shore, and only my second day on the water since winter had melted from the woods. I was practically shaking with eagerness as I rigged up my rod.

My shaking quickly took on an added source of frenzy: the black flies and the mosquitoes on the riverbank were much fiercer than I had anticipated, and their persistently swarming, eyelid-crawling, ear-auguring, stinging presences set all of me in motion. My tortured skin rippled like a horse's. I thrashed blindly into the river, thinking I could get away from them. *Wrong.* They were just as persistent over the water—crawling down the neck of my shirt, up my sleeves, into the whorls of my ears, under my sunglasses, and into the creases around my eyes. The only advantage to being in midstream was that I could now look back through the haze of them and see that they were even thicker on shore. They looked like an inversion layer over Los Angeles.

Northern spring and summer are brief, between sixty and ninety days, depending on the latitude, and they are usually wet. These conditions spawn an unholy proliferation of insects, enough of whom seek a bloodmeal to spell acute discomfort to their involuntary donors. I had not forearmed myself with the toxic miracle DEET or a bug jacket, foolishly believing that no biting insects would be found on spring's fast-moving Sucker. But now they clouded my vision, spinning before my eyes as I had seen them do on so many videotapes about subarctic fishing. My friends and I were savvy to the savagery of the North Woods' spring bugs—to a person, we avoided inland canoeing and camping between mid-June and late August, when innocents from other parts of the country entrusted themselves to our not-so-gentle woods. We had often sat around the TV hearth and laughed ungenerously at the swarms of insect extras crawling across the lens during In-Fisherman's *Water Wolf,* sniggered at the valiant efforts of Larry Dahlberg to ignore the insects hazing his image, hummed along with the audio track's subarctic ground bass, *whinewhinewhine,* as it caromed from channel to channel.

And now? My comeuppance.

So I tried to adjust my opinion of the invertebrate hoards by imagining them as a beneficent hatch—say, a fog of juicy mayflies or caddisflies. No such luck: they remained what they were, tiny biting insects who failed to fall accommodatingly to the water's surface and be slurped down by pale trout lips.

But wait: mosquito and black-fly larvae fed trout, did they not? They did. A point in their favor.

And were not mosquitoes the chief pollinators of many northern plants, including our native orchids and blueberries? They were.

And were they not the favorite food of yellow jackets, that occasional late-summer trout fodder? Yes. They were also marvels of ingenious adaptation: high Arctic black flies, for example, are all females, reproducing parthenogenetically. Was it not therefore niggardly of me to begrudge these small creatures the motes of protein they needed to lay viable eggs?

That was as far as I could take such reasoning just then. Slacking away from the positive, I imagined my face as it might look by the time I returned to the truck: bloated beyond recognition, a mass of bloodworm-red welts. I had seen that face before, and it had not gazed back at me with a certain alienated majesty.

All this while, I was wading slowly upstream, looking for suitable trout water, whining very unbecomingly and ineffectually. I finally settled into a spot downstream of a nice riffle and began casting. Each backcast sucked a fresh convoy of black flies up my right sleeve, which crawled now like living cloth. Ouch. *Ouch.* This was not the Zenlike, concentrated fishing I had hoped for. But it was, after all, what the North Woods, in this first warm stretch of spring, had to offer.

So I decided I had better get used to it, sans DEET. After all, hadn't generations of anglers and woodsmen managed to get by without high-tech solutions? I recalled the smudge fires we had built during the unusually wet summer of 1994, when I had attended log-building school up near Sand Lake. We had built mounds of wet wood, then added damp grass, moist sawdust— anything to make our fires gutter. And when they began to smolder, we huddled around them, eyes streaming from the smoke, throats scoured raw by the smoke, but grateful, *so grateful,* for temporary relief from the mosquitoes.

Well, no possibility of a smudge fire midstream . . .

—Wasn't it a fact, though, that if *enough* biting insects exsanguinated me, I would develop a certain immunity to their bites? I recalled old settlers' tales about woodsmen who achieved complete indifference to the swarms who settled grayly over their skins. I can't say this was a very consoling thought, but it did take the edge off my present horror. Indifference, apparently, could be learned.

A fish threw my hook at this point. My last glimpse of him was of a white throat and lips heaving above the riffle, a strong tail cartwheeling beyond them. Clearly I was paying too much attention to the bugs and too little to my fishing, so I turned once again upstream and tied on a new Pass Lake, then went back to casting into the riffle. As I did so, a curious thing happened.

The swarms of bugs no longer felt like an assault by hundreds of individuals, maddening in their separateness, their everywhereness. Quite suddenly, they felt instead like a fan or a feather being drawn slowly and lightly across my skin. I leaned forward into what I now sensed as a delicate blowing veil of bugs, and they no longer seemed like demons to be fought. Instead, they became creatures to be endured, even to be fed. I stopped struggling against them, stopped swatting at them. Crazy as it may sound, I even rolled up my sleeves. *Take me,* I thought.

Besides: having been on the stream for close to an hour now, I had noticed that, quite mysteriously, my thoroughly bitten hands, face, neck, and ears exhibited no signs of swelling. I couldn't even spot the familiar red welts rising rangelike along my inner wrists.

My spot in earth and time was already rolling away from the sun, the water beginning to give off a tangible cold, the air to blue. I fished through two more pools and riffles, and because I was not an adept at wet fly fishing, I broke off or failed to set the hook in five more fish who lunged at my fly, spring-eager to feed.

10 Flyover Country

WHEN I WAKE TO MORNING'S LIGHT, it's to the sight of a slow, mazy spring creek fringed by fall-gold willows, cottonwoods, and grasses. Beyond the worm fence that keeps livestock away from the water, a flat broad valley of hay pastures rolls toward the blue foothills of the Bitterroots. The light is low and dramatic and ignites the tips of streamside willows to red-gold. A few patches of early snow, pink with alpenglow, cling to the bony ramparts of the mountains. On the sweet inside curve of the creek, the willows lie deep in shadow, unlit, subdued. The creek itself is an opaque gray-green, cool and smooth; a single rise form dimples its nacreous surface at the bend, turning the water there to beaten gold. Near the outside bank, a lone angler lowers himself toward the water, awaiting a strike.

Ah, Montana!

It's all right there, on my bedroom wall.

Like its predecessors, this year's Sage pinup poster for Western trout fishing celebrates big water, big land, high mountains, powerful rods. Lying here in my snug Minnesota bedroom a thousand miles east of the Big Waters of my childhood, I reflect upon how much Western lands and Western angling dominate the imaginations—and pocketbooks—of Minnesota anglers who can afford to fish wherever they want in the Lower Forty-eight.

As it happens, I cannot. But most relatively poor Minnesotans can fish Montana because it's only an eleven-hour drive away. Just the same, I prefer to cast my lot with the generally smaller and distinctly bushier waters of the Upper Midwest, which instead puts my fishing squarely in the rainshadow of Eastern angling traditions and techniques. Out West, standard rods are heavier and longer to contend better with wide rivers, powerful currents, and equally powerful winds. Back here, rods are shorter, like our modest valleys, and gentler, like our little alder-lined creeks. In Minnesota, if there's a very powerful wind, we don't usually try to cast through it. It often comes accompanied by or portending a thunder-and-lightning storm, so prudent anglers get off the stream. Ten-foot rods aren't unusual on the huge tailwaters and the steelhead rivers of the West; hereabouts, most streams are no more than seven to fifteen feet across, so light, short rods work just fine. But our creeks' diminutive size and claustral surroundings seem to rob them, in many anglers' opinions, of dignity and value. You've got a long search to find a rod poster featuring one of the North Woods' tiny freestone creeks. It seems generally agreed that the austere, almost illimitable sweep of the Rockies, Sierra, or Cascades are necessary to confer nobility on trout waters.

Having come from the West, I see things differently. I spent my childhood not in the land of sky blue waters and tiny brooks but in California, Nevada, and Oregon in a time when only sandy two-tracks led down to Lake Tahoe's north shore, when the McCloud and Feather rivers raced unfettered down their canyons, when Bonneville Dam's fish ladder on the Columbia was still being touted as a miracle of engineering. (As a child, I wondered aloud how the poor fish could negotiate such seeming mazes without harming themselves. Forty years later, we know the answer: THEY CAN'T.) In short, the West's brawling rivers may be my true homewaters, but as fishing experiences go these days, they leave me pretty unimpressed.

By the time I had grown up, almost none of Northern California's waters still ran free. By the 1970s, the federal Bureau of Reclamation, the State of California, Los Angeles Department of Water & Power, Pacific Gas & Electric, and a score of other organizations and agencies had built twelve hundred major dams, the world's two largest irrigation projects (the Central Valley Project and the State Water Project), and "rehabilitated" more arid acres in California than anywhere in the world. I am old enough to remember the death of two places condemned by the state's rainmakers: the Berryessa Valley, just east of the Napa Valley, and a nameless green cleft in the Sierra foothills above the town of Folsom. Both were drowned by new dams. My father took us to see the little Mormon settlement that would soon be covered by the rising reservoir behind Folsom Dam. Its residents had resisted the drowning of their homes, of course, but in those days California dams waited for no man, never mind other orders of creatures. The white clapboard houses and oaks and manzanita were duly folded beneath dark waters.

Months later, in August, we visited the new reservoir that had risen above the Mormon crossroads. Folsom Lake, as it was disingenuously called, had become only partially filled by that time, but already no signs of the village and roads remained. The reservoir's picnicking grounds and beaches had not been built yet. All that was visible were opaque brown waters slapping against chaparral-covered hills, soaked hillside vegetation, and the mud where the two mixed. Numberless frogs warbled from their temporary hillside marsh, while around them summer built toward brushfires.

The public rationales for the dams, appalling as many of the consequences were, seemed noble enough: irrigation of homestead farms and control of periodic flooding. In fact, B-Wreck, as the federal Bureau of Reclamation is known in some parts of the West, built projects that worked in favor of agribusiness and developers careless enough to build on centuries-old floodplains. But scratch the experience of anyone who has lived in the arid West for more than twenty years, and you will find anxiety about boom-and-bust, drought-and-flood cycles, declining groundwater supply, and agriculture's increasing demands for water. Dams, it now seems clear, are not the answer they were touted as in the 1940s to 1960s. By creating cheap, subsidized irrigation and flood control, dam builders encouraged agriculture in regions that couldn't otherwise support cattle, never mind cotton. By moving water from northern watersheds to the arid Southwest, dam builders helped to create unsustainable, artificial population growth at terrible cost to northern river systems. The over 90 percent decline in the Sacramento-San Joaquin river system's salmon and steelhead runs are just one of the most conspicuous prices that California's dam-happy water brokering has caused. Few mourn the equally ruinous extinction or near-extinction of other native fish like the squawfish and Dolly Varden. I do, and that's why tailwater fishing holds all the appeal for me of shooting elk at a game farm.

———

AS I WRITE THIS, Duluth is having one of those Minnesota summer days that I probably shall never get used to. Outside, the temperature is about 70 degrees; the humidity in the house, according to my hydrometer, is 90 percent. A fine haze hangs over the wet green trees and lawns and softens the outlines of houses, cars, and sidewalks as if a scrim has been stretched across my windows. Not a breath of air stirs; the atmosphere simmers delicately. This is as close to entropy as I can imagine climate coming; the air has the same feel and taste as my own skin, as if the margins between self and not-self have melted. Grayed-down as the day is, its tree, shrub, lawn, and sharp-bladed iris greens nonetheless stand out with hallucinatory richness.

Water in the North Woods of Minnesota, Wisconsin, and Michigan falls effortlessly from the sky throughout the summer months. There is usually enough water swelling the streams in the forms of groundwater and snowmelt, clear and cold, to support trout. To my lately Western eyes, the mostly narrow, winding, slow-moving streams of the North Woods are miracles simply because they flow during June, July, and August—months when so many of the West's natural streams dry up entirely. I cannot understand why Midwesterners value these abundant waters so lightly, but they seem instead to regard a week on the Madison, Bighorn, or Upper Missouri, those rain-shadowed Western rivers pounded by arid winds and surrounded by yellowing fields, as the height of summer romance.

Give me the Brule or the Siskiwit. After two decades of moving around the States, I treasure the opportunity to stay in one place and learn to care for and protect it. Getting to know a few streams well enough to have some idea about how to fish them means committing myself to them, admitting my ignorance, and accepting the certitude that I shall never know enough. Good disciplines.

In "Bad Pool" (1989), Nick Lyons wrote movingly of Michigan writer John Voelker (Robert Traver):

> I often think of the old judge Robert Traver, and his exclusive love of bright, wild brookies in nearby water that he knows and loves. Not for him excursions to far-flung corners of the world for one-week stands. Not for him the itch of newness. He likes the simple quality of what he knows well and has lived with—consistently. He likes the solitude and the texture, the expectation of returning to his familiar "Frenchman's," the gentle variations, the constants, the tin cup and the bourbon, morels in the woods, intriguing rock formations back among the trees, the smell of Upper Michigan cedar, days that brush the heart with their intimacy.

I can think of no better goal for myself than to emulate Voelker's content with his homewaters. Learning to fish well means looking hard at what's in front of me, being willing to take in what I hear and observe without filtering it first through the baleen of intellect. This is invigorating in the root sense of that word: angling, which I am learning through my senses, charges me with new life and purpose. Submitting myself to the tutelage of waters, weather, and fish doesn't lead only inward; it also leads toward the immense, seemingly intractable problems of logging, sewage disposal, and mercury deposition—problems that no one can escape on the streams of the North Woods, where mining and logging seemingly wait around most bends. Perhaps this explains in part Minnesotans' zeal for fishing Montana: problems there belong to someone else and look different. Perhaps they aren't always recognizable to us outsiders.

The dams that have made fishing in the Northern Rockies world-famous are a case in point. To Midwesterners, the fabled tailwaters on Montana's Missouri, Madison, and Bighorn and Utah's Green are simply givens. To a Westerner like me, the dams that created them are so politically and culturally loaded that I can take little joy from the prospect of fishing below them. Floyd Dominy and B-Wreck changed Western watersheds' warm, turbid rivers into cold, clear ones, thus giving rise to the region's now-celebrated tailwater fisheries for West Coast rainbow, European brown trout, Upper Mississippi drainage walleyes, and Great Lakes/Rainy River basin lake trout. In the process, their dams killed off native squawfish, bonytail, humpback chub, and razorback sucker, all of which depended on the Colorado basin's silty waters. Except for the razorback sucker, all of these fish have been listed as endangered species in their native drainages by the U. S. Department of the Interior.[1] For me, these tailwaters are haunted waters.

Here in the North Woods, native fish have fared somewhat better. Brook trout were suffocated by sawdust, turned to fish paste by logging drives, steamed by heightened temperatures behind driving dams, chased out of their holds by introduced browns and rainbows and smallmouths. But despite these griefs, they have not been entirely supplanted. This is due in no small part to the fact that they live in flyover country—this vast stretch of north-central North America that apparently interests populations of stream anglers on the East and West coasts not one whit. Our trout may not be the hog-fat animals of Montana's spring creeks, but those of us who fish for the Black's and Ontonagan's more modestly proportioned creatures don't have to share the water with scores of other anglers, either. Although

---

[1] See Paul B. Holden, "Ghosts of the Green River: Impacts of Green River Poisoning on Management of Native Fishes," in W. L. Minckley and James E. Deacon, eds., *Battle Against Extinction: Native Fish Management in the American West* (1991). Two useful books on the politics of Western dam building are Philip L. Fradkin, *A River No More: The Colorado River and the West*, revised edition (1995) and Marc Reisner, *Cadillac Desert* (1986).

I live in the town with the largest percentage of fishing-license holders in the Lower Forty-eight states (the champion license holders are residents of Anchorage and Fairbanks), I can't recall a single outing in the past three years when I've spotted more than one other angler along any stretch of river I fished. (*True, part of the reason may have been that in my ignorance I wasn't picking very promising stretches to fish, but still...*) If you can stay off the water on weekends up here, you can pretty much have any stream to yourself in flyover country.

The other mitigating factor, of course, is the popularity of lake fishing in the North Star State. Improbable as this may sound, Minnesota runs neck-to-neck with Arizona for the record for boats-per-capita of all fifty states: talk about the power of wishful thinking . . . Though they're useable here only from late May until sometime in October, boats are the primum mobile of northwoods angling, the link between fishermen and the walleyes and muskies most of them pursue so singlemindedly. Walleyes (Minnesota's official State Fish), of course, can also be found in small rivers, but because size is the name of the game in most fishing, huge walleye "factories" like Lake of the Woods, Mille Lacs, Leech, and Rainy lakes attract most of the fishing action. Everybody else, it seems, is busy pursuing muskies (Wisconsin's official State Fish) and their slightly smaller cousin, the northern pike, both of which are also celebrated chiefly as lake fish. So while Minnesota's annual average of two million anglers rock on the waters in their Lunds and Alumacrafts (both manufactured in Minnesota), I join the scanty, dispersed pod of stream anglers who wade or canoe waters too cold for walleyes and muskies and pike. And I am happy to say that the fishing is both good and, for the most part, goes a-begging. No Trout Unlimited fish-porn calendar art touts our northwoods streams, no full-color bleeds in Tom Rosenbauer's *Casting Illusions* highlight our two-foot-wide border creeks winding between streamside corridors of white spruce and balsam fir. It's as if we're off the official map.

If this sounds like a complaint, it is, and it isn't. Local anglers everywhere are jealous lovers of their favorite fishing spots. We suspect them of inconstancy, worry about their other suitors, resent those who would strike up their acquaintance and despoil them, particularly if the would-be suitors are outlanders. I'm no different. The fact that these waters are routinely passed over—quite literally, usually at an elevation of 30,000 feet—by anglers from the East and West coasts and the big midcontinental cities to the south bothers me not at all. What does disturb me, however, is that local streams seem almost equally ignored by the only people in a good position to protect them, namely local anglers.

The almost fetishistic devotion of some Minnesota anglers to Montana tailwaters represents just that much less time, money, and action that can go into protecting streams here. I'm not saying this is strictly an either/or situation: at least in theory, it's entirely possible for someone to spend two weeks each summer fishing for mammoth rainbows below a Western dam and then spend the other fifty worrying about, and supporting, his or her local stream back home. But in practice, often it doesn't work out that way. Plenty of local anglers even brag about their ignorance and distance from local streams. "I haven't fished a Minnesota stream in years," I've heard anglers say proudly, one too many times. "I only fish Montana and Alaska." People who haven't fished a local stream recently are unlikely to work to protect or better it, either.

So the poster on my bedroom wall is bittersweet: it reminds me of the expansiveness of Western country, the specialness of water encountered in the West's dry places, the sense in which that rugged young country remains for some people what Wallace Stegner called it—"the geography of hope." But it also reminds me how much easier it is to embrace what is distant, exotic, and Somebody Else's Problem. Here in flyover country, forest and urban creeks need friends, too, and often they've been orphaned for distant tailwaters.

11 Nights in the World a Woman Can Walk[1]

The kind of woman fisherman I mean is a . . . lone, perspiring, hair straggling, mosquito-haloed creature wading up to her whizzle string in rough water, all the while casting like crazy and wearing a beatific expression that proclaims to the world what a ball she's having and all but shouting pee on society . . .

—Robert Traver (John Voelker), *Trout Magic* (1974)

FISHING HAS TAKEN ME PLACES I wouldn't have otherwise considered going past the age of thirteen: through culverts, down slick clay slopes facing sewer outlets, into fens and bogs and swamp forests, onto the drowned bottomlands of broad river valleys. Not so long ago, it took me scrambling mountain goat-style over bedrock cliffs alongside the North Shore's Brule River, where the only hand- and footholds are the steplike exposed roots of old spruces. It occurred to me as I heaved myself upward, favoring my bum knee, that angling involves a great deal of play, reviving or extending the part of my nature that engages passionately in activities lacking practical ends. Fishing's about pure pleasure, about total engagement in sensuous, serious play. As much as anything, it's about physical fluency in the dark.

Before I moved to Minnesota, spending time in the woods alone, never mind after dark, did not even occur to me. It seemed, quite simply, too dangerous: California's state and national parks are frequently the scenes of violence—most of them, by all reports, visited on campers and anglers innocently hunkering around evening campfires or slumbering in their tents.

---

[1]With acknowledgment to Janet Kauffman, whose wonderfully titled book *Places in the World a Woman Could Walk* (Graywolf Press, 1993) inspired the title of this chapter.

Whether my change of heart was occasioned only by the relative cultural mildness of Minnesota, by newfound confidence in my senses, or by other things, I don't know, but I began venturing alone into the North Woods' forests and waters shortly after moving here. The first time I did so, I was filled with self-recrimination and doubt: was I entertaining some *Liebestot,* some flirtation with mortality?

The occasion for such gloomy questions was a canoe trip I took with my two dogs on Bear Head Lake, just outside the Boundary Waters Canoe Area Wilderness in northeastern Minnesota. We had paddled about an hour down the west side of the lake on a late September afternoon, watching for the post that marked the campsite from the water. By sunset, I had set up our camp, the canoe was safely pulled up on the beach, and the food pack stowed well back in the woods. Everything went fine until late evening, when the jack pines began to shiver, cold and warm air collided thunderously overhead, and the sky opened.

The storm rocked us all night long; I realized then that I hadn't known how magnified the sound of rain could be when stretched across the tympanum of a tent. My otherwise fearless bull terrier Rita trembled and repeatedly attempted to breach my mummy bag, while stoic Bumper lay, snout buried between his considerable paws, as if resignedly awaiting our painful end. Over the howl of wind, I waited for the slow, toothy parting of tree tissue, the rushing descent of a spindly jack as it gathered speed to crush our defenseless nylon dome. My body hair bristled with electricity. As we lay in the dark, I reflected that I had overlooked some Significant Details: I hadn't bothered, for example, to bring raingear or to check weather forecasts. We were now about to pay for my oversights. The only things I had apparently done right were to put up the rain fly and to register at the ranger's station. At least I had the satisfaction of knowing that the DNR could locate our lightning-charred, tree-crumpled bodies days from now, when the storm finally lifted . . .

None of us slept. I can't speak for the dogs, but I lay in the dark, every sound hugely amplified by my inability to see, tensed tight as a bow string. The sheer excess of every sound, each blow to the tent's walls, carried the force of revelation. Like it or not, I was moored there in the dark, unable to make the storm pass any faster, incapable of halting the wind or the distressing creak of the jack pines. But this very helplessness eventually worked a kind of magic in me: I felt forced to adapt myself to the storm and the night's pace. When I finally relaxed—anxiety is very exhausting—I was enchanted by the sounds I could distinguish, by the variable speed of the wind, the tidelike rhythm of rain.

At dawn, the storm swept east toward Lake Superior, and a delicate stillness filled its place. The sun ascended slowly in air so soft and moist that the apricot light diffusing water and sky left them horizonless, unbounded. In this pink-goldness, spires of spruce and stanchions of jack pine hovered above the faint floating islands. Loons, much bigger than I had imagined they would be, hung dark and doubled in the water-air. I felt as if the storm had birthed a miracle, and I wanted to get out onto the water to witness it up close. Once we had shoved away from shore, I paddled silently among the loons, thrilled by them, by the mist, by the near-tactile presences of trees and air, by the white-tailed deer who saulted along the narrow beaches, by the baldy who fanned her short white tail overhead. I paddled up to the dock on the opposite side of the lake about 7 A.M. as anglers were launching their noisy aluminum boats into the water, and I enjoyed their startled looks: a woman with two dogs in a side-lit Kevlar canoe that glowed like a stained-glass window, prowing out of the golden mist.

Later, as the dogs and I drove out of the park, an immense doe streaked across the road like a portent through a dream. I felt blooded. A hunger I hadn't known I possessed gripped me, and I could hardly wait to sink my teeth into *meat*. That morning in Ely, I ate flesh for the first time in three years, knowing that I had passed a milestone: the North Woods were a place I felt good in, comfortable and alone. Not only that: I felt rocked and protected in them, even after dark. And feral.

Since then, I've camped in the North Woods of Minnesota, Wisconsin, and the Upper Peninsula in all four seasons. These are nourishing places for me, places where I like putting up a tent and anticipating the fall of dark for the opportunity it offers me to hear fellow creatures at night: the deep consumptive rumble of great gray owls in December, the liquid sex call of saw-whet owls in late February, the night cough of a white-tailed deer. Someday, I (mostly?) fantasize, I'll wean myself from the tent and carry only a sleeping bag, my late twentieth-century version of the three blankets Thoreau took on his camping trips to the Maine woods, the thinnest possible barrier between me and the night woods. Why settle for becoming a Transparent Eyeball when I can instead become a Transparent Ear, a Transparent Skin?

———

I MENTION ALL THIS because the way I fish is mostly an outgrowth of those first northwoods experiences. Because I feel secure in forested country, I enjoy following streams toward their mouths back there in the trackless, boggy bits that commonly give rise to them. This means walking anywhere from a quarter to several miles offroad on those fine old fishermen's paths that grace most Northern streams. It means moving lightly and alone, and it usually means traveling after dark.

Except in cold early spring and very late fall, the North Woods' spate streams offer the best fishing after twilight, when skittish stream fish can feed near the surface without fearing Death from Above in the shape of kingfishers, herons, and mergansers, and when many of the biggest hatches of mayflies occur. Frequently I walk in amid the fast-falling light of early evening, and as I head upstream into progressively more claustral country, I watch for markers along the usually faint paths—downed trees, doglegs leading toward the water, tiny tributaries, beaver dams, distinctive instream boulders—so I can retrace my steps long after dark.

Once in late August, I threaded my way through the alders to a slow, sandy stretch of the upper Wolf in northeastern Wisconsin, hoping to witness an evening hatch or spinner fall and the resulting mayhem on the water as fish rose to the insects. I was too green to know *which* hatch I was longing to intersect, though in the back of my mind I was hoping for the North Woods' most famous hatch of all—the hex *(Hexagenia limbata)*, a mayfly about the size of a blue darner dragonfly.

I slipped into the water about ten in the evening. Though the sun had long since set far to the south, light still illuminated the soft pale air, and the river's slow flow still held the faintest bit of color. For what seemed like a long time, I fished the limpid water upstream in a leisurely, almost dreamlike way, casting to the occasional subsurface commotions near the banks.

Then all hell broke loose. They flew in like Hueys, immense and silhouetted against the afterglow in the western arc of sky: three-tailed flies who rose and fell in the air like bubbles in a column of boiling water. They scritched through my short hair and brushed my earlobes, feathered my exposed neck and plummeted down my shirt front. Fish bobbed up like surfacing subs, then sank with wet, noisy gulps. Suddenly they were everywhere around me, the water animate with dark fish snouts and the crosshatchings of spreading rises.

I had stumbled into a hex hatch, not expecting to encounter it and not prepared to fish it, so after a few casts with my short rod and the biggest dry fly I had with me, I reconciled myself to mere watching. I had to: the fish all but curled their collective lips at my modestly sized flies, as if to say, "Is *this* the best you can do?" *Well, okay, that's the best I can do,* I thought, and relaxed. I spent a few futile minutes trying to swipe mayflies from the air to look at more closely back in the truck, but they were too—I won't say fast: they were too heavy for that—*unpredictable* in their flight to capture. Though they touched me, even invaded me during the time I stood in the river, their flight was random, at least as far as this human animal could detect, so I had to content myself simply with watching the shadow play of their dark forms against the waning light.

And then, about half an hour later, they were gone. The fish knew it, and sank from sight. The water became smooth as a platter, and soundless. I saw no more mayflies until I caught a hex hatch at an all-night service station about a week later on the U.P. There the flies clung to gas pumps like bark to a tree, and the concrete apron was slick with their bodies.

―――――――

IT S ABOUT 6:30 P.M. in late September as I head down the embankment to the fishermen's path above County Road 33 on the French River. The path leads through a tangle of small deciduous trees—alder and dogwood, mostly—and balsam firs. On the bank opposite me in the deepening dark, black spruce march up the hill in soldierly ranks; backlit by the downed sun, they've become *black* black spruce. On my side of the river, there's still enough light to make out the pale flutter of big-toothed aspen and the tangle of grasses along the water. In the short while I've been walking, the stream has turned from something quick with sky reflections to a smooth, laminar pewter flow. Even its riffles have gone soft and gray.

Somewhere off in the distance, the *pok pok* of a shotgun erupts, muffled by the moist cold air. *Great,* I think, *tomorrow another angler finds my perforated body along the trail.* Will my rod sock get mistaken for a—what? deer? grouse? woodcock? What hunting season has opened, anyway? Such questions may betray some residual fear I still have of the dark woods, displaced now onto a poacher, but I suspect they arise more from my fear of firearms in the wrong hands (out of season, after sunset). Just the same, I decide I'll be better off in or near the water, where my movement is less likely to be mistaken for that of prey.

The light has fallen so far to the southwest that only the tops of trees are still distinguishable from the night sky; the rest of the woods and water are wrapped in a comforting gloom. Down the throat of the stream, a faint bubble line marks the fast current, but I have to bend to the water in order to see it. Looking toward the left bank, I can barely make out the flat darkness that spells a little back eddy where current reverses itself below the mouth of a tiny feeder creek. Here the water is probably deep and fishy, and I cast cautiously toward it, hunched beneath the almost imperceptible silhouette of overhead branches, trying to avoid a hangup that I can't possibly see to untangle. I feel a tug in response to my cast, but it hasn't the electric, animate quality of a fish. In the low water of a rainless autumn, most such hook-ups are with the cobble streambed.

Upstream on the left, the sky still glimmers faintly, not with color but with enough light to make visible a maze of flat black that spells water curving toward the riffle just above me. Everything I can make out now is some shade of gray-black—a Whistlerian landscape, soft and suggestible.

But as the sighted world shrinks, the audible one expands, and I relax into the dark. I can still hear a soft *pok pok,* now thankfully moving to the west of me, where the poacher sightlessly pursues his quarry. The riffle pours its braided waters over boulders, making a higher sound where it slides over and around protruding rocks and a deeper, more continuous hum where it meets submerged ones. Downstream, something *plinks* in the long smooth pool: perhaps it's a brookie surfacing. A flutter in the trees on the east bank may be wings moving the still air or leaves shaken by the passage of wings. A car or truck crunches on the gravel road a quarter mile away. Then there's only the sound of water sliding over stone. My ears feel as if they are growing, covering my head, swiveling like fleshy dishes in the dark.

I can no longer see to cast, so I regretfully reel in and slide my Warden's Worry into the hookkeeper by touch, then wade to shore. I find the fishermen's path in the dark as if by radar: a sensed trough of black in the rustling foliage, a hollowness threading itself through occupied space. I follow its twisting path, and it leads me away from and then back toward the sound of the river, softer, now louder, now softer again. Once, twice I lose the path, stumble toward the mounting volume of river sound, find the path again. Each time I come to the edge of the stream's sound, I unhook my streamer and toss it back over the black water. I know that if I hook a fish, I won't be able to see to unhook it cleanly; if I snag my line, I won't be able to see to untangle it. But I can't resist the temptation to fish by sound, to interrupt the river's featureless flow. Night fishing is pure sensory play, an opportunity to live by ear as other animals do, and I don't want to stop.

But eventually I run out of river and arrive at the first hard human light: a small rectangle burning through the trees on the far bank, doubled waveringly in the dark current below—a north window in the last house above the bridge. I am almost out of the woods.

In a few more minutes, I can hear the inert wall of the embankment straight ahead of me, an audible flatness where before the air had seemed lively and open. The trees stop abruptly, and tall grasses ascend the grade almost vertically. Above them, I can make out the faint spires of black spruce across the road, and above them, blacker still, the clear night sky, punctured by stars. I scramble up, clutching handfuls of strong-rooted grasses to help me climb. Across the county road stands my fishmobile, another home.

The night air is chill and my left arm sops from groping underwater to unsnag a fly, so I don't bother to break down my rod or take off my waders after I reach the truck. Suddenly I am shivering. By the dashboard's glow, I see that I've been out in the dark for a little over two hours. It feels like twenty minutes. Heat cranked up and windows open, I barrel homeward through the night, listening to John Prine. The fact that I caught no fish bothers me not at all. I have just given myself what I most value: time in a place I love spent tempering my senses, deepening my experience of night in the woods and on the water. That I can walk these woods in what feels like safety, touch the trees under darkness and know who they are, wade these waters I cannot see, yet know what fish they hold and what small bottom-dwelling creatures they give life to, confers a kind of sympathetic magic on me. I feel strong as these trees, timeless as these waters, sexless, no longer a human woman but a human animal.

But this is a luxury, an old friend tells me: I am able to enjoy this sense of boundlessness, this lack of gender-consciousness, of self-consciousness, because by background I am sufficiently privileged to dare my nights out-of-doors. What, she asks, if I were a woman who had grown up where night sang only of terror in the keys of rape, muggings, break-ins—would I still view the fall of darkness as a source of pleasure? If I had dwelled only among crummy city streets and learned only streetwise ways, would I see the North Woods, with their wild sounds and movements, their cloistering trees and open bogs, as comforting?

Probably not. Even as a middle-class single woman in San Francisco, I had good reason to fear the fall of dark, and I did, but I wasn't conscious at the time how much such fear governed my movements, informed my caution. Moving to Minnesota was like letting the genie out of the bottle: my first solo camping trips showed me how straitened my life had been, or become, how thoroughly I had learned to associate the fall of night with danger. Once I had shed those associations and felt the freedom that night offered me here, I knew I would never willingly return to a life that inscribed dark with danger. I am lucky enough to be able to make such choices, yes, but I'm not at all certain that this has much to do with the class I was raised in (middle of the middle), much less the class I now belong to (as the old saying goes, genteel poverty).

I think there's a larger issue at play in my fondness for night fishing, and it has to do with what value I choose to assign to physical risk. Why take risks when you don't have to? One of my editors is a whitewater canoeist; her idea of a good time is to form that most tentative of temporary alliances with Class V rapids, moving downstream on them like a leaf riding a torrent. "It calms me in a way that nothing else can," she says. "I feel incredibly peaceful afterward." A close friend canoes the Far North, in places where she carries pepper spray, in case she meets brown bears. Being in such open, untrammeled, bear-ruled country relaxes her.

I'd as soon pitch my tent at the corner of Sixteenth and Mission as brave the rapids that calm these women, but I take their point: there is something driving self-selected risks that has very little to do with recklessness—a fine word derived from the Middle English *recce* (care, heed): "deliberately courting danger, foolhardy, rash"—and a great deal to do with living down fear.

Last summer, nursing a bum knee, the result of a bad ligament tear, I hobbled down to the Manitou River on the Superior Hiking Trail to see what I could see and to scare up some fish below the cascades. It was late afternoon, and I was alone. I limped-scrambled around the misty bottoms below three-tiered falls, seeking out good spots from which to cast up and through the fast water. I fell down a few times in side eddies, clanging my injured knee on the streambed's formidable cobbles, and each time, I wondered briefly *what I was doing here,* miles from anyone who could help me if I wasn't able to climb out of the streambed or back up the trail on my own. Nobody knew where I was, other than somewhere on the Manitou (its main stem is about eighteen miles long). I had a 1.6-mile walk back to the park's entrance, all of it uphill, and I was ill-prepared to spend the night on the ground.

Did this make me reckless?

I open myself to physical danger not because I am interested in that sort of testing but because sometimes I like to fish alone, meaning with no companions and in places obscure enough to pretty much guarantee my solitude. Quests fraught with uncertainty for me are almost all bodily ones, whether they are explorations of another's waiting body or of a new river. The physical world leaves me both tremulous and ardent, fearful of how little I understand it, fearful of how my desire may misinterpret it, but I do not fear semiwild places themselves—only myself in them.

I'm no ancestor worshipper, but as far as I can see, the narrator of the Viking saga *Snorri's Journey* got it right: "Fearlessness is better than a faint heart for any woman who puts her nose out of doors. The length of my life and the day of my death were fated long ago." I think of my westering paternal great-great-grandfather, crossing the Missouri into the West with Brigham Young and the other persecuted Mormons, all of them headed into the back of beyond—they didn't know where—just that Zion was *out there* somewhere, in a place sere and unfamiliar. Would you call their journey reckless? It certainly offered plenty of physical danger, but it also seems to have been suffused with spiritual certitude. What about my maternal grandfather, sent alone to Minnesota from Hamburg, age eleven years, a note pinned to his jacket—was he reckless, too?

Danger, not so long ago, meant mostly this: a person was entering unfamiliar territory in which her experiences and skills might not be what the place called for. Now we mostly talk of danger in more internal ways, as if the scariest turf were within us. A friend tells me that one of her AA sisters says, "My mind is like a bad neighborhood: it's a dangerous place for me to visit alone." A lot of people go armed into memory these days.

But my questing turns toward the outer world—a lover's body, a stream. And the only way I can learn either of these is to put myself within it physically, take a measure of its heat and cold, its planes and curves, its gradients. Streamside plants, snatches of body hair: worlds to root around in. Is this, I ask you, reckless behavior, or is it not the only way to learn certain things, by wading into them—wading in alone—and seeing what I can see?

As I grow older, I realize that such questing becomes physically, if not emotionally, riskier. I am staking the strength and elasticity of a body no longer very strong and elastic against the considerable forces of rock and current and cold, and increasingly there are moments when this makes me feel afraid. But I can't see how else I can learn what I want to know, be where I want to be. And I cannot imagine what will take the place of this form of questing once I am too frail to undertake it.

Knowing has become a sensual path, a trail through the senses leading to a grail that is itself immaterial. I have to stick my nose out-of-doors, along with my legs and arms and back, have to use them and my hearing and sight and smell to people the world—or rather, to apprehend what creatures make up that world—and through these perceptions to find what they mean to me. Extending myself physically is the only way I know how to do this.

———

"JUST ONE MORE CAST," I muttered for the thirtieth time. I had already lost two Mickey Finn and one Blacknosed Dace streamers to the Manitou's snaggy bottom, had already connected with several fish but lost them around rocks and drowned trees. The shadows now sprawled most of the way across the big pool below the falls. It would be dark soon, and I still had that 1.6-mile hike out to the park entrance. *Just one more.*

I could call this behavior reckless, full as it was of possible dangers. But it was also the only way I could learn how the Manitou's current worked below the falls, how deep its runs were, where the rainbows living there held. For me, learning those habits of the river at this one spot was something worth knowing. How worth knowing it would be if I ended up chattering my way through the night on the bank, jacketless, mosquito-bitten, laid up by my bum knee or a broken ankle, and wondering if morning would bring sun and hikers to help me out of fog and killing solitude, I couldn't have said. But we earn our knowledge by sticking our noses out-of-doors, literally or figuratively. The knowledge of place that I want most of the time demands, as one of my self-imposed conditions, that I conduct my explorations alone; to learn such places in company would be not to learn them in the same way. You could argue that for me, recklessness would be taking on a quest under conditions that narrowed my range of perceptions, that made learning the place less likely. This could mean a physically less risky exploration—one made in the company of five other people, say. But the likelihood of such a trip yielding the experiences, the illumination I was seeking would be very low. Foolhardy, in fact.

I hobbled back up the Superior Hiking Trail to Crosby-Manitou's parking lot. It took me only an hour. Along the way, I saw two other people, both women alone. They seemed as pleased to encounter me as I them, though the reaction of the younger one was a little too effusive for my taste: "Oh, I think it's *just so great* that you're still getting out here," she gushed, tall and bronze and Amazonian, clearly prepared for any physical emergency. Compared to her, I looked like someone AWOL from adult daycare, but yes, I was *still getting out here,* distended knee and all.

Back at the trailhead, I limped directly to the bumper of my old Toyota fishmobile and sagged gratefully against it, waiting to cool down enough to drive home. My injured right knee had swollen to softball size. I was poking at it gingerly when, as if by magic, two more women materialized from the woods. These two, unlike the hearty Girl Guides on the trail, looked as if they'd been teleported from some urban fastness: both wore black-knit halter tops, short swishy skirts, city sandals, and most of their pale skin lay exposed to the hoards of mosquitoes and no-see-'ems that clouded the nearby woods. One of them even wore a small crocheted black shoulder bag.

"Where's the water?" one of them asked.

I imagined them traipsing down the hiking trail to the Manitou in their thin-soled shoes, armed only with lipsticks. "The water?" I pulled out my trail map. "You want to take the Middle Trail down to its intersection with the River Trail. That'll take you along the ridgeline north toward the falls—"

"No—*the water,*" she interrupted me impatiently, waving a

grape-colored plastic Slurpee cup in my direction. "Where's the *water faucet?*"

I stared back pityingly. "This is a walk-in park," I said gently. "It doesn't have water faucets. It doesn't have campgrounds."

They stared at me skeptically, as if I might be the Trickster himself, then turned on their pert heels and disappeared back into the woods.

Over the next few days, I watched the local newspaper closely, steeled to read a report about two seemingly unprepared women who had become lost or dehydrated or injured, crazed with bug bites and sunburn, evacuated from the woods on rescue litters. But whatever adventures those two encountered in Crosby-Manitou State Park were apparently not newsworthy. Reckless by my standards, perhaps by their own they were merely having an evening fling in the woods.

Paradoxically, the more you learn, the higher you climb up the ladder of seeming recklessness. I believe that fishing alone at night poses no profound risks when I choose to do it. I carry a hunting knife, a light jacket, and, that day at the Manitou, a map and compass. The trails I walk are traveled frequently enough that someone will find me if I cannot get out on my own. I've no idea why those two young women felt well enough provisioned to set out on the Superior Hiking Trail dressed for a night on the town, but danger probably has a different address for them than it does for me. Perhaps for them a dangerous neighborhood is internal, not external. Perhaps they are two women who feel armed in each other's company.

12 Midsummer Eve

I HAD SPENT THREE DAYS with my feet up, slowed by a knee injury, and now it was Midsummer Eve. This is no idle matter here near 48° North latitude: our longest day occurs while spring flowers—lilac, crabapples, tulips—are still blooming, and from here it's all, you might say, back downhill, toward the trough of winter.

I was not going to waste this longest and sweetest evening of the year, a twilight as mild and soft as this one, particularly after two days of rain and high winds. So despite my bum knee, I limped out to the Toyota fishmobile and drove up to the Lester River, the farthest northeast of the ten trout streams that course down Duluth's basalt and gabbro hills, scoring the town.

The Lester's headwaters arise some thirty-six miles north of where the river meets Lake Superior below the Highway 61 bridge. By the time the river flows under the bridge, it has been fed by Amity Creek down a long steep canyon visible from Seven Bridges Road for several miles, rarely more than twenty feet wide at high water. Just before its final few hundred yards to the lake, the Lester levels off and widens, and the river begins to flow like shellac, dark and almost undetectably slow. Here it makes a right turn and spreads—you can no longer dignify its movement with the term *flow*, it's more like the simple tug of gravity—between rocky escarpments to its meeting with Superior. Long after the Lester leaves its mouth, it's visible on Superior's surface as a transparent brown tongue, clean-edged, which laps at the clearer, colder water.

When I arrived at the Highway 61 bridge, it was eight in the evening. Armed with binoculars, I limped painfully from the truck to the first of several observation points the city has built overlooking the river. Staring almost straight down into the water's dark coil, I saw occasional rises and rarer arcs where small Kamloops flung themselves out of the water and into the atmosphere we humans occupy. This behavior always enchants and puzzles me, for often it seems to have little to do with surface feeding; it's as if the yearling fishes' high animal spirits simply cannot be contained, and they must jump.

But the slow advance of twilight brings predators, so while the fish may be safer near the surface in the dimming light, the number of their would-be slayers increases. Kingfishers, in their curiously formal plumage, rattled and flitted from branch to branch, occasionally plunging into the stream after their prey. A commotion in a tall streamside poplar on the opposite bank disclosed a dusky bird so big I assumed it was an owl. A few minutes later, when it flew across the river toward me and alighted in a nearby white pine, I saw that it was a juvenile American bittern, gawky and green at the new task of eating on its own. Soon it lifted into the air and flapped back to the far bank, where it joined the kingfishers at streamside, bunched against the gorge's rock wall, wavering on yellow stick legs, its murderous beak hovering close over the water.

Of course, the long dusk brought out human predators as well. These stationed themselves below the bridge, where they lined the round shallow pool above the river's mouth on a narrow spit of gravel and cobble devoid of any life save that of the fish who passed up and down the pool from lake to river. It was a peculiarly joyless place to fish, to my mind, lacking the complexity of trees and shrubs and the creatures they housed.

Two adult anglers were fishing sinking lines, casting, casting, casting, casting impatiently, then stripping in line with hasty jerks. I tried to imagine myself as a fish presented with their flies, which plummeted into the water, then only nanoseconds later tore back to the surface. The exercise seemed almost fantastically doomed; in the dimness of twilit, tannic waters, no fish, however fit, was likely to spot such flies in time to lunge for them. There at the bottom of the pool where the water barely flowed, small preyfish and invertebrates would in all likelihood hover or crawl, not plunge down in the equivalent of concrete overshoes. Nearby, a young boy fished bait, and he hooked 'looper after small 'looper. I noticed how he flicked out his spinning line, let it sink, let it stay. Let it stay some more. Gradually, as if with great reluctance or regret, he wound in a bit of line. Then a bit more. A flurry of white water at the surface: yet another small 'looper.

I returned to the upstream side of the bridge. The sun was now below the horizon, the water below had turned black, and beneath its lacquered surface floated what were apparently two immense, wavering pink dildoes. These proved to be reflections of high clouds in the northwest—priapic, hectically pink, seemingly embedded in the still water. Above them rose a transparent darkness broken by overlapping rise rings that formed dizzying moiré patterns across the surface. Fish broke through the river's cap, their white bellies sudden startling gleams where they leapt and disappeared. Their appearances offered the weird elegance of stochastic theory: while the overall probability of another leap was 100 percent, it was impossible to know *where* the next one would occur or to focus attention on more than one spot at once. Trout would rise where trout would rise.

A deep V spread across the silvering surface of the pool at the base of the bridge. At its apex bobbed a boxy head fitted with improbably small ears—opercula, perhaps, for they hardly seemed like mammal ears. In the low light, the creature looked anything but reddish—frosty, in fact—and I assumed it was a muskrat. But as it glided downstream toward where I stood, low in the water, growing steadily huger, the waning light winked back from the animal's wet gleaming tail, and I saw that it was a beaver. The tail—very good eating, a local trapper tells me—floated like a canoe paddle or lily pad in its wake, as if the beaver were towing a small barge. The creature disappeared under the bridge, swam back within sight, then lodged itself amid small drowned shrubs, where it chewed concentratedly on twigs it held in its small front paws. Finally, it swam away upstream in a random, undulant pattern dignified by the chromed trail it carved, and then disappeared. Meanwhile, the young bittern had not melted from its frozen crouch along the rock wall.

These little dramas unfolded themselves over the space of two hours. A full moon rose gold as field corn in the east, then hoisted itself higher in the deepening dark above the lake. I saw all these things while semis and the visitors' traffic for Grandma's Marathon thundered by fewer than six feet from where I stood. I missed the sensation of casting into the Lester's slow, reluctant waters, missed the tug and twitch that signaled the arrival of an animal I had sought and then conned from his holding spot, missing the summer warmth of the water separating around my bare legs, then closing downstream of them. But fishing isn't merely about catching fish, as almost every angler will tell you. Although drawn to the river by the fish who lived there, I did not need to handle them—but on days like the three I had spent feet up on the couch, under orders to stay out of streams, I had dreamed about the powerful acrid scent of living fish and their sleek mucousy bodies.

I felt newly grateful for being middle aged, for the patience I had finally learned, which helped me stand alongside a busy highway for two hours on one leg, heronlike, watching the network of lives in the river below. A decade ago I could not have done that—it would not even have occurred to me to try.

In withholding myself from the water, I found that I had entered it in a different way, seeing the water animals from a heron's point of view, a kingfisher's, a certain kind of angler's. I watched fish vault from the river for the hell of it. I watched more and more of them leap as night deepened, until the water was hatchmarked by the rings of their passage.

13 Lie Down with Strangers

Wait, I see something: We come upstream in red canoes.
Answer: The migrating salmon.

—Koyukon riddle[1]

PEPSI AND BEER CANS, liter Coke bottles, a big spaghetti jar, yards of snarled monofilament, a Kiss T-shirt, chunks of bloody suet, M&M wrappers, on and on. The banks of the Big Manistee looked like the aftermath of a funny car or Monster Truck showdown.

When I emerged from the scanty woods on the bluff overlooking Suicide Bend, the river was already lined with anglers. It was a late September dawn, and the sky was low and broody, lit only near the horizon, where it flushed Mercurochrome red. The far bank had attracted a full crowd, few of whom ventured into the water; instead, they stood on the sandy shoreline and flung bait toward the fast current in midriver. In their winter motley and the low, muted light, they looked like a chain gang condemned to wield rods in the murk and cold as a penance.

Fishermen had camped on the bluffs overnight, and their tents were ringed by family-sized tins of Spaghetti-Os and Dinty Moore Beef Stew, Old Milwaukee and Schlitz cans, and enough nests of Trilene and Spiderwire to ensnare all of us. Coleman stoves, nylon webbing chairs, big friendly mutts and Labs, the occasional child. I had never fished such a big river before, and I had never fished amid such a carnival atmosphere.

This was not a crowd grounded in any collective code of

---

[1]Quoted in Richard K. Nelson, *Make Prayers to the Raven: A Koyukon View of the Northern Forest* (University of Chicago Press, 1983), p. 69.

angling conduct. People were treading on the fishes' redds. A flotilla of Western drift boats, aluminum skiffs, even rubber rafts bobbed in midriver. Smokers lit up in the water, and the brief sizzle of cigarette butts hit the water around me like static. Most of the anglers were spinner and bait fishermen who cast regularly across my line. In five hours on the river (6:45 A.M. to 11:45 A.M.), I saw only two actual landings. A third was missed when the angler's husband reached over to net her fish and instead knocked the animal off the hook. The salmon slid underwater so quickly that he seemed almost to have been a dream: a dark, large male, barely glimpsed. This was fishing not as introspective ritual but as revel. It reminded me of a D. W. Griffth or Cecil B. DeMille set piece: us the cast of thousands, code name RABBLE.

Beneath three feet of water, along the edges of pale gravel straits tossed up by female chinook, the dark streamlined shapes of steelhead hovered. They had come upstream from the safety and fecundity of the big lake to station themselves nearby while the chinook hens swept aside gravel with their tails. Clouds of eggs buried earlier in the week, stoneflies, caddisflies . . . the steelhead, waiting, waiting like small sharks.

———

THIS WAS MICHIGAN'S BIG MANISTEE below Tippy Dam, a Western-sized river flowing into Lake Michigan about halfway down the west side of Lower Peninsula. Until 1995, snagging was a legal method of taking fish on the Manistee, and in a way, this still showed in fall 1996. Snagging had consisted of throwing out heavy treble hooks on forty-pound test line attached to big saltwater reels, then hauling the lines in through the water with short, jerky strokes. With human luck, some of those hooks would find their marks in the backs or sides of fish. It was an ugly method, random and devastating, less likely to hook fish cleanly than to injure them. Many of the anglers now hurling bait into the river did so with no particular method or direction—like snaggers, they simply hauled back and flung their lines as far out as they could.

"Snaggers are your basic food gatherers, little more. They don't care about the environment, they invariably consume large quantities of beer, and their courage comes in twelve-ounce doses," a Michigan Department of Natural Resources (DNR) agent told me later that morning. "They're not territorial—they'll get right up into your face."

Snagging is efficient only when fish run almost flank-to-flank, but then that's what they did each fall on the Manistee for many years. Back in the bad old 1960s to 1970s, chinook had first been stocked in Lakes Michigan and Superior to control alewives—small oceangoing fish who had made their way into the lakes, creating dramatic die-offs along shorelines in summer—and to replace the lakes' big native predators, the lake trout *(Salvelinus namaycush),* who had died off. In the years that followed, Lake Michigan's fecundity, mainly a result of pollution, created legendary runs on the Manistee. In good years like 1996, Michigan's fall chinook runs gave anglers in the Lower Forty-eight the next best thing to fishing native runs in Alaska or British Columbia: the sight of huge silvery fish fresh from big water heading upstream, planing across the shallows, then hovering ghostlike over spawning gravel in a couple feet of water. The number of these animals is almost incomprehensible: imagine a herd of 25,000 twenty-pound dogs invading a narrow gorge en masse. That's something like the number of chinook who entered the Manistee in fall 1996, far fewer than the historic high in 1986. After 1986, when the big lake became overfilled with top predators, lethal Bacterial Kidney Disease (KBD) struck Lake Michigan's chinook. Then the exotic alewives mysteriously died off, en masse. Both declines prompted salmon fishermen to appeal to the Michigan DNR to "restore" these exotic introductions, which probably says more about anglers' zeal for big gamefish than it does about the inconstancy of collective memory. "Big fish," says Michigan DNR conservation officer Tom Rozick, "do strange things to normal people."

The Great Lakes, even more than northwoods streams, have

been the site of persistent and extreme ecological tinkering. Chinook were imported from the West Coast to deal with an ecological disequilibrium so profound that controversy still exists about the hierarchy of problems in the big lakes. But chinook and lake-dwelling rainbows (aka steelhead), which flourished in such dazzling numbers in the lakes' most polluted years, haven't proven to be as hearty and enduring as the lakes' original inhabitants. Right now, thanks to human-created mobility and technology, the Great Lakes are a weird aquarium of species, some native, some not, all of them fluctuating in size. "Vacant niches," fisheries biologist Peter Moyle observes, "by and large do not exist in nature." Today, the Great Lakes' top predatorial niches are being contested by a deMille-sized cast of species.

With the exception of my day below Tippy Dam on the Lower Peninsula, most of my Great Lakes fishing has taken place on Lake Superior, so what follows describes the changes that have occurred there. As the highest, coldest, and largest of the Great Lakes, Lake Superior has benefited from a delay in the changes that have occurred on the lower lakes. It's quelling to realize that hindsight did so little for so long to protect the greatest of the Great Lakes.[2]

Like the almost warp-speed movement of HIV around the world, the arrival of animals who didn't belong to Lake Superior's waters was the result of Western technologies. The Erie Canal brought the sea lamprey into Lake Ontario, the lowest of the Great Lakes. Those jawless, scaleless, highly predatory fish attached themselves to their prey with big, toothy, hickey-making mouths and sucked out what these days are called *precious bod-*

---

[2] My sources for information on the changes in Lake Superior are drawn from many sources, but I owe a particular debt to Professor Emeritus Thomas F. Water's *The Superior North Shore: A Natural History of Lake Superior's Northern Lands and Waters* (University of Minnesota Press, 1987). The aptly named Professor Waters knows Minnesota's streams, as well as its great lake, intimately, and he writes about all of them knowledgeably and feelingly. My other debts are acknowledged in the afterword.

ily fluids. The Welland Canal, built to move boat traffic around Niagara Falls between Lakes Ontario and Erie, was completed for the first time in 1829 (it's been rebuilt repeatedly); sea lampreys used it, too, to move westward. In only a few decades, they had killed off the big lake trout in the lower lakes. Lampreys were found along Lake Superior's Minnesota shoreline in 1946; by 1953, lake trout populations here were falling by 25 percent a year. By 1960, only 10 percent of the former commercial catch of lakers was being taken. In 1962, Minnesota closed Lake Superior to commercial lake trout fishing.

Sea lampreys were the most thorough and visible destroyer of Superior's fishing, but they were not the first. This largest expanse of fresh water in the world is also one of the most impoverished; its cold and its depth do not support the rich invertebrate and preyfish life of the lower lakes. Seventeenth- through nineteenth-century accounts by European explorers and settlers spoke wonderingly of the lake's supposed fecundity, but observers like Sieur de Lhut, Louis Agassiz, Henry R. Schoolcraft, and Robert Barnwell Roosevelt witnessed Superior at times of year (spring through fall) when fish moved into the shallows and tributaries to spawn. Such observers made the quite understandable but devastating mistake of believing that the entire lake held populations as large as the ones they observed during spawning seasons at the mouths of rivers. Once dispersed throughout the lake, however, the principal species—lake trout, lake whitefish, and lake herring—were in fact fairly scant compared to their numbers in the warmer and more fertile lower lakes.

By the late 1880s, lake whitefish were in serious decline; the logging industry had smothered their shoreline redds with sawdust and bark. Commercial fishing almost finished the job; lampreys later delivered the coup de grâce.

Lake trout, the mammoth predatory char of Lake Superior, had been on the decline even before lampreys arrived, for they, too, were overfished: roughly 4,000,000 pounds of them were taken from the lake each year between 1885 to 1960. Because commercial fishermen consistently removed the largest (and therefore the oldest), breeding-sized fish each year (the average female laker does not become sexually mature until she reaches the age of twelve), the animals could not reproduce fast enough to replace the number who were being slaughtered. Lake trout, too, crashed in Superior, though not as badly as they did in the lower lakes, where they disappeared entirely.[3]

Lake herring filled the gap for commercial fishermen after lake whitefish and trout had entered serious decline. The North Shore's "herring chokers," as the mostly Norwegian immigrant fishermen called themselves, began settling on the North Shore between Duluth and the Pigeon River on the Canada-Minnesota border in the late nineteenth century after the Lake Superior & Mississippi Railroad (1870) and the Canadian Pacific Railroad (1885) opened new markets for Lake Superior fish. In 1890, only fifty commercial fisherman fished on the North Shore. In 1917, the state received 273 North Shore applications for commercial licenses. Soon this number swelled to 400.[4]

As the number of commercial fishermen increased, their impact on the lake's fisheries increased even faster. Hand-lined linen gill nets were replaced first by steam-powered nets (1890) and then by nylon nets (1940s), which increased gillnetting's efficiency threefold. Catch records for the North Shore mirrored the patterns seen earlier for lake whitefish and lake trout: first a steady increase in catches (10,000,000 to 15,000,000 pounds each year between 1915 and 1965), then precipitous declines. It is a

---

[3]Efforts to recreate breeding populations of lake trout in the lower Great Lakes have so far been unsuccessful. University of Wisconsin Sea Grant researcher Richard E. Peterson has found that levels of TCDD, the most toxic form of dioxin, are still too high in the lower lakes for the sac fry of lake trout to survive.

[4]A fine account of this era in Lake Superior's history is the late Ted Tofte's "Wonderland of the Herring Chokers," which appeared in *Lake Superior Angler* (1996), pp. 32–42, the annual magazine of the Lake Superior Steelhead Association. Since publication of Tofte's memoir, the North Shore Commercial Fishing Museum has opened in Tofte, Minnesota.

tale dishearteningly familiar to anyone tracing the technologies of mining, agriculture, fishing. We recent immigrants seem incapable of regulating extraction once we've the means to increase it; it's as if there's a technological imperative to see just how far we can take it.

Overfishing and lampreys played the chief parts in the herring's decline, but a third factor also contributed—another exotic newcomer, the rainbow smelt. Smelt were first stocked in the St. Marys River at the southeast end of Lake Superior in 1909. They made their way into the body of the lake in 1930. This was undoubtedly good news to lake trout, whose native prey, the whitefish, had declined; it was bad news, however, for lake herring, who were already seriously overfished and who now came under assault by an exotic who favored herring fry for breakfast. Rainbow smelt rapidly grew in numbers, creating the legendary smelt runs of the 1950s to 1970s, when North Shore residents happily waded into nippy lake tributaries during the tiny fishes' spring spawning runs, scooping them unceremoniously into plastic garbage pails, lawn bags, and laundry baskets. Then the smelt, too, crashed. Their peak year was 1976, when 4,000,000 pounds were caught. Now you can stand on the bridges overlooking the mouths of the Lester and Talmadge and French rivers in spring and almost miss seeing the little chromed fish, no longer than butter knives, as they swim upstream. The few diehard netters who still pursue them sit sprawled on the gravel, cleaning their scanty catches one by one. North Shore communities that still hold annual spring smelt feeds have to import block-frozen smelt from Canada.

You see how it goes. And these are only the fish native or inadvertently introduced to the lake. Factor in the deliberate introductions to Lake Superior by fisheries folk in Ontario, Minnesota, Wisconsin, and Michigan—never mind the anonymous contributions made by individual anglers—and you can see what a hodgepodge of beings now inhabits this cold, relatively inhospitable lake. Here's the run-down on gamefish introductions alone:

1883 Rainbow trout introduced by Province of Ontario
1889   "   "   "   " Michigan
1895   "   "   "   " Minnesota
1956 Pink (humpy) salmon accidentally introduced by
      Province of Ontario
1966 Coho salmon introduced by Michigan
1967 Chinook salmon introduced by Michigan
1969 Coho salmon introduced by Minnesota, Province of
      Ontario
1974 Chinook salmon introduced by Minnesota
1980 Atlantic salmon introduced by Minnesota

Is there any end in sight? Lake Superior's states and provinces, under the international U.S.-Canadian Great Lakes Fishery Commission, agreed in 1956 to cooperate on a long-term plan to control sea lampreys and to restore Superior's native fish. Even so, each spring, the Minnesota DNR invites anglers (*stakeholders,* as we're called under the agency's current "just-say-yes," feel-good ethos) to say which of the finny tribe we'd like to see next year in Lake Superior and its tributaries. It's as if the DNR is an uncommonly solicitous waitstaff and we, the anglers, are diners choosing from an elaborate menu:

"I'll have the steelhead, please."

"Give me a healthy order of chinook—and make that *big* chinook."

Naturally, this invitation to specify fish-of-choice means many things to many people. The big-game fishermen of the Lake Superior Steelhead Association, for example, want maximal stocking of the fish that thrived in the lake during the polluted sixties and seventies to ensure that such "naturalized species" (their term for the Pacific and Atlantic salmon and rainbow) regain their historic highs. If I had a dime for every good-hearted North Shore fisherman who has groused to me in the past two seasons about the DNR (aka DOES NOTHING RIGHT)'s failure to provide them with enough big salmon and steelhead to "bring back" the conditions of the 1960s to 1970s, I'd be a modestly affluent woman. Members of conservation organizations, on the other hand, view chinook, steelhead, and Atlantic salmon as "exotic introductions," with all that such a term implies of distrust and distaste for such animals. Both groups pay for the same state-stocking and habitat-improvement programs. So whose, if anybody's, view should prevail? What should be done about Lake Superior's crowded top-predator field? Significantly, the creatures who have to live with our capricious human decisions are the fish themselves, and they have no voice, no vote, other than to vote with their bodies: shrink in number, wash up dead on beaches, succumb to diseases.

Right now, thanks to effective sea lamprey control throughout most of the lake and the limits placed on commercial fishing, Superior's lake trout restocking program seems to be working—60 percent of the catch now coming out of Superior is lake trout. In 1996, the U.S.-Canadian Great Lakes Fishery Commission declared that restoration of self-sustaining lake trout populations had been achieved. But the introduced chinook, steelhead, and coho are also top predators in their ecological niches; in fact, some of their niches overlap those of lake trout. Is it showdown time at the OK Corral?

———

WHEN I COULD NO LONGER FEEL MY FEET, I left the Manistee. Up on the bank, looking down over the broad river, its crowd of boats, their blue-fuming motors, and the anglers who rimmed the shore every three or four feet, I felt sorry for the fish: the summation of their life's purpose enacted not amid the solemn rush and solitude of big water but amid such throngs—1,200 pairs of human legs, lines and hooks raining upon them, propellers grinding across their backs. A human marriage consummated midfield during a destruction derby would approximate the pathos of it.

Yet many of the anglers clearly loved the fish—the sight of them, the alien being of them, the idea of them. Others just as clearly viewed them as a mere commodity, a resource to be "harvested." On the river that day, one of the only two salmon I saw netted was caught by a man who didn't even want the fish. "Anybody wanna keep him?" he had yelled as the salmon thrashed frantically in his net.

"Yeah," a friend shouted back, and that reply ended the fish's life, just like that: fate wielded arbitrarily by the more powerful.

When I got back to the inn, another angler was sawing open a buck chinook at the fish-cleaning station. I went over to look at the fish. White mouth, black gums, sharp, recurved teeth, a staring golden eye. Gill covers the size of earmuffs; behind them, gill rakers that still glowed red and plush.

"What are you going to do with the head?" I asked.

He looked up from his work as if I might be mad.

"*Do* with it? I'm gonna throw it in the garbage can."

"Can I have it?"

"What do—? Nope: I don't even want to know. Sure."

I went to get a big Ziploc bag out of my truck and brought it back to him.

About two hours later, he sidled up to me in the knotty-pine Liars' Lounge. Looking down abashedly at the linoleum, he whispered, "I left your, uh, *head* out at the station."

I crunched across the frosty lawn. A room light beyond the cleaning station lit the chunky package lying next to one of the posts.

I picked it up. Heavy, heavy with bone, yet fishbone is lighter than mammals'. I took the bag out to the car and put it carefully in a two-gallon bucket. The gill covers flared over the rim. I thought about the chinook as a living element of the river, brought here by terrible need, and caught, you could argue, by his urgency to complete something. Such a fish is no longer attuned to food or territory, his stomach and crop diminished to nothing so his gonads can swell to immensity and shoot streams of white milt through the water above a redd. Side by side, he and a hen fish, their mouths agape, their bodies straining. Even before he was killed, he was already dying, his tissues oxidizing, darkening, necrotizing. Salmon die so quickly after spawning that it's difficult to get them on ice before they implode.

And the fish's killer?

"I hate to kill them," he had told me while filleting. "But I just have to take *one*."

———

"THIS IS NOTHING to what you saw when snagging was allowed," yet another conservation officer told me over breakfast the next morning. Snagging, he claimed, had attracted "a lower class of anglers" who left sixty-pound test in snarls on the banks, Dacron, beer cans . . .

"But they're all still there," I said.

Still, the number of people fishing was fewer now, he countered. "They come from all over the country," he told me proudly. "If you look at the license plates on the trucks down in the parking lots, they're from all over." (They were not, at least at the Tunk Hole, where I had parked; mine was the only non-Michigan plate.) "Everybody knows that this is the biggest run in the Lower Forty-eight."

And, very sadly, he was right: salmon are extinct on at least 40 percent of their native rivers in California, Oregon, Washington, and Idaho, while on the rest, the number of wild fish has been reduced from the hundreds of thousands, even the millions, to straggling bands of twenty-five, one hundred. Over 97 percent of California's runs are now gone.

In 1990, the Shoshone-Bannock Tribe of Idaho petitioned to have the Snake River clan of sockeye salmon declared endangered under the federal Endangered Species Act. Back in the 1950s to 1960s, the Idaho Department of Fish and Game, believing that sockeyes no longer ran into the lakes and that the lakes could be "rehabilitated" as sport fisheries for hatchery rainbows, dammed and poisoned the sockeyes' spawning waters to remove "trash" fish. The sockeyes who still managed to swim up from the Pacific through the Columbia's elaborate system of dammed and laddered impoundments to their native lakes declined to almost nothing. In 1991, a lone female sockeye made it through the eight dams lying between the Columbia's mouth on the Pacific and the lower Snake. When she finally straggled into Redfish Lake, she was immediately captured by waiting Idaho conservation officers and taken to a hatchery, where she was named Eve.

Eve's successful battle up 970 miles of warded rivers did not end her struggles. Her natural fate would have been to enter the lake, dig her redd, deposit her eggs, and shiver alongside one or several of the male sockeyes who had made it upriver with her while they fertilized her eggs. Instead, the few males who returned were also transported to a hatchery. Eve was stripped of her eggs, the males of their milt, and the fertilized eggs incubated for eventual release to Redfish Lake and the Snake River. Had the fish spawned in Redfish Lake, its waters would have reabsorbed their dissolving bodies and fed the parents to their offspring, then prepared the fry for their eventual long journey to the sea and their own reenactments of their parents' fates.

We humans put an end to that. In 1990, the National Marine Fisheries Service listed Snake River sockeyes as endangered. The next year, a lone male sockeye, dubbed Lonesome Larry, made it upstream to the same point. He was captured, stuffed, and then mounted on the office wall of Idaho Governor Cecil Andrus, who pointed him out to visitors as the victim of the dams that had ruined Idaho's fishing. Today, Idaho's ragged sockeye runs are maintained solely through hatchery releases. Only ten sockeyes reached Redfish Lake from the Pacific between 1993 and 1997. Returns are almost as dismal for Idaho's steelhead and chinook: only 1.2 percent of steelhead and less than 0.01 percent of chinook who leave the river and the hatcheries return to their native gravels to spawn. Ninety to 95 percent of those are hatchery-raised fish genetically less adapted to life in wild waters. Idaho is now suing the federal government for the destruction of its salmon fisheries.

Today, the largest runs of wild salmon in the Lower Forty-eight swim upriver into Lake Michigan tributaries—planted fish gone wild, arguably naturalized, like so many human immigrants whose former homes were wracked with violence, soiled and ruined, and who thrive now in new places. The salmon, of course, are not consulted about their relocation, and the humans who ruined their homewaters are often the same ones responsible for resettling them to new streams thousands of miles away. Much like young children, the fish have proven dumbly adaptable; lacking nothing needed to thrive—clean, cold waters; suitable prey; gravel and cobble streambeds for breeding—they settle in and make themselves at home. Released to distant waters since the 1960s, Pacific salmon have found their way downstream to Lakes Superior, Michigan, Huron, Ontario, turning the silver of free-ranging ocean dwellers, re-ascending their new home rivers in fall for spawning, darkening there to die and blend with the tannic waters of the North Woods.

Most of the steelheaders and salmon fishermen I meet on the North Shore's tributaries don't care much about the fishes' origins or the big lake's carrying capacity: like so many Americans, they seem to believe space is limitless, the environment so expansive that it can absorb newcomers indefinitely, just so long as they are ones they can fish for. The peculiar irony in all this is that despite the big lake's demonstrable instability over the past hundred years, it is now more stable—more recovered, if you will—than the Pacific Northwest from which these fish have come. Compared to the genocide visited on animals besieged in their native streams by overfishing, logging, and road building, Pacific salmon are doing comparatively well in our impoverished waters.

The North Woods is a region that the rest of the U.S. has more or less forgotten. Our climate is sufficiently exacting that we aren't high on most people's list of desirable places to live; the Great White Wall of Winter (annual average snowfall on the U.P.:

246 inches; in Duluth: 60 inches) keeps them away. We've few precipitous slopes, so logging and road building haven't been as devastating to our streams here as in the Northern Rockies and the coastal ranges of the Pacific Northwest. Superior's commercial fishing is regulated more closely than Pacific Ocean fishing. For all these reasons, transplanted Pacific salmon have found more secure homes half a continent away in the Great Lakes than in their native waters.

THE NEXT DAY IN MICHIGAN was everything that Suicide Bend was not. I spent the morning on one of the Manistee's tributary creeks, narrow, overhung with basswood, willow, and poplar, uncrowded, clean. The fish hung beneath transparent coppery water upstream of the road. Around a bend that looked like the very back of beyond, cottages abruptly appeared and crowded down to the water above eroded banks. Nonetheless, the spot was surprisingly lovely in its combination of unkempt, deeply lived human spots and roiling creek, dark with suspended salmon.

Downstream, I walked through one of three side-by-side culverts, feeling the odd closing in of sound, the invagination of space. At the far end, a salmon flipped his tail, and the wet smacking noise rolled down the water toward me. I saw his dark back, gilt sides, and white belly. Beyond lay bright water, the colors of high fall that had not yet appeared on the Manistee.

The creek flowed out of the culvert onto a shallow, sandy flat where watergrasses streamed brightly toward a bouldered drop-off fringed by maples wearing coral and gold. Salmon thrashed upstream through the riffles, finning onto the flats like so many torpedoes. They reminded me of the grainy old black-and-white navy combat footage shown on *Victory at Sea*: chinook as depth charges, raising wakes higher than their dorsal fins, cutting between anglers' legs, veering through waters that didn't even cover them.

It was like stepping on an anthill: sudden, frenetic activity at ankle level, and myself unwittingly caught in the midst of it: shake-ass frantic tailing (their other fins didn't help them in water so shallow), entire bodies swithing to attain maximum torque, and then they were gone upstream, shot through the dark culverts like rockets.

Along the outside bank of the broad flats lay a little pool shaded by white cedars. Fish fortunate enough to run upstream along that side of the creek found their way into it, and they stacked up there to rest. Those who came up the center or the inside bank were less fortunate and were probably startled by their sudden arrival in sunstruck, barely negotiable water. You could almost see their surprise and quick recovery as they flailed frantically upstream toward the safety of the culverts and the deeper water beyond.

———

I HAVEN'T BEEN EAGER for a repeat of Manistee Madness, but I did look forward to my first autumn on the North Shore and the return of its chinook to their homewaters on Lake Superior's tributaries. One of the closest to Duluth is the French River, where the DNR has placed a trap to capture returnees swimming upstream to spawn.

The trap lies some hundred yards from the river's mouth above two small, deepish pools and two modest bedrock falls, all of them shaded by swaying curtains of northern white cedar. The trap is eighty-six inches deep, forty-eight inches wide, and barred on sides and top. The downstream side stands at the lip of a drop-off. Current from the river flows through the trap. If fish power their way up the falls, they swim into the trap through a narrow door the height of the trap and thirty inches wide. There they remain until a fishery worker comes to take them out. Some mornings in the fall, twenty fish await liberation from the trap.

Until two summers ago, getting to the trap on weekends and evenings involved swinging out over the river to avoid a chain-link fence erected to prevent exactly that sort of rashness. Then John Spurrier, the French River fisheries supervisor, decided that if *that many people* were risking their lives to reach the traps when the hatchery's gates were closed, the agency should probably help rather than hinder them. The fence came down, replaced by a footpath. COME ON IN, the improvements beckoned.

After that, my early-morning and late-evening attendance on the fish became much easier. I found myself staying longer each time I visited, now that I no longer had to propel myself out into the dark over the river to get to the trap. Other people's attendance picked up, too, particularly retired people and people with children, lots of whom probably hadn't had the body—or the nerve—to urge each other to vault out over the river.

Being a regular at the fish trap, and a quiet dresser always decked out in uniformlike khaki pants and no-nonsense boots, I soon found myself being mistaken for a DNR officer or someone else of vaguely official capacity. An expert. This case of mistaken identity allowed me to conduct an informal and thoroughly unscientistic survey of people's reactions to the chinook and Kamloops (a race of rainbow trout) who swam into their ken.

Most people seemed touchingly interested in the fish. They wanted to know *who they were,* why they had swum into the trap, how long they stayed there, what happened to them when they were sprung. Most people were not anglers—those guys were downstream in the surf off the mouth of the French, casting into Superior's autumnal northeasters. Few of them ventured upstream to visit the fish in the trap.

Those few who did usually offered a rote commentary: "I'm surprised to see you got anything in there at all, the way you've cut back on stocking." (I would nod seriously.) "Fishing's been lousy since this Lake Trout Thing's started. What's wrong with salmon? Returns are lousy. What're my license and that stamp paying for, anyway? We need more hatchery releases. What're you, closing up the hatchery or something?"

I smiled, I sympathized, I should have been paid for this, like a greeter at Target. The shore fishermen grumbled away, delivered, for the moment, of their deep pain. I would never file a report. (A DNR creel surveyor told me that at least half the fishermen she interviewed last spring exploded at her, berating her for the DNR's current "prejudice" toward lake trout over salmon and steelhead in the big lake.[5])

The fish trap and the DNR bring out the best in us when strangers lie down together atop the fish trap, shading our vision from the light above with hands and caps. We press our noses against the grating, our stomachs, knees, and breasts flattened against the cold, iron-smelling bars.

"You see anything?" a nine- or ten-year-old asks me impatiently.

I point out the long dark body just below us, but the boy can't see it. "Lean out over the back of the trap and look back in from there," I suggest, and as he scuds forward, I smell that peculiar human child amalgam of light sweat, denim, and old food— schoolroom smells. He flops regardlessly near the back of the trap and peers over, down, and then inward and backward. I know what he's seeing: a deep, wavering ceiling of light-shot water, a floor of steel and sky, and in the watery heights, a huge, upside-down fish.

"I see him! I see him! Why's he all black?"

"He's dying," I say. "As soon as they come in from the big lake, they start dying."

"So why'd you trap him?"

"Every morning the hatchery guys come down and take the fish out and bring them up to the concrete tanks and strip the females of their eggs and the males of their milt—"

"What's milt?"

---

[5] In spring 1998, at a public hearing on Minnesota's chinook-stocking program, Dave Koneczny, president of the Western Lake Superior Trolling Association, informed DNR staff, "People who fish Lake Superior have the right to fish for the species of their choice."

I look around furtively for eavesdropping parents. "Fish cum."

"Oh."

"—then they mix those in a big pan and hatch the salmon in big tanks to put out in the river again next spring."

"Oh." A long pause. "But what happens to *these* fish, then?"

"They die."

"Oh. *Cool.*" I can feel the grate bounce under me as the boy draws backward, jumps up, and rattles across the trap to the stone stairs on the riverbank. "Hey Dad! They *die!*"

I have lain down with many strangers atop the fish trap, some of whom needed help first to lie down and then to get up, some of whom arose with swimming eyes and walked away silently, some of whom laughed and rubbed their hands together like villains in a melodrama. I've lain down with one stranger who promptly tumbled headfirst into the pool above the trap. Most people behaved as if they were awed by these immense creatures who swam from the huge lake. But how can I say I really know others' hearts?

Only once have I been troubled by a stranger's reaction. That time, I was seated below the trap on the bank, watching chinook mill about in the lower pool. The fish were close to a yard long, most of them already dark with their own deaths, but a few were still lake pale—water-colored, really.

Below them, wedged between two large rocks, lay one of their dead. Fall 1997 was exceptionally dry on the North Shore, and the French received so little water until early November that fish died offshore while awaiting enough current to run upstream.

Here was a chinook who hadn't made it. He lay on his side, leached of all color, a silver-dollar fish. The pale clear water's refractions magnified and distorted him, so I couldn't say how big he really was, but he looked immense. His telltale kype (the hooked jaw that male salmonids grow during the spawn), his sharp, inward-facing teeth, his great staring gold eye shimmered clearly through the current. Dark torpedo shapes surged upstream above the dead fish. It's almost impossible to resist the human temptation to metaphorize salmon, so I had no difficulty at all in wondering what, if anything, those living/dying salmon made of their bleached comrade lying there on the bottom.

Just then a young father with two sons, boys about five and seven, started noisily down the path toward me. I saw immediately what was about to happen. The older child spotted the dead fish in the water and reached down to pick up a big cobble from the pile of riprap along the bank. He gathered it close to his chest with both hands, like a bowler about to roll a ball.

"DON'T STONE THAT FISH." My voice was very low and scary, a severe voice I didn't recognize.

He spun around and stared at me.

My heart boomed in my chest and ears. I could not explain why it had become so important to me for the dead fish to be left intact, undisturbed there at the bottom of his pool, but at the moment that felt more important to me than whether or not I scared the boy.

His father and brother approached.

"But it's *already dead*," the child said, as if perhaps this fact had escaped my notice.

"Then why stone him?"

The boy looked back at me blankly. Just then his father came up from behind and drew the boy close, as if I might hurt him. All of us froze for a few seconds, and then the man pushed both his children lightly down the path toward the river's mouth, where they soon busied themselves stoning the waves.

My inconstant heart thudded in my ears.

———

I NAILED THE CHINOOK'S SKULL to my fence when I got home from the Manistee so the birds and flies could pick it clean. I didn't know yet if I wanted the immense ivory skull for the animal altar that was steadily piling up on my mantel or if I'd leave it on the fence, one dead being pinioned to another, hoping that they'd eventually grow together into a new form—a weathered, green skull emerging like a dream from a greening gray fence, as they do in Alaska.

What I did know was that the chinook's head deserved a proper ending, and that didn't mean a garbage can. Traditional coastal peoples of the North Pacific bury the skulls of their kills or return them to the waters they were pulled from. Such endings honor the animals' magnificence, treat them as fellow beings deserving of respect. Fish are individuals with their own fates, their own histories and traits, and I believe it defiles them to speak only of "harvests" and "populations."

I fish for them because it's the only way I know of to tap on their door and receive a reply, but I see such encounters as essentially tragic: hard on the fish and shaming to me because our powers are so inequitably distributed. I am reminded constantly of the lonely position we Western humans have chosen to assume via à vis the rest of the planet's creatures. I am trying to change my own relation to fellow beings, but I'll always bear the peculiar burden of my people's tradition, which places humans outside the province of nature and celebrates our estrangement, which sees a fish's life as nothing to celebrate or, once taken, to mourn.

14 Ephoron Leukon

IT WAS A LATE-SUMMER or early-fall evening. At first, they hovered palely above the black water, visible against the dark undercarriage of the highway bridge, but few in number. Then their ghostly shucks began drifting by, white as chalk. Just before dark fell, they so covered the western sky at river's edge that the streamside trees looked pixillated—small bytes of green deepening to black against an almost solid wash of blue-gray wings.

They were *Ephoron leukon,* evening mayflies who live up to the name of their order, *Ephemeroptera,* by hatching into adults, taking flight, mating, laying their eggs back in the water, and dying, all in a single night, and their species name, *leukon,* by their color.

When I entered the Cloquet River on that mild late August evening, the pale creatures, known to anglers as white mayflies, were still streaking toward the surface in the eddies along the riverbank, their bodies angling upward like rocket tracers against the dark water. Once at the surface, they trailed their shucks behind them while they dried their wings, riding the current like spinnakered boats. Then they took to the air, two-tailed males, three-tailed females, joining in midflight, sometimes falling back toward the water as one, then fluttering skyward again, mounting in a near-solid bank four to five feet in height and extending as far up- and downstream as I could see.

The sky was alive with them. They entered my ears, the neck of my shirt. I felt them flutter up the loose legs of my shorts and bat around in my crotch. They crowded behind my glasses and shot up my nostrils. Despite the mosquitoes, who were also out by the millions, seeking their motes of blood, I unbuttoned my shirt and opened the neck wide to funnel mayflies toward me: I wanted to feel them flutter against my breasts, my throat, my sternum, their touch delicate as single hairs.

By the time I stopped at a gas station an hour later for water and looked down my shirt front, shoals of dying mayflies had pooled at my waist, wings still beating feebly, their translucent bodies fitted together like stacked spoons.

15 Industrial Fishing

*We humans tend to see things in the human time scale
because that's all the time we get.*

—Paul Schullery

IF THERE'S ONE TWENTIETH-CENTURY literary chestnut
known to virtually all fly fishermen, it's the late Michigan
Supreme Court Judge John Voelker (Robert Traver)'s "Testament
of a Fisherman," the preface to his 1974 book *Anatomy of a
Fisherman.* I don't recall ever attending a class, lecture, or workshop on trout fishing that hasn't included a pious, even a teary-
eyed, recitation of Voelker's manifesto, which begins like this:

> I fish because I love to; because I love the environs where trout are
> found, which are invariably beautiful, and hate the environs
> where crowds of people are found, which are invariably ugly; be-
> cause of all the television commercials, cocktail parties, and as-
> sorted social posturing I thus escape; because, in a world where
> most men seem to spend their lives doing things they hate, my
> fishing is at once an endless source of delight and an act of small
> rebellion; because trout do not lie or cheat and cannot be bought
> or bribed or impressed by power, but respond only to quietude
> and humility and endless patience; because I suspect that men
> are going along this way for the last time, and I for one don't want
> to waste the trip; because mercifully there are no telephones on
> trout waters; because only in the woods can I find solitude with-
> out loneliness . . .

Voelker's words elicit snuffling responses from listeners, too. Like
the patter of Lab puppies' feet across a kitchen floor and ducks silhouetted against a late-fall sunrise, "Testament" seems to whisper
to outdoorsy men in the tones of creation. By the time the

courtly old curmudgeon died in 1989, though, the distinctions Voelker had drawn between invariably beautiful, trouty places and places crowded with people had broken down significantly, even on his beloved Upper Peninsula. But then, "Testament" was always more fustian than fact.

Not all trout streams flow through beautiful surroundings. Some of them are emphatically industrial. The trout don't care. As long as water offers fish the food, shelter, dissolved oxygen, and spawning sites they need, their earthly surroundings are of supreme indifference to them. It's we anglers who long for banks and trails more congruous with the free-swimming lyricism in the waters.

Industrial fishing is a necessary corrective for me to all the "natural beauty" that Traver bards about in "Testament." Quite simply, most of our lives get lived in settings less idyllic than the tiny U.P. trout streams, beaver ponds, and glacial scour lakes that old Judge Voelker craftily misnamed and deliberately misplaced in *Trout Madness* and *Trout Magic*. We would do well, I think, to learn to love the waters that flow through our workday lives, suburbs, and industrial landscapes.

Three cases I know firsthand are the lower Nemadji River in Superior, Wisconsin; the St. Louis River and Bay, where their waters flow into Lake Superior near Duluth; and Eagle Creek above Savage, Minnesota. All flow through or toward resolutely glum surroundings. The Nemadji winds at an almost glacial pace through the outliers of Superior's warehouse, ore dock, and grain elevator district. Yet in spring and fall, beneath the protective opacity of its red clay surface, the river's mouth teems with walleye, steelhead, salmon, and pike. Eagle Creek erupts from a boiling spring on a hilltop above the small town and emerging suburb of Savage in the Minnesota River Valley, its narrow, winding headwaters bounded by willow, oak, and dogwood, by water hemlock, wild carrot, and marsh marigold. Beyond this screen of streamside greenery, however, you can glimpse the bright flash of car doors and hear hammering from a machine shop. On lower Eagle Creek, Highway 101 trembles with traffic from and to the nearby cement plant, and industrial castoffs—old tires, plastic antifreeze jugs, oily rags, anonymous bits of metal and plastic—line the creek's banks. Yet for all that, Eagle Creek still has its fish, brown trout last planted there in the 1970s and managing on their own ever since. St. Louis Bay is the site of two Superfund sites, but it's also a superb walleye, pike, and smallmouth bass fishery offshore of the Twin Ports' grim satanic mills.

I like to go fish watching in such places. It's peculiarly moving to me, a reminder that surface beauty is no guarantee of healthy waters and that surface homeliness—industrial landscapes like those through which Eagle Creek and the Nemadji flow—is no guarantee of sterility. It is also a reminder that fishing used to be an everyday, at-the-end-of-the-local-road sort of experience for most anglers. Ordinary people—not today's long-distance-commuting "sports"—walked down to the nearest pond, lake, or river to relax after work and maybe pick up something for dinner. Fishing near home fitted the temper of daily life not so long ago: it was something you could walk or bicycle to instead of hauling a trailer behind a truck or driving 900 miles to do, like so many Minnesotans on their annual fishing treks to Montana.

Fishing is still that way on the St. Louis River and Bay. Many of their anglers are bank fishermen who work the shoreline from Superior's city forest, the public fishing pier at Boy Scout Landing in Gary-New Duluth, and the other access points along the river's long estuary.

The people whom I meet fishing along Superior and Duluth's industrial waterfronts, like those fishing Minneapolis's city lakes and the Mississippi River shoreline, are mostly what some fly anglers dismiss as "meat fishermen," meaning that they angle to catch and eat fish. It's true: the odor of fishy shore lunches floats from boat ramps and landings along the St. Louis River more often than along trout streams these days, and the big Dumpsters lining parking lots near the landings are redolent of rotting fish skin and guts. The St. Louis's anglers are a mostly unpretentious lot, dressed in workday clothes, sporting serviceable but distinctly unflashy tackle, plying the water in banged-up aluminum skiffs and runabouts, Grumman canoes, and the occasional rowboat. Wives and children settle into the bayside parks to prepare meals and do a little shore fishing from old web chairs. Odd that such customs should be regarded as suspect or second class.

Early last spring I headed down to Boy Scout Landing on the St. Louis to see how pier fishing was coming along. It was close to sunset on one of those impossibly sweet and mild spring days that carry in their soft air the promise of summer. Swans and geese called on the sedge islands in midriver. Onshore, a group of five elderly men sat in a circle of lawn chairs, socializing. Canada geese strafed the area, honking loudly. Down on the little sand beach, a middle-aged couple in lawn chairs sat casting spinning lures, seemingly without expectation that anything would come of it.

A worn, rickety wooden pier jutted out over the water, and on it three teenagers—two boys and a girl—were fishing with $19 Zebco outfits. On a stringer tied to the pier hung their five plump yellow perch, pectorals red as arterial blood. The kids caught fish continuously—perch, a fourteen-inch walleye, a northern—using nightcrawlers. I realized *I wanted to catch fish that way.* And promptly had a hot flash.

Across the water, popple and birch were shyly greening up. The water was the same della Robbia blue as the sky; the air stirred, faint as baby's breath. Redwinged male blackbirds chirred from the tops of trees. To the west, the St. Louis rolled toward us as the faintest of currents, pooling across an ancient beach of glacial Lake Duluth.

But this was no watery paradise. Signs planted before the fishing pier: EXOTIC SPECIES ALERT (Eurasian ruffe, zebra mussel, spiny water flea) and FISH ADVISORY (warnings that fish taken from the river were seriously polluted and polluting). Sylvan and urban-bucolic as the place looked, it was toxically "hot"—a century-old site of heavy industries that had left the river's bottom sediments almost hopelessly contaminated. The handsome condo development downstream from the pier stood on the site of a paint factory that had dumped lead and arsenic and coal tars into the St. Louis for close to a hundred years, turning the river a different hue each time a new batch of paint was mixed. Farther downstream, U.S. Steel (now USX)'s 600-acre site stood empty and fenced, but still soiled and dangerous, its tiny clogged creek sending PCBs and mercury down into the river basin at the foot of Morgan Park.

It was difficult to summon up such horrors on an evening as sweet as this and the following one. The light was dipping quickly, and the birds stepped up their mating calls. The grass took on a deeper green, and the water, where current moved through it, became a deeper blue. The woods to the west and south fell into shadow and darkened. Soon there were plenty of people out on the pier, all of them fishing for walleye. A boy had just caught a ruffe[1], which everyone called a *ruffy*, and after the crowd had peered at the offending alien, the boy twisted off its head and threw it back into the water.

The ten- and eleven-year-olds seemed enormously self-assured and matter-of-fact about their fishing. I solicited advice from them, for I wasn't able to set up the new spinning rig I'd acquired that morning properly. My self-elected tutor expertly adjusted the drag, admired the reel, waggled the rod sagely. "That oughtta fix ya up," he said. "I'll watch to make sure you're doing okay. It's easy. Just takes a little patience." His eyes narrowed critically as he watched me cast. "Just keep it up. That's it."

A tall, hard-ridden blond man in his forties had just rolled himself a cigarette when his line began to tug. "This always happens to me as soon as I've rolled a smoke," he sighed. "I

---

[1]The ruffe is a small, perchlike eastern European fish unintentionally introduced into the bay in 1985 when an oceangoing ship pumped contaminated bilge water into the Duluth harbor.

started wearing a patch, but I forgot it today." He paused; whether he was talking to himself or me wasn't clear. "On the other hand, I suppose you could get addicted to patches, too." He looked over and smiled.

"Maybe you should offer your tobacco to the water," I said.

"Oh, *I did,*" he replied. "I always do that before I start fishing."

He began reeling in, and it became apparent that he had caught a very large fish. When the fish saw the dock and the man's net, it panicked and tried to run back out, but it had swallowed the hook very deeply. The ten or so of us on the pier gathered around to watch the deeply bowed rod and the water for the next sight of the fish. Collectively we emitted the kindly energy of baseball fans when their team is doing well.

When the fish finally thrashed over the side of the pier inside the man's net, we all cheered and crowded close to look at it. It was a big male walleye, twenty-five inches by the tape. His weird luminous eyes glassily reflected back the evening light at us from the *tapetum lucidum,* the vast retinal layer at the back of the eye that allows walleyes to see well enough to feed after dark. The fish's sides were a brassy gold-green, his belly white and vitreous.

Tuli threaded the fish onto a big galvanized steel stringer and plunged him back beneath the water. The fish was intended, he told us, for his failing eighty-two-year-old neighbor. Now he hoped to catch a few more to make pickles from. The rest of us returned to our stations after slapping Tuli on the back, high-signing him, offering congratulations. It wasn't as if he had done anything remarkable; the fish, after all, had caught himself on an unattended line while Tuli was describing his work in a group home for developmentally disabled adults to me. What we were saluting was his good luck, his good nature, and the great doomed fish. Tuli soon became absorbed in trying to catch another fish and telling me about fishing for suckers up on the Leech Lake reservation, and then it was time for him to leave and tuck his son into bed. He left without catching another fish, carrying away his five-pound walleye.

How was he going to kill him? I asked. I hoped that he wasn't going to make the fish suffocate. Was he going to smash in his head?

"I want to eat the cheeks," he said. "I'll bash him over the head. It'll be quick." The fish gasped on his stringer. I hoped that death would come swiftly.

A few minutes later, another man caught an eighteen-inch lake sturgeon, a pink, shapely creature with sharp scutes, who had been neatly hooked in the corner of its mouth. The children on the pier and I stroked its barbels and fingered the recurved scutes before the guy unhooked it and tenderly put it back in the water.

Little flotillas of Canada geese floated on the water, and an eagle pounded upstream above the river. ("I know," one of the men said when I pointed out the bird. "They have a nest over on that point.") Long shadows began stretching eastward from the pier across the wind-riffled, marine blue water. A party of aluminum canoes paddled up to the landing where the ten of us stood on the pier, laughing and chatting. The kids played with Lunker, my Lab-cross pup. As the spectrum of light compressed, I noticed a shallow eddy about 150 feet upstream of the pier. I thought to myself, *Hmmmm—that looks like a likely spot for fish of some sort.* One of the men fishing on the pier told me that I should try the upstream side of the Highway 23 bridge for channel cats. That seemed like a worthy journey, too.

Lots of anglers won't eat a fish like Tuli's twenty-five-inch walleye. Its color, they say, marks it as a river fish too polluted to consume. Better, they believe, to keep only the pale walleyes who enter the river just long enough to run up to the Fond du Lac Dam to spawn. State fisheries biologists regard this as a mostly folkloric superstition; the real danger, they say, is in eating fish large enough to have built up dangerous concentrations of mercury. According to their recommendations, Tuli's twenty-five-inch walleye would be a one-meal-a-month fish for anyone eating local fish regularly, thanks to its probable mercury load.

I DON'T WANT TO ROMANTICIZE fishing in industrial settings. Certainly it lacks the powerful sort of solitude that forested stream fishing offers as well as the opportunity to spend time within a place that's still largely intact. But it provides something that's perhaps equally important: a deeper integration into the everyday, an appreciation of the intricate give-and-take between waterscapes and large numbers of people. That's something you don't learn much about when you walk three miles off-road to do your fishing, unless you're also doing it in the midst of a clear-cut.

St. Louis Bay south of the Western Lake Superior Sanitary District (WLSSD) treatment plant is a hallowed northland site for warmwater fishing, and while you mightn't want to *eat* many of the larger fish you pulled from the water here—the Minnesota Fish Advisory is pretty emphatic about the need to limit oneself to a few meals a month from small individuals among the bay's top predators (pike, walleye, bass) and bottom feeders (carp, catfish)—*catching* these luckless genetic time bombs is probably a fairly responsible thing to do. No one seems to know how high a concentration of PCBs fish have to consume before they become sterile, but the Minnesota Pollution Control Agency (MPCA) continues to report more details on what local people already instinctively know: high levels of PAHs, mercury, other heavy metals, coal tars, and PCBs have been found in harbor sediments.

The bay is rife with scary biologic hot zones: Superfund sites at Interlake and USX (formerly U.S. Steel) industrial plants, and heavy concentrations of toxins at Duluth's Howards Bay, Grassy Point, Unnamed Creek Basin, and ship slips, and at Superior's Newton Creek/Hog Island and Fraser shipyards. In summer, parts of the south bay are posted with NO FISHING and NO SWIMMING signs. Below the mouth of the St. Louis River, this is a decidedly gray and industrial waterscape, rimmed with oil-grimed concrete slips and rusty iron docks, towers of aggregate, dusty concrete plants and grain elevators, switching yards, and the belching Lake Superior Paper Industries plant. But I see it this way mostly when I drive around it in my truck; by land, it looks grim enough.

Seen from the water, however, particularly at first light, the bay and harbor are beautiful. When not frozen, the water is a smoked mirror, the arched center span of the Blatnik Bridge reflected below, forming a pale circlet of steel. The red Pokegama to the east and the St. Louis to the west pour their highly colored waters into the gray harbor, and along their mud lines, fish feed. At dawn, the lights along the docks and on Duluth's hills blink out, one after another, and the starred water slowly gains visible color and movement. Until that happens, though, you fish mostly by sound.

Sometimes the harbor's big air-powered foghorn wauls out its warning, and the two notes roll over the water like living creatures, panting as they move closer. In summer, the foghorn booms on even the sunniest of days for the enjoyment of tourists. Sometimes an incoming ship bleats pertly three times to signal its arrival, answered once by the operator of the Aerial Lift Bridge.

These aren't waters I'd care to explore in a bellyboat; the wakes kicked up by ore and grain ships and sea lice—I mean Jet Skis—could capsize me. And they aren't waters I'd care to fall into, either. For all the success of WLSSD's celebrated cleanup of the bay, I'm not eager to expose my waders—much less my skin—to the alchemical unknowns dissolved in that water. I'm not saying that anyone unlucky enough to slip in would bob back to the surface transmuted into the monster from *Swamp Thing*, DNA permanently and horribly rearranged by the streambed kiss of PCBs and PAHs, but I can't *not* think about such possibilities: the waters beneath me have been exhaustively and apocalyptically described.

The WLSSD was built in the 1970s to clean up emissions coming from Duluth and the paper mills over the hill at Cloquet in response to the 1972 federal Clean Water Act. Before the treatment plant came on line in 1978 to 1979, the St. Louis River stank so badly and ran so high with foam that visitors to Jay Cooke State Park below the Cloquet mills avoided going near the water. From the state park, the river flowed over the Fond du Lac Dam and past the paint factory at Boy Scout Landing, past U. S. Steel, past Interlake, past a dozen other sites that pumped wastes directly into the river or bay, where they joined sewage waste from the City of Duluth.

Those bad old days still live on in urban legend. Local anglers continue to solemnly repeat the tale—always involving a "friend of a friend"—who fished off the wlssd's plant, "reached his hand into the current to unhook his bass, and the next day his hand was all blistered and red." Bass who glow in the dark possess an imaginary half-life independent of the wlssd's and the mpca's current readings. That's understandable: for too long, St. Louis Bay's fish *did* all but glow in the dark.

Or simply disappeared. By the 1960s, the bay was so polluted and warm that the only fish who could survive there were black bullheads, fish who can live in water almost devoid of dissolved oxygen, fish that one Minnesota Department of Natural Resources document describes as "the next thing up from mud." For decades, the dnr didn't bother to conduct studies of the bay's fish or creel surveys of its anglers. The bay was considered dead.

"It was like a sewer out there," recalls John Spurrier, dnr fisheries chief in Duluth. "Oh, in spring a few die-hards would fish for the walleyes who swam in from the lake to spawn upriver. They convinced themselves that walleyes with white bellies were lake fish and safe to eat and that ones with yellow bellies were resident river fish and too polluted, but that was just rationalization." By summer, the bay and the St. Louis River smelled so bad that nobody ventured out to fish on them, anyway.

But for all that . . . Watching this river where big strong fish swim again despite the damage-dealing bottom sediments, I witness the resilience of the waters and the cleanups that people can achieve. Despite the horrors detailed in the MPCA's latest harbor waters assessment, the industrial waterways of the Duluth-Superior waterfront are far healthier now than they were back in 1977, when they barely supported aquatic life. Some of the worst sites have been cleaned up, and something close to zero emission has been achieved at other still-active sites.

As soon as the runoff from Cloquet's mills began flowing over the hill by pipeline to WLSSD in 1978 instead of down the St. Louis River, fish started returning. "We saw the walleyes make a big comeback almost immediately," says John Spurrier. "The changes we're seeing today are still repercussions from the cleanup. As late as 1986, 75 percent of the fish we found in the bay were only three species: perch, black bullheads, and white suckers. In 1994, bullheads and perch were less than 10 percent each of our samples, and channel cats, lake sturgeon, walleye, and Eurasian ruffe were all more than 10 percent each. If you accept the idea that diversity is a sign of health, then the bay is a much healthier place today."

To some extent, how we choose to view an industrial waterscape like the St. Louis Bay depends on how resilient we believe natural systems are and where we fall along the cup-is-half-full, cup-is-half-empty spectrum. A dear friend of mine says, "We have to *choose* to be happy," and the choice between half-empty, half-full strikes me as a case in point: do we choose to be overwhelmed by the amount of cleanup remaining to be done, risk the paralysis and despair that go with that emphasis, or do we take heart from the cleanup that's already taken place, gain confidence from it, and risk the complacency and overtrust in technology that accompany it?

For the late Judge Voelker, a place like the St. Louis Bay might well have seemed a hellhole, its once thick rim of boreal forest long since logged off to build charmless port towns and railroads into the interior, its once renowned coaster brook trout fishery reduced to hatchery-bred populations of nonnative fish.

I could choose to look at the river and bay that way, but I don't. The fish who swim here now are different from those whom nineteenth-century anglers exclaimed about; you certainly won't find three- and four-pound brook trout nudging up the Nemadji anymore. Warmer waters have probably permanently displaced the coasters from this part of their old range. But introduced Pacific salmon surge up the Nemadji each spring, reinventing home. And after being hunted to near-extinction in the bay and Lake Superior a century ago, lake sturgeon have returned. Today, they're regularly taken by deepwater lake trout anglers on Superior and by bank fishermen at Boy Scout Landing. State fisheries biologists find them in their catch nets miles out in the lake. Northern pike, black bass, and walleyes spawn in the river while the lavish pollution visited on this place gradually silts over or (maybe) gets dredged out.

Aldo Leopold, the great Wisconsin game manager-turned-ecologist, believed that "we can be involved only in relation to something we can see, feel, understand, love, or otherwise have faith in" *(Sand County Almanac)*. Industrial fishing offers that tangibility—it is more visible, more constant, and far closer to where most of us live than the wilderness fishing we dream of and long for.

The resilient fish of a place that "we can see [and] feel" did not attract angler-protectors or weekend habitat-restoration workers until fairly recently. The first efforts to clean up the St. Louis occurred in the late 1960s, when local residents and business people began calling for restoration of the river. As late as 1989, the hardy, mostly warmwater inhabitants of the river and bay's industrial waters had to fend for themselves. Anglers intent on restoring fishing waters preferred to work on Voelker-style streams deep in the North Woods.

Stream preservation and rehabilitation had become part of the Wisconsin DNR's fisheries management program and an academic discipline at the University of Wisconsin by the early 1960s.[2] These were matched at a volunteer level by the organization Trout Unlimited, a coldwater environmental group that was founded in northern Michigan in 1959. Between them, state and volunteer agencies were able to accomplish a lot on northwoods streams, whose chief problems often lent themselves to successful remediation: inadequate cover for fish, bank erosion, and channelization. Working in beautiful, Voelker-like surroundings was gratifying to anglers, and the improvements they made on diminutive streams became almost immediately visible.

Meanwhile, the St. Louis River and Bay sat and stunk. Its contaminants—chlorines, dioxins, PCBS, mercury, and coal tars—were substances so toxic that even the federal Environmental Protection Agency hasn't decided yet whether to dredge them up or allow them to silt over. The latter seems unlikely: Lake Superior doesn't take in a lot of silt, except where the Nemadji, St. Louis, Pokegama, and Red rivers enter its southwest end, swollen with iron red clay that cleaves the blue lake each spring and summer like a tongue. But the bay is huge: almost nineteen miles long, with a surface area of 11,495 acres. Restoring something so huge and abused still challenges the federal government, so it shouldn't be surprising that citizen volunteers were slow to take on such a project.

But they have. Since 1989, the St. Louis River Citizens' Action Committee has chipped away at what is remediable: monitoring ship wastes, down-ramping rates on the Fond du Lac Dam, feedlot inflows, and silvicultural practices; acquiring land for buffer zones; educating citizens and golf-course managers about lawn chemical and yard wastes; protecting heron rookeries and habitat for bald eagles, terns, plovers, and other waterbirds—the list

---

[2] See, e.g., Sid Gordon, *How to Fish from Top to Bottom* (1955, repr. Stackpole Books, 1996), Ray White and Oscar Brynildson, *Guidelines for Management of Trout Stream Habitat in Wisconsin* (Wisconsin DNR, Technical Bulletin 39, 1967), and Robert Hunt, *Trout Stream Therapy* (University of Wisconsin Press, 1993).

goes on and on, a daunting and magnificently complex vision of what makes up the health—and sickness—of a semi-industrial, semiwild place.

———

AT DAWN ON AN AUTUMN MORNING, I canoed near the bay's southern end at Boy Scout Landing, and through steam curling into the cold air, I saw Gary-New Duluth bobbing on the horizon, a little diorama, nothing but lights: first a whole chain, then a few, then none. The water rocked rhythmically beneath me; no tide here, just the steady, one-way current of the St. Louis flowing toward the bay and the faint chiming of young ice as it drifted by on the surface. The air smelled sharp with winter, its undertone fishy, watery. On either side of the river, where the water fell away, stood palisades of leafless birch and popple. I tried to imagine what this place looked and smelled and sounded like a hundred years ago when booms of white pine floated here, bound for Duluth and Superior mills. And what it looked and smelled and sounded like only thirty years ago, when it ran foam-crested, almost lifeless. On three sides, I could see some of the bay's hundreds of miles of shoreline: northwoods forests of conifers and popple that crowded down to shallow, weedy bays, and sand-and-gravel yards where not a blade of grass waved beyond the chain-link fence. In one way or another, most of the river and bay offers anglers uncanny solitude, considering that both are sandwiched between busy industrial ports. Downstream at the WLSSD's treatment plant, a current of 80° water poured steadily into the bay, attracting walleye, pike, and smallmouth to the invertebrates and small fish who gathered and grew there in the warmth. I could imagine the gulls fluttering overhead, attracted to the abundance.

I don't prefer the bay to less human-mediated surroundings, but to exclude it seems an odd denial of where most of us North Americans now live, which is to say within sight of cities. Better, I think, to acknowledge and spend time on such waters. Doing so

may be the first step toward repairing the damage earlier generations of settlers have done here. Ecologists, Aldo Leopold wrote,
live in a world of wounds, mindful of all that is damaged and
missing from the land, air, and water. But the corollary is also
true: we can live mindful of the world's resilience, and honor
what becomes, once ruined land and waters are given a chance to
repair themselves.

A noisy splash off to my right, and I saw the faintest of large
forms, a deep sunburnt shape rolling just beneath the surface,
behavior I associate with the North Woods' great lake sturgeon,
once again a living part of this river. Na-me, as the Ojibwe call the
sturgeon in their origin tales, is a powerful spirit who controls
other water beings. As first light slid across the water, coursing
upstream, I waved to the rolling fish. This ancient being, and my
little petroleum-derived Kevlar canoe, and the human industries
down in the harbor that dishonored this bay, and the human
technologies that are now partly restoring it, and the few diehard bank anglers off to my left on the fishing pier—together
these wove together a dreamtime harsher than the ones I have
found on northwoods streams, but one as true.

16 Shocking Natives on the Split Rock

I am Salmon Fontinalis,
To the sparkling fountain born,
And my home is where oxalis,
Heather bell and rose adorn
The crystal basin in the dell,
(Undine the wood-nymph knows it well,)
That is where I love to dwell.
....
Noted oft in ancient story,
Erst from immemorial time,
Poets, anglers, hermits hoary
Confirm my vested rights sublime.
All along the mountain range,
'Tis writ in mystic symbols strange:
"Naught shall abrogate or change."

—from Charles Hallock, "Baptism of the Brook Trout" (n.d.)

WE WATCHERS OF THE WILD all have our unicorns—those animals, plants, geological formations that seem near-mythic, almost unattainable, and emblematic of the places we seek out. These differ, of course, depending upon where we happen to find ourselves. Here at 48° North, the animal that most stirs my imagination that way is the coaster brook trout.

At this point in our human history, very large brook trout are almost exclusively creatures of the Far North: Labrador, northern Ontario, and Manitoba. Little more than a century ago, brookies of five to six pounds could be found in the Rangeley Lakes of northern Maine, the Upper Peninsula of Michigan, and along the shores of Lake Superior, where they were known as coasters. Coaster-sized brookies still swim the Nipigon River of northwestern Ontario, but otherwise they have been all but eradicated from the southern end of their range—if, indeed, the remaining big fish of the South are genetically similar to the trout of the Far North.

This is only one of the questions that humans can't answer about these unicorn fish. Nineteenth-century writers who observed big coasters—so called because they hovered along the coastlines of Lake Superior and its largest island, Isle Royale—when they'd come into the shallows to feed during spring months, and during fall, when they'd ascend rivers to spawn, believed that the fish were plentiful year-round, and fished for them as if they were. Newspapers and guidebooks made coasters sound like everyday creatures, and no doubt they were less rare before their spawning rivers were scoured of holes and debris and gravel, and widened and slowed by logging. But the anecdotal accounts by anglers more than a century ago who claimed to have caught two hundred pounds of five- to six-pound fish should be taken with the same grain of salt as contemporary accounts of record walleye and pike catches.

Fish biologists theorize that the almost fabulous size of northern brook trout is a result of living in cold lake waters that promote slow but long growth. Farther to the south, brookies rarely reach the age of three. Here at 48° North, in scantily nutritious streams whose temperatures become near-lethal in hot summers, the fish seldom get much bigger than six to eight inches. But the farther north the fish live, the cooler the summers, the more even the river levels, and the colder the waters. If fish in such latitudes also are lake dwellers who use streams only for spawning, they are guaranteed fairly unstressed lives; the lakes provide them with a constant food supply and relatively even temperature year-round. They grow to be five, ten, even twelve years old—basketball-sized fish as gaily and improbably marked as their hand-sized creek counterparts.

Anyone who has seen such a brook trout, particularly a male in his spawning colors, knows what I mean by calling him the unicorn of fishes. His back is crazy with vermiculations—jagged dark traceries like forked lightning or beetles' tree galleries—that drape over his sides like a short cape and spread across his tall dorsal fin. Below the vermiculations, his sides are speckled with jolly red, yellow, and blue spots (accounting for the Canadian term for him, the *speck*), a gilded goldfish belly during the spawn, and fins tri-striped in white, black, and red. His tail is almost square (accounting for the old Yankee term for him, the *square-tail*) and his body deep. So successful is his cryptic coloration from above that when suspended beneath the surface of northern waters, such a trout is all but invisible. In spring and fall, when the light is so low that the water appears black, you look not for the fish but for the telltale leading edge of white on his tri-colored pectoral and pelvic fins. In summer's bright broken light, you look not for the fish but for his shadow on the streambed.

The biggest remaining population of coaster brook trout in the Lake Superior drainage live offshore of Isle Royale, a national park in the big lake near the Minnesota-Ontario border. Seventy percent of the park is under water, and there the coasters—roughly 200 breeding-age fish of each sex—swim the basalt shoals eleven months of the year (five under ice), searching out minnows, chubs, troutlings, and, in season, hatching mayflies. In October, after the park is closed to visitors for the winter, they swim into the island's harbors to feeder creeks and spawn. Some die from the rigors of spawning; most swim back to the relatively shallow waters surrounding the island and spend the remainder of the year there, at the edge of the big lake.

These are much-studied creatures, for they constitute the shape and genetic material of human hopes to restore their kind to all of the upper Great Lakes. Here, in this plan to restore coasters to the lakes, these water animals' unicornlike qualities become most visible, for restoration seems as much a matter of wishful thinking as of plausibility. The reasons for my saying this are everywhere evident around the lake. Its tributaries are eroded and degraded, with water temperatures approaching the inviable for brook trout. Scores of fishermen line the larger tributaries during the coasters' fall spawn, waiting for the chinooks. The lake itself is crowded with other large predators, some of whom may have taken over the coasters' feeding niche.

It's axiomatic that you can't restore an animal unless the habitat he needs is still (or again) available. Not much evidence exists, unfortunately, that what coasters need can be found elsewhere than around the shores of Isle Royale and a very few North Shore streams.

AT 8 A.M. WE WENT OUT TO ELECTROFISH the Split Rock River up to the first natural barrier, a series of imposing waterfalls that rear up twenty-five to thirty feet, a mile above the river's mouth. The Split Rock River is unusual in having its first barrier so far upstream: most of the North Shore's waters run only a short distance from their mouths at the lake to the first high fall or height of land.

The Split Rock's two branches drain a watershed of some forty square miles, joining a mile above the falls, where the river drops 400 feet to the falls in a grade of almost 8 percent. Below the falls, the river meanders downstream through a broad, flat valley to its mouth below Highway 61. The last half mile is surrounded by marsh, its banks deeply cut back in spots, the water crowded by the root wads of willows and alders.

Here Jeff and Christine, DNR fisheries specialists, and I, DNR volunteer, donned neoprene waders, linemen's rubber gauntlets, and Corkers (steel-cleated wading sandals wound ineffectually around our Schmoo-footed boots). Jeff shrugged the portable forty-eight-pound electroshocking unit onto his back, picked up the long-handled shocking probe, and stepped slowly into the stream. Christine and I followed with salmon-sized nets, stirring up clouds of silt that floated trainlike in our wakes. Poking the probe here and there beneath undercut banks and downed roots, Jeff sent electrical currents racing through the water. Christine and I lingered behind him, ready to net whatever fish became temporarily stunned by the shock and sent upward onto the current. In a twenty-minute walk, Jeff managed to bring up—quite literally: electroshocking sends the largest fish belly up to the surface—one steelhead parr and one big chinook. The fishiest-looking spots didn't prove to be very fishy: a few suckers, a creek chub, some lovely, quicksilver minnows that Jeff heaved over his shoulder with a fine nonchalance which horrified me.

We were searching for coasters as part of a project to determine whether or not they are genetically distinct from their stream-run cousins. Since 1991, Nipigon-strain coaster eggs have been donated each year to the Grand Portage Chippewa Band by the Dorion Fish Culture Center for culture and release into reservation rivers. In fall 1995, the first sexually mature fish from these stockings returned from Lake Superior to reservation streams. By 1997, three successive year-classes had returned. The three-plus-year-old fish were returning to spawn. "They were crowding three pounds. Some of them were over twenty inches," recalled Lee Newman, a U.S. Fish & Wildlife Service fisheries biologist who worked with Grand Portage conservation officers on coaster restoration.

Newman views the project he co-administers with the Grand Portage Band's John Johnson as a model of "low-tech, state-of-the-art" reproduction: "This was a shoestring project that could be done on a few hundred dollars a year, but it was so ingenious! The [fish]eggs were placed in the gravel of reservation streams that had been home to coasters fifty years ago, and then we let nature take care of them.

"The band went into this knowing that they wouldn't be harvesting any 10,000 pounds of fish," Newman says. "But tribal elders used to catch coasters on reservation streams fifty years ago, so the band wanted to restore them." Newman gets dreamy when he talks about the big coaster brook trout of Nipigon and Isle Royale that the band and his agency are trying to bring back.

"When brook trout go down to the big lake," he says, "they get very silvery. The outer surface of their scales acquires a layer of guanine that coats them like spray paint. After they come back into the streams in fall, their normal color returns. But when they first come back in, some of them are iridescent orange and silver and sort of purple. They just *glow.* Even people who've seen them before—they're speechless for about thirty seconds. Coasters attract fanatics as bad as muskies do.

"And there's nobody better able to restore and protect these fish than the tribes. Nobody. Because the key to restoring coasters, or sturgeon—or any fish, for that matter—is to keep them alive until they reach maturity. The Grand Portage Band leaves them alone, so the net result is 2.5- to 4.5-pound fish—and we're finding them in *very small* streams.

"I ask you: Where else could those vulnerable, beautiful animals expect better protection than on a reservation?"

———

FARTHER UPSTREAM, WE FOUND our first brook trout, a twelve-inch, half-pound fish that Jeff thought might be a coaster. It was pale as a hatchery brown, its skin either sun-bleached or the silvery cast of coasters just after they've come in from the lake, where silver and gray is useful cryptic coloration. Jeff couldn't determine its sex. I wondered if the fish's paleness mightn't simply mean that it spent a lot of time near the Split Rock's mouth, which offered no shade except beneath undercut banks.

"Well, it's certainly pale, and coasters are supposed to be pale," Jeff said wistfully, hope hanging in every word.

Christine clipped the little conundrum's adipose fin and carefully tweezered it into a plastic Baggie, followed by a scale scraping. We released the brookie, who disappeared with fine dispatch into the brown murk.

Gradually the stream's meanders straightened and gained grade and speed, then making occasional right turns instead of lazy curves. Upstream the water was shallower, rifflier, with deep pockets and pools along the outside bends. The vegetation changed, becoming more forested; birch, white cedar, black and white spruce, and balsam fir lined the banks. At the head of a riffle forking into a broad, shallow run bottomed by cobble and a narrow, deep side channel crowded by alders, Jeff shocked a chinook who had been finning quietly in the shade of a huge downed white cedar. He was a male fresh in from the lake, still pale and green, and he floated lifelessly downstream to me. I gently scooped him up in a net and then carried him down the run, away from Jeff's electro-probe, so he wouldn't get shocked a second time.

He lay belly up in the net, gills barely moving, as I stumbled downstream. At the bottom of the run, I stopped, and by then he seemed to have stilled entirely. I touched him with my wet glove; he didn't respond. I remembered the DNR electroshocking instructor's warning: "Some of the bigger fish are going to die—there's no way around it. If that would really distress you, you should probably think about working on a different project."

I stared down at the thirty-inch fish in my net, his white belly narrow and unmoving. *Please don't let him be dead,* I prayed to nothing in particular. He didn't stir. I bent down and laid the net on the stream bottom. The fish lay loglike in the bottom of the bag beneath the glinting current. *He's dead,* I thought despairingly, and reached out to touch him.

In that second of contact, he rolled onto his side, righted himself with an immense flail of his tail, and surged out of the bag. I had never seen a fish swim downstream before, and I'm not sure that I did then, exactly—the water in the riffle wasn't as deep as the fish's lateral line, and this chinook was a big, deep-bodied fish, so I'll say instead that he *shimmied* his way downstream, torquing across the cobbles with lashes of his tail, his body well out of the water. The speed of his going plowed a high watery furrow that curled over on itself and glowed in the midday light. Even after the great fish had finned away far downstream, I could still follow his progress by the snaking course he cut.

IN THE MEANTIME, Jeff and Christine had found another brook trout, this one bigger than the twelve-incher they had measured downstream. We took it to a gravel spit alongside a nearly dry tributary to weigh, measure, and clip. This one, too, was pale and silvery. It—they couldn't determine its sex—weighed 340 grams and was 375 mm long. Christine clipped its adipose fin for DNA analysis later; Jeff scraped off some flank scales and sealed them in an envelope. The scales would be scrutinized through a microscope for their telltale annular rings, which yield the same stories as those in a tree's trunk: age and seasons of faster and slower growth.

We stared at that fish for a long time. It hung in four inches of water near the bottom of the plastic bucket, finning quietly, its mouth opening and closing in small, neat pops. At that time of year, male brook trout commonly sported gilt bellies the hue of domestic goldfish; this fish's belly was white. Stream male char in fall have tiny kypes, the hooked jaws that male salmonids develop during the spawn. But this fish's jaws were neat, small, and shapely, those of either a female or a nonspawning male. Stream brookies' backs are often so dark that they're almost black, lit only by paler vermiculations, which imitate so precisely the appearance of broken light on moving water.

Thoreau, in *The Maine Woods,* called brook trout "the fairest flowers, the product of primitive rivers . . . these bright fluviatile flowers," yet he fished enthusiastically for "the foolish race" in quantity, until "a good blanketful of trout, ready dressed" had been caught. It was Thoreau's generation that presided over the dramatic decline in native brook trout throughout their range. Perhaps not coincidentally, that generation invested brook (or *speckled,* as they were more likely to be called) trout with a fully developed character. Anglers who valued the speck highly attributed a variety of virtues to it: sagacity, dignity, and ennobling beauty. Genio C. Scott's accolade in *Fishing in American Waters* (1869) was typical:

[The brook trout] is an intellectual kind of creature, and has evidently a will of his own. He looks sagacious and intelligent—sedulously avoids thick, troubled, and muddy waters—prefers the clear spring stream—displays an ardent ambition to explore streams to their source—is quick, vigorous, and elegant in his movements—likes to have the exclusive command of the stream—keeps up a rigid system of order and discipline in the little community of which he is a member—exhibits a remarkable degree of nicety and fastidiousness about his food[1]—is comparatively free from vulgar, low and groveling habits—entices his pursuer into the loveliest scenes of Nature's domains—calls forth from man his utmost ingenuity and skill—and, in a word, in every stage of his existence preserves a dignified demeanor, unattainable by any other living occupant of the streams.

Brook trout, unlike pike, fed on foods that ennobled them, wrote Charles Hallock in *The Fishing Tourist* (1873): "They mingle voluntarily with none but the select coterie of their own kith and kin, and carefully avoid the contamination of groveling bottom-fish." Anglers who admired the brookie saw in its decline and usurpation by "German" (brown) trout an end to all that was graceful and natural in fishing—the democratization of what had been choice and exclusive by what was crude and popular (or populous).

By the time *The Speckled Brook Trout* was published in 1902, its essays on stateside brook trout fishing were mostly elegiac and looked back to the 1870s, the last decade in which New England stream fishing held up fairly well. Those of the book's essays concerned with contemporary brook trout fishing focused on streams north of the border, where "Canadian forests are yet undesecrated, and are likely to remain so": Newfoundland, Labrador, northern Quebec, and Ontario. There large brook trout, like those described a generation earlier by Thoreau, Scott,

---

[1] *Grubs? insect larvae? dead flies?* Love is indeed blind!

and Hallock, could still be found. Thus was the brookie's twentieth-century "character" set: *In wildness is the preservation of the
world.* Like the gray wolf, the brookie became emblematic of
wilderness, of remote, untrammeled places.

  By 1920, when the brown trout had mostly replaced the
brookie in the streams of New England and the mid-Atlantic
states, anglers had yet another reason to despise its usurper: the
brown trout was a Hun, symbol of the hated enemy of the recent
Great War. Those anglers who welcomed the importation of
European brown trout or the planting of native smallmouth bass
into new watersheds viewed the speck's passing as one of the inevitable prices of human progress. Waters that could no longer
support brook trout could, at least, support these industrial-age
fish. In his *Book of the Black Bass* (first published in 1881, and
then repeatedly revised for the next 30 years), James A. Henshall,
the chief lyricist of the black bass and one of the original members of the U. S. Fish Commission, dismissed the brookie as a fish
whose time had passed:

> [The bass's pre-eminence], I think, is inevitable; if for no other
> reasons, from a force of circumstances occasioned by climatic
> conditions and the operation of immutable natural laws, such as
> the gradual drying up, and dwindling away of the small trout
> streams, and the consequent decrease in brook trout, both in
> quality and quantity; and by the introduction of predatory fish
> in waters where the trout still exists.
>
> Another prominent cause of the decline and fall of the brook
> trout, is the erection of dams, saw-mills and factories upon trout
> streams, which, though to be deplored, can not be prevented; the
> march of empire and the progress of civilization can not be
> stayed by the honest, though powerless, protests of anglers.
>
> But, while the ultimate fate of the brook trout is sealed beyond
> peradventure, in open, public waters, we have the satisfaction of
> knowing that in the black bass we have a fish equally worthy, . . .

and which at the same time is able to withstand, and defy, many of the causes that will, in the end, effect the annihilation and extinction of the brook trout.

The gradual healing of public forests and waters in the North Woods has been accompanied in the past thirty years by an interest among state and federal resource agencies and some anglers in restoring native fisheries, a movement paralleled among Chippewa bands, which are trying to reconstitute pre-invasion fisheries by reintroducing "heritage fish." These complex cultural aspirations were now embodied in the fish lightly finning in the bucket at our feet—a wild brook trout whose parents might be coasters, the football-sized specks described by so many travelers and anglers to Lake Superior in the second half of the nineteenth century.

This trout would have stood out, had it ventured into the darker, more shaded channels of the Split Rock River, because of its paleness. Its back was ocher sprinkled with the usual vermiculations, these of almost a pure yellow. The red on its fins was a bleached red-orange. Nothing was vivid about this fish's coloration, and nothing was cryptic, either, for the dark, tannic stream stretch of the river where we found it. If you could design a fish to look as unlike a stream brook trout as possible and yet *be* a stream brook trout, the result would probably look like the fish now swimming in our bucket.

And yet . . . Thaddeus Norris, in *The American Angler* (1864), saw nothing remarkable in pale stream brook trout:

> All observing anglers have noticed the effect of water and light on the color of Trout; those taken in streams discolored from having their fountains in swamps, or flowing through boggy grounds where hemlock and juniper trees grow, are invariably dark, their spots less brilliant, and their sides and bellies frequently blurred; while those of bright streams flowing through open meadows or cultivated fields, are as remarkable for the deep vermilion of their spots, their light color, and delicate shading.

So had we found any coasters? Nobody knows yet. DNA analysis will establish whether or not the fish we and other teams found are genetically similar to the coasters of Nipigon, and whether or not they are similar to the stream brookies above the North Shore's barrier falls. These are separate questions; one does not necessarily lead to the other. The fish may be coasters, they may be a native strain of below-the-barriers stream-run fish, they may be a third strain, or they may be hybrids.

———

COLD AND TIRED, WE DROVE BACK from the Split Rock shortly after noon that fine fall day. I lay against the backseat, thinking about Norris's angry eulogy to the northern forests' big brook trout. He wrote it almost 150 years ago, but happily only the first part is still true:

> In the rivers and brooks of the more settled part of the country, Trout have decreased both in numbers and size. This is to be attributed to many causes; to the clearing up of forests, exposing the surface of the ground to the sun, which has dried up the sources of sylvan brooks, or increased their temperature, and consequently that of the larger waters which they feed, rendering them less suitable for Trout.... Streams which once had few fish besides Trout in them, now abound with Chub and other inferior fish. The saw-mill, with its high dam obstructing the passage of fish, and its sawdust filling the pools below; the tannery, with its leached bark, and the discharge of lime mixed with impure animal matter extracted from the hides, flowing in and poisoning the Trout, have done more to depopulate our waters in a few years, than whole generations of anglers. It is an old story everywhere along our mountain streams, of how abundant Trout *once* were; and the angler is shocked and disgusted on every visit.... Any law against such vandalism in the United States is seldom or but feebly enforced.

17 Hooked

*The Morrison is a small dark fly noticed by Colonel Morrison upon the
waters of a little lake in the Northern woods, and before observed in
many other places, always eagerly seized by the trout. He preserved no
specimen, but described it as a tiny black fly, having a dark red body
ringed with black. The color in the body he thought was due to the blood,
which in the light shone through the delicate dark skin; the wings and
feet were black. The fly was made after this description. He tried it, and
found it all he had hoped, and not knowing the name of the insect which
it represented, allowed it to be called the Morrison.*

—Mary Orvis Marbury, 1892

EVEN BEFORE I OPENED IT, the package from Hunter's announced its contents by an escaping whiff of mothballs. I hefted
the box: it was almost weightless, an airy reliquary of feathers
rare and common, but ones that my regular hunting and gathering seldom yielded.

The package's contents took my breath away. Words don't
exist for most of the colors found on a cock pheasant's skin,
much less on the living bird. There are subtle, dusky teals; burnished, deep coppers; iridescent, inky greens and purples; deep,
oxidized blood reds. The patterns include crescent moons, stip-
ples, delicate scallops, chevrons. This one pheasant skin would
help me construct hundreds, if not thousands, of wet flies and
streamers suggestive of spiders, water striders, emergent mayflies
and caddisflies, small baitfish like dace and sculpins to lure trout
to my line and from thence into my supra-aqueous world.

Three nights ago, I tied for five hours. I know that because *The
Jazz Image* is a three-hour show that began, ended, and was
replaced by chamber music while I tied. This isn't unusual: tying is
as good a way of losing track of time as fishing in a stream. Even

writing that phrase, *losing track of time,* tells me that there's something woefully wrong with the way I was taught to think about nonfishing time, as if it were something to be meted out and controlled.

Tying has an unbounded quality to it—an underlying sense that time is not linear, with a past and a future, but only a now. *Now* I am filling the shank of this hook with a collation of animal and synthetic bits that will behave like a living being in next spring's running waters. I can see the quirky, twitchy behavior of this streamer as it eventually darts, stops, darts through the dark waters of the upper Sucker, attracting a hoard of tiny admiring brookies. Trial-and-error, plus traditional dressings, have taught me what materials will create the kind of movement I hope to impart to this streamer, what colors will translate in the dark, tannic stream into plausibly shinerlike appearance. I occupy simultaneous nows—the one of a day vividly known through all my senses on a creek and the one of my fingers working over this hook.

Dressing a fly is a ballet for fingers. They rotate, forming elegant cat's cradles, stretching and swooping around each other and the hook, stroking and ruffling materials, behaving like the flexible tools they are. Dressing a fly offers two kinds of pleasures. There's the sensuous one of watching floss flow onto the hook's shank like paint, tinsel brighten and formalize the floss, hackle produce either a fly as light and resilient as thistledown or as soft and creaturely as spider's legs. And there's also the intellectual pleasure of interpreting a living creature in dead or inorganic materials, of *building* these confections and then watching them flutter or twitch improbably to life in a clear cold stream.

The whole of my attention is focused now upon a tiny curve of steel wire somewhere between an eighth of an inch (#26) and an inch and a half (#4XL) in length. On this shank of wire, I try to create an entire, miniature world. Depending on the species of fish I am planning on presenting my fly or streamer to, the season, and the sort of water (fast or slow, clear or turbid, stream or river), I can choose to tie an imitation of a specific insect or fodder fish or an attractor whose color, size, and action in the water are designed as a general provocation.

Dressing a fly can be as simple as following the time-honored patterns in the scores of pattern books available or as complex as playing a three-dimensional chess game. I can use local samples of the various stages of invertebrate stream or streamside life as models; I can concoct fanciful attractors based on no more scientific principle than how certain colors and materials please me. Many of North America's oldest attractor flies are what were once called "lake and bass wet flies." Most of them, wrote angling historian J. Edson Leonard in 1950, "are just beautiful creations and look no more like living creatures than a traffic signal or the grille of a new Buick."

I concocted one such gaudy "fancy fly" the other night that rather pleased me: it had a red wool tag (the terminus of the body); a yellow floss body ribbed with fine oval French tinsel; a throat of red ostrich herl; a tail of iridescent green-blue peacock sword; a wing of white calf's hair, golden pheasant crest, and peacock herl surmounted by an iridescent green-black neck feather from a golden pheasant, and a red ostrich herl collar behind its black thread head, the whole of this busy business tied onto a #8 6XL streamer hook, which is about three-quarters of an inch long.

This is the way such fancy flies were tied during their heyday, through World War II: Carrie Stevens, one of the most celebrated tiers of fancy streamers, for example, whipped up the General MacArthur during the war chiefly as a tribute (its head was wrapped in bands of red, white, and blue thread, and the feathers used to wing and hackle it were also red, white, and blue). The late fishing historian Joseph D. Bates, Jr., says of the General, "Although the fly was designed from a patriotic point of view, rather than because the colors suited accepted angling standards, the fly has proven very successful for trout and landlocked salmon in Maine waters." George and Helen Voss devised a successful streamer they named the Atom Bomb (not, as you might anticipate, consisting of melted plastics, but a standard confection of red-white-yellow-black feathers). Such gruesome whimsies will take the fish they're intended for, allowing their makers to make their cultural point and have their fish, too.

Such flies probably take brook trout readily enough, not so much because of their gaudy excesses as because the brook trout's local range is mostly bedrock streams, where the fish cannot afford to be terribly selective about what they eat. Throw fancy flies like these at brown trout, however, and you can all but hear the raspberry being blown at you through the water. But since I'm fonder of brook trout than any other salmonid, their naive avidity does not condemn them in my eyes. Rather, it offers me the license to play with fancy flies, knowing that in this case they are also practical ones.

My last concoction at 11 P.M. was another streamer for my brookies: purple floss body, silver oval tinsel rib, peacock sword tail, wing of red ostrich herl, ring-necked pheasant rump, and black dog hair, collar of golden pheasant tippet, cheeks of iridescent black starling shoulder feathers. Outside, the snow fell quietly, a Schubert oboe fantasia played on the radio, and my old wall clock ticked away all that invisible time. In the charmed circle of illumination on my cherrywood table, the soft plunder of hen necks, pheasant skins, peacock swords, flosses, tinsels, and hairs surrounded the vise and my glass of beer like the spoils of empire, which, in a sense, they were: human dominion over the rest of creation. But that wasn't how I viewed these glowing, almost indescribable feathers and hairs then: they were the relicts of life, testimony to a passing we all share, one that I am as bound up in as the creatures that passed that night through my hands, and I was inventing new lives for them, new beings compounded out of their unlikely conjunctions on tiny wire shanks. Like Mary Shelley's Doctor Frankenstein, I was inventing life, or at any rate initiating it, using the spare parts of birds and beasts otherwise cast away, twitching them into new patterns.

As I tied, it seemed as if I could see down time through all those generations of anglers and tiers who bound such hope and pleasure into their own, similar tyings. Only three generations ago, fine North American tiers prided themselves on tying without the help of vises, which they viewed as the crutches of clumsy novices. I think about that. It is like a nest of Chinese boxes, this business of tying, for each act, each material, is resonant with the long folk history of craft. Each half-hitch knot is both my particular act and one in a seemingly endless succession of knots tied not so much by individuals as by a tradition: a succession of mostly anonymous folk artists with peculiarly intimate relationships to the bodies of dead animals, mortuarists who honor the dead by recycling them.

My mind evacuated itself of all other concerns, concentrated utterly on building up a tiny mimetic world on a bit of carbon steel finer by far than the edge of a dime and in length about the span of my index fingernail. *A little world made cunningly,* if indeed I became at all good at it.

I tied off the final wind of a thread head, anointed it with a crown of clear nail polish, and surveyed my creation from all angles. Perched at the tip of the vise's jaws, it looked oddly alert and alive—a bit like a bird, an insect, a tiny fish. It glowed with the refracted light from a half dozen different beasts' and birds' coats. A fancy fly, a reliquary of history as well as of specific lives.

I turned out the light.

———

ONLY FOUR GENERATIONS AGO, most North American tiers used the feathers and furs that came to hand from their own barnyards, fields, and woods. Sometimes I try to imagine their collections, the preciousness of materials gathered personally rather than purchased. Six generations ago, anglers on North American frontiers made their own blind hooks from nails or had them forged by the local blacksmith, then bound them with imported gut or horsetail leaders before tying on flies or streamers. I imagine them doing that, the patient work of a long winter evening that gathered the sweet expectation of spring and another season of open water. Thaddeus Norris, in his 1864 *The American Angler's Book*, wrote, "There are some materials, in the way of feathers and dubbing, described by English writers, which cannot be had here, unless imported to one's order." Household materials and native animals, he suggested, could provide all the findings an American angler would want:

> [The angler] does not see a bird—a wild duck, a cock, an old hen, a turkey, or a peacock, without suitable feathers being presented to his eye. He will see dubbing everywhere: his wife's muff, the cat, or a lapdog, or a gray or red squirrel, or a hare, or a pile of mortar and tufts of cow's hair lying about it, or the place where there has been a hog-killing, with the refuse, down, or furze cast heedlessly by, a buffalo-robe, a bear-skin, a foot-rug, all suggest *dubbing*. Old pattern-cards of moreen in the store of his dry-goods friend are begged for. . . . All these are garnered up with miserly care, and stuffed into the dubbing-pocket of his book or wallet of fly materials. He need be in no hurry to collect them, for if he has the bump of acquisitiveness, he will in good time stock his wallet to repletion, without sending to Demarara for green monkey's fur, or to India for the feathers of a golden pheasant, or to England for a starling's wing[1] or the fur of a water rat.

Before America's ascent to trading and diplomatic power, fly tiers improvised most of their creations from the feathers of North American robins, bluejays, wrens, wild turkeys, barnyard fowl, and waterbirds. Many improvised flies from materials at hand while fishing. One Minneapolis angler, W. P. Andrus, wrote to

---

[1] How quickly nonnative species can acclimate themselves! When Norris wrote this in 1864, the European starling was still a rarity in North America. Its third deliberate introduction by humans occurred in 1890 to 1891 when the American Acclimatization Society released sixty starlings into New York City's Central Park as part of the society's goal of establishing all the bird species mentioned in Shakespeare's plays and poems into the United States. From those sixty birds, the population of starlings in North America has increased to over 200 million.

Charles Orvis in the 1880s that he had devised his Parker fly " 'on the spot' to . . . great success." Clearly Andrus carried some materials with him when he fished, anticipating the making of flies. After several hours of fishing on an Adirondacks lake, Andrus wrote, he sat down, unraveled some thread from the red flannel lining of his coat, wound that onto a hook, bound the body with silver tinsel, added guinea hen for wings and a tail, and wound on a brown chicken hackle: "Well, to make a short story of it, I proved conclusively that my new fly was a sure 'killer.' "

Such streamside creations are a purist's dream: flies tied in direct response to present conditions ("[We] had used nearly every sort of fly we had in stock, but with very poor success . . . the sky became slightly overcast and the trout began jumping") using the materials at hand. This approach is enormously appealing to me, and I never approach a stream without looking for suitable tying materials (bird feathers, tufts of fur, milkweed silk). To concoct a fly on the spot using what comes to hand is an improvisational art that bows to the fact that fish will bite, or not, on the basis of more than mere imitation.

These days, however, to build such flies is to court possible penalties from the state DNR and the USFWS, who may prosecute those who use the feathers of roadkill migratory species. About six years ago, an acquaintance of mine who lives on the Fond du Lac reservation in northern Minnesota was charged by USFWS and DNR officers with trafficking in forbidden feathers because she gathered roadkill birds and beasts to use in her dreamcatchers, which she then sold. Eventually, her case went to trial and she was exonerated on the basis of her band's 1852 treaty rights, which guaranteed that members could hunt and gather throughout Minnesota's Ceded Territories. The feathers of migratory roadkill birds are officially verboten for me to gather, never mind use. However, since most of them are also impossible to distinguish from purchased feathers, I sometimes gather and incorporate them into my flies, reasoning that my use of them honors their bearer's death or moult as well or better than being nibbled up by mice or flattened into jam by an ATV's tires. Suitable feathers for the purpose are almost generic: dark and webby or speckled and webby, long and wild looking. I fish more confidently and happily with them, convinced that the fly I am casting is made up of what is local and peculiar to the place.

———

THIS BUSINESS OF "FLY, FEATHER, AND HOOK" is almost as old as recorded human history, but its modern origins start with the Red Hackle fly described in the fourteenth-century English *Treatisse on Fyshynge* attributed to one Dame Juliana Berners, in which we read,

> In the begynning of Maye [use] a good flye, the body of roddyd wull and lappid abowte wyth blacke silk; the wynges of the drake of the redde capons hakyll.

The Red Hackle is what fly anglers today call a soft hackle. It has a sparsely tied fly consisting of a body of wool yarn ribbed with black silk thread wound around a hook with stiff, reddish feathers wound around the yarn body so that each barb stands out, encircling the hook like an Elizabethan ruff.

Five centuries later, Mary Orvis Marbury, daughter of Charles F. Orvis, founder of the American angling supply house that still bears his name, included a history of the Red Hackle in her magnum opus, *Favorite Flies and Their Histories* (1892). Marbury compiled her book to ensure that

> the associations connected with artificial flies ... so many and so pleasant[,] ... should neither be lost nor ignored, since they constitute one of the charms of angling. ...

> That these "veterans of many a fight" are not forgotten and thrown aside, but are carefully treasured, inspires the belief that their histories, so far as may be repeated, will be gladly welcome.

We desire so earnestly to indicate the identity and personality of each one . . .

By the time Marbury wrote this, she had been in charge of fly production at her father's company for sixteen years. She and her staff of six young women worked in an upstairs workshop of an Orvis building on Union Street in Manchester, Vermont, which now houses, appropriately, the American Museum of Fly Fishing.

Favorite Flies was the outgrowth of Charles Orvis's interest in regional fly patterns. Far more anglers requested custom-tied flies in the late nineteenth century than they do now, though the Orvis Company still fills such orders. In the late 1880s, Charles Orvis wrote to his scattered clientele in the U.S. and Canada asking for samples of their favorite flies and information about them. It became Marbury's job to collate and make sense of the more than two hundred replies her father received. Marbury framed the letters that flowed back to the Orvis Company between 1890 and 1892 with essays on the history of that transhistoric fly, the Red Hackle, and on the relationship between orders of aquatic insects and the flies that inspired or imitated them.

Marbury and her father were trying to rationalize the names and patterns of flies and to provide customers with tested patterns for use in their travels to new waters. These were formidable, if miniature challenges. Men, Marbury noted matter-of-factly, lacked an acute sense of color, which made tying up flies from their written descriptions difficult:

> It is surprising to find how many men call blue green, or *vice versa*. Experience shows us that most of them call chestnut brown a red; drab, a gray; purple, a blue; with no distinction at all for the various shades of olive, claret, maroon, and yellow.

Perhaps men simply lacked the vocabulary of sewing stuffs and of the dizzying array of colors made possible by the new aniline dyes. In any case, male vagueness about a fly's colors presented one of the problems the Orvises faced in creating standardized patterns. Colored plates in *Favorite Flies,* Marbury wrote, "have seemed to remedy this in a marked degree."

The Orvises' second challenge was to sort out regional differences in naming flies:

> Until recently, but few fishermen felt that they could designate artificial flies by names; it was only now and then that you would meet one who spoke with confidence in his knowledge. You would hear him describe his favorites, and such descriptions! He would declare, "For an all-round fly, give me a Professor with a green body!" meaning a Grizzly King. The next might say, "Now I tell you, the best fly for black bass, every time, is a large-sized Ferguson with a green body and a speckled wing"; again a Grizzly King was intended. One who wrote the above to us pitifully added, "But I can no more get the right Ferguson; I have ordered of many dealers, and they always send the wrong fly." A specimen of the Grizzly King was sent to help him out of his dilemma, and he wrote back gratefully, saying, "You are the first I have met in a long time who knew the real Ferguson."

Marbury thought this problem could be solved by naming flies in color plates and providing their origin and history "so that in the future these records may be consulted when claims conflict." She urged readers to give each new pattern "a distinctive name" and to "avoid giving old flies new names, or old names to new flies."

The 300 flies in Marbury's book represented two schools of thought on fly design that still mark the craft of tying. There were imitators—flies designed to look or behave like foods that trout, bass, and salmon actually encountered—and attractors— flies that might provoke a strike because of their novelty of movement, color, size, resemblance to an enemy, or other threat.

Fly tiers clearly have greater scope for fancy in designing attractors than imitators, but not all fish species or individual fish are equally seduced by attractors (or, for that matter, by imitators). Attractors work best on fish who habitually make what anglers think of as indiscriminate strikes—brook trout and black bass, for instance—which happen to have been the species who graced the waters of the northeastern U. S. and southeastern Canada, where North American fly fishing had its origins.

The waters that brook trout inhabited are usually swift, very cold, and not very fecund, for they flow over the bedrock of the ancient Canadian Shield and the equally ancient Appalachian mountains. Fish living in such thrifty waters strike at just about anything that looks edible. Black bass, on the other hand, are native to slower moving, warmer waters than brook trout, but they are highly territorial (they are nest builders) and aggressive feeders, so big, flashy flies work well with them, too. Marbury noted, "In America, 'fancy flies' [attractors] are more numerous than the imitations, especially since their introduction as a lure for black bass."

When native brook trout began to die out because of the warming and polluting of their waters, they were replaced by imported European and British brown trout, and fly styles changed in response to their introduction. Browns, particularly big ones, did not rise as readily to flies as brookies did; the largest of them were fish-eating, cautious night feeders. Big, brightly colored streamers put brown trout down. Marbury noted,

> As streams have become depleted, and the fish more shy, they need to be fished with greatest caution and skill; there is, therefore, a demand for smaller flies, delicately tied in colors less gaudy than those needed for the flies used on wild, unfrequented rivers and lakes.

By late twentieth-century standards, many of the "smaller . . . delicately tied . . . less gaudy" flies that Marbury described seem anything but sedate. Flies like the Orvises' Silver Ibis or Carrie Stevens's Gray Ghost, a streamer popular about thirty years later, employed materials as exotic as any but the gaudiest of today's salmon and steelhead flies.

The materials used to concoct the flies in *Favorite Flies* seem only slightly less exotic than those included in British salmon flies of the period. By Marbury's time, the humble materials advocated by Thaddeus Norris had given way to those of a nation active in world trade. Marbury's list of tying materials, besides the fur and feathers of native creatures like loons, wild turkeys, bobwhites, and deer, included all the spoils of empire—feathers of Mongolian pheasant, African jungle cock, Indian crow, European bluejay, Asian bustard, South American blue macaw, furs of black seal, polar bear, grizzly bear, Indian dog, and Asian monkey.

This importation of skins and feathers from the world's wild creatures did not cease with the rise, near the turn of the century, of the Catskill tiers, a school of fly tying whose aesthetic was radically simple, even minimalist. Although Catskill tiers were widely admired and discussed for their trim imitations of mayflies and caddisflies, their influence seems to have exerted itself chiefly on those Eastern streams where their methods were invented.

In the Midwest, Herter's famous annual catalogues of tying materials provide an index of what anglers had at their disposal. Materials for tying gaudy, exotic attractors were as popular at Herter's after World War II as before. The 1948 catalogue lists, in addition to the cock and hen hackles,[2] marabou and peacock, domestic turkey and ring-necked pheasant that make up the majority of feathers used today, the following exotics: "indonese" and Bali duck skins; Reeves, Lady Amherst, golden, and argus pheasant; cock of the rock; tropical kingfisher (blue chatterer); raven, coot, florican bustard, swan, condor; Scottish moorhen, snipe, grouse, and plover; English woodcock, starling, and bluejay; European curlew; North American mallard, pintail, canvasback, teal, and scaup; jungle cock. Herter's also offered twenty varieties of squirrel tails (Himalayan, Bangola, Haido, Hudson Bay, Kenya, Kashu Pini, Eluela Tropic . . .); African rolla and

---

[2]Interestingly, hen hackle has been recently (re)"discovered" as a material for tying soft-hackle flies. Typically about one-eighth the price of cock hackle, it is now being praised for its webby, streamerly qualities and its "discoverers" hailed for their canniness in recognizing a good but overlooked material—never mind that it's been around all along.

jackal tails; coyote, Canadian and European wolf tails and pelts; lynx, fitch, skunk, seal, Malayan mountain goat; African monkey and baboon skins (sacred long-haired, black long-haired, silver; barred orange baboon); Siberian, Kodiak, grizzly, polar, and black bearskin pieces.

It's chilling to think of the number of tropical birds and Northern fur bearers who died to supply the fur and feather trade not so very long ago.[3] International treaties like the 1918 Migratory Bird Treaty, the Convention on International Trade in Endangered Species (CITES), and the U.S. Endangered Species Act (ESA) have slowed the traffic in most of these materials because the animals who wear them have become protected—or, in a few cases, extinct. But according to environmental and angling writer Ted Williams, the illegal traffic in exotic skins and feathers for the tying trade continues to this day, fueled by the growing market for fancy traditional salmon flies. Writing in the *Atlantic Salmon Journal* (Winter 1995), Williams reported that recent undercover stings by agents of the USFWS's Division of Law Enforcement found that of "more than a dozen prominent fly shops ... at least six [are] knowingly dealing in black-market materials for classic salmon flies."

One well-known tier told Williams, "I've tied flies for twenty-five years and met a lot of nice people. But lately there's this cult—this whole thing of ownership of rare materials. You go to any antique show or sportsmen's show, it's like a nightclub. You whisper and you can get the stuff, just like you can get cocaine. Chatterer, Indian crow, toucan, macaw. . . . There's lots of muffled talk, deals going down all the time. . . . We posture ourselves as righteous sportsmen and go into fits if we see a spin fisherman squeeze a six-inch brook trout. But we can put the kill order on birds in Venezuela."

---

[3] Herter's eventually went out of business after being twice convicted and fined for importing illegal tying materials.

AMONG MY MOST PRIZED legal materials are porcupine quills. The quills, which I use to wrap Catskill-style dry fly bodies, are unhappily all too easy to gather: porcupines are not fast movers unless there's a dog involved, and their bodies can be found bristling along most roads in northern Wisconsin and Minnesota. I stop whenever I spot a not-too-overripe victim, pluck out some quills with the tweezers I keep in the glove compartment of my truck, and seal them in Ziploc bags. The porky's belly fur is another fine material, with an electric frizzle to it that moves languorously in the water.

The other legal local I enjoy using is my dogs' undercoats. Although not waterproof like a muskrat's, it has the same soft, fine texture and gray coloring and is very easy to dub for fly bodies. And if I snip off an occasional lock of long, coarse, hard, badger-tipped fur from their ample manes for a streamer wing, they're probably none the more damaged, either.

A devoted tier comes to see the material world in ways radically different from other people. Austin Hogan and William Tapply created beautiful streamers using milkweed floss for the wings. Hogan's had an orange floss body, a tail of lemon wood duck, and throat of barred wood duck; Tap's Milkweed Fly had a body of flat silver tinsel, a thick tail of golden pheasant tippets, a throat of red hen hackle, a long wing of milkweed floss dyed burnt orange, and an eye of jungle cock.

I spent two Augusts amid the haunts of goldfinches, who nest later than any other songbird in northern Minnesota and Wisconsin, searching for their chosen nest-building material, the down of the common thistle, which does not seed until August in these latitudes. Goldfinches weave nests of thistledown so tight that they are waterproof. Thistledown makes an excellent tying material, both for winging small wet flies and streamers and for dubbing bodies, a process that involves felting a fibrous material—hair, fur, down—onto waxed thread and then building up a body from winds of the dubbed thread. So in mid-August, I was out among the goldfinches, gathering down for tying flies while they gathered it for building nests.

I also discovered a use for those otherwise superfluous fabric-softener sheets that folks owning dryers use to lard their wet clothes. Standing lost in thought in my daughter's dining room, I noticed a spent sheet of Bounce wound about her Levi's and T-shirts. I picked it up. Aside from its gaggingly sweet scent, it seemed to possess all the qualities requisite in a fine dry fly wing: translucency, porosity, ease of shaping. I stuck it in my pocket and brought it back to Duluth.

The next night I tied some blue duns and fiddled around with the dryer sheet for wings. It tied up beautifully. Next I dropped the #16 fly into a mug of water and watched fitfully through the rest of the evening as the fly ebbed lower into the surface film, then sunk slowly, then bobbed back to the surface, its wings seemingly hyaline but utterly intact.

Bingo. For $1.35, I could own enough suitable winging material for the rest of my life; all I needed to do was buy a box of Spartan SCENTLESS dryer sheets and give it to my dryer-owning daughter with pleas to use and return to me.

Then there were rubber bands. I knew that maggots were singularly succulent morsels from a trout's point of view; eighteenth- and nineteenth-century British and American angling books are full of detailed instructions for husbanding maggot collections throughout the winter so that these "gentles," as the grubs were called, would be available for spring fishing. Anglers were advised to bury meat in barrels of sawdust or bran. Gentles were clearly a Big Deal to my fishing ancestors, as were the adults—Mary Marbury, for example, offered a pattern for "The Bluebottle, or 'flesh fly' . . . [which] deposits its eggs upon decaying animal matter; from them are hatched the maggots that fishermen call 'gentles.'" Leonard M. Wright, Jr., whose manic attempts to increase the trout population in his stretch of New York State's Neversink River are recounted in his charming (and, unfortunately, out of print) book *Neversink* (1991), once hung several dead woodchucks from a tree whose branches sprawled over one of the river's pools:

> In a few days, a steady supply of maggots began trickling out of the carcasses—especially during the heat of the day. A school of trout assembled below each one, and I could almost see them putting on heft with each passing day.

Wright's experiment came to a shuddering halt when his wife and two children came upon the swarming biofeeder when they went down to the river for a swim.

I thought I could go gentles one better: I decided to try building some maggot flies. These must have the look—appropriately succulent, vitreous, and ivory colored—but not the quickness of live maggots. One of the newer plastic tying materials is called Nymph Rib; it comes in the predictable colors of most subsurface larvae—rockworm green, bloodworm red, crustacean pink and orange—but it also comes in a hue the manufacturer forthrightly calls Maggot Ivory. Wimpish tying catalogues customarily deny this material the gruesome dignity of its full name and refer to it merely and mildly as Ivory.

But ivory Nymph Rib is just that—conspicuously ribbed—and I wanted a material that possessed the same smooth, undulant surface as the real creature. Herein, of course, lies the true irreason of tying: *the fish don't care* how close most imitations are to the real thing—the angler does. If a fly won't take fish, it arguably isn't much of a fly, but if a fly takes fish and yet isn't much fun to tie or to look at, then arguably it isn't much of a fly, either. The Nymph Rib Maggot was a soulless fly because it didn't look maggot-y enough to me.

"Rubber bands," suggested John, an angler who worked during the Thanksgiving holiday at a suburban tackle shop. He told me he'd fished maggots constructed from round white rubber bands during the school year in Colorado.

So I tried rubber bands, and while they had a somewhat more— how shall I put this?—*biotic* quality than the hard-surfaced Nymph

Rib, they lacked the repellent gleam of the living animals. The Rubber Band Maggot possessed the requisite whimsy and gratifying ingenuity, but it didn't look much like my idea of a maggot.

Short lengths of cooked udon noodle seemed like the model to aspire to. But noodles themselves wouldn't do for several reasons: first, any genuine edible would prompt the fish to swallow the hook, and I did not want to induce such an act; second, noodles do not cast well, and fishing for me is no fun if I must cast something resembling a wet sock or cold pasta; and third, angling, like any other way of organizing a life, proceeds by a set of self-devised rules. Fly angling proceeds by the rule of casting only artificials, not true edibles. An arbitrary rule, perhaps, but an iron one, for all that.

But the *appearance* of a cooked Japanese noodle . . . yes. Thus began the second phase of my search.

In his book *Fly-Tying Methods*, Darrel Martin demonstrates how to make a fly whose body extends beyond and above the rear of the hook. It is an imitation of a subadult mayfly. The method Martin describes uses 3M double-stick tape that is first rolled into a tubular body shape, then covered in dubbing fur, and finally affixed to the hook's shank. The tape, I knew, was of a suitable shade of ivory and possessed of a pleasingly satiny glow. Off to OfficeMax to buy a roll for experimenting with maggot making.

This is how obsession operates, though I can claim little enough of it compared to the Darrel Martins and Arthur Flicks of the world. In fact, one of the unexpected reassurances angling has offered me is proof that my fixations are mild compared to those of many anglers. But of course obsession has its charms as well, not least of which is the way it helps me see the materials of our culture in unexpected ways.

Contemporary tiers eye the world covetously. The men you see wandering in a seemingly dazed fashion through fabric stores, the women prowling craft shops with distant looks in their eyes—chances are that you have sighted a fly tier bent on finding new materials. Entire tying industries have been built around annexing materials from other manufactories to our own tiny but fanatic backwater. C. Boyd Pfeiffer, who charts weird tying materials in his column "Strange Stuff" for *Fly Tyer* magazine, has been sent flies made with Velcro, Velox blankets, dryer lint, Saran Wrap, dust mops, "fuzz balls from new carpet," plastic trash bags, and foam hair rollers. Nothing, it seems, is off limits.

———

A TEMPTATION IN TYING, as in so much else, is to want more and more sophisticated equipment in order to make the job easier. This, I think, is a weakness of novices like me. Seasoned tiers, I've noticed, use whatever equipment is at hand and often revere wobbly, primitive old vises simply because they're comfortable with them and have trusted them for years. At the point that I find myself drooling over new vises or weird, intricate single-use tools, I remind myself that the beautiful early twentieth-century flies on view at the International Center for Fly Fishing in Livingston, Montana, were tied, for the most part, with no vises at all or with hand-held pin vises similar to the sort used to glue laminates together. No one has improved on the workmanship of those early flies, so I'm left wondering why we humans have such a predictable urge to make all our tasks—in particular, our *chosen* tasks, like fly tying—easier.

And faster. For me, tying at its best is an opportunity not only to work with beautiful natural materials but to do so at an unhurried pace amid unelectrified surroundings offers me hints of the sensual and temporal worlds occupied by anglers five, six, seven generations ago. The hard winter light nails a bolt of chilly gold to the oak floor, throwing a frieze of tangled shadow from the naked vines outside the windows. No halogen bulb illuminates the work beneath my hands. This is slow, painstaking work, each turn of thread bound up with speculation about the creatures whose feathers and fur I am reusing, with wishes for the cunning of my creations come open water next spring. Tying is a form of hope, of subtle malice, of deceit. And for me it is slow, unaided by rotary vises and gallows attachments. Whenever the acquisitive lust that fuels our national economy takes me over, I try to remind myself that I tie for continuity with past times and people, to know something of their world.

Tying many of the old northwoods patterns connects me both imaginatively and materially to earlier generations of anglers. These flies can't be called truly timeless, for the conditions that gave rise to some of them are no longer present—for example, northwoods waters have fewer or more beaver ponds; warmer or cooler water; more or fewer fish species competing for the same habitat; more or less logging in the watershed; and, almost always, more fishing pressure—but several have hung on for more than fifty years, like the Pass Lake, a simple black fly with a white, usually calf-tail wing that anglers think triggers brook trout strikes because it resembles the leading edge of a brookie's fin. (Early anglers on northwoods streams sometimes baited hooks with brook trout fins and caught brookies on them.) Depending on the weight and size of the hook and the material used to concoct Pass Lakes, they can be fished as swimming baitfish (streamers), insects floating on the surface (dry flies), nymphs struggling up to the surface, or drowned insects (wets). Between its versatility and its ease of tying, the Pass Lake remains firmly entrenched in northwoods fly boxes.

Other old regional favorites have gone the way of silk fly lines. The chief factor in their disappearance seems to be the time they take to tie. In a world where time has become arguably a scarce medium, a fly that takes most amateurs more than five minutes to make isn't likely to stay in favor. John Fowles, in *The French Lieutenant's Woman* (1969), commented that the dilemma for his upper-middle-class, mid-Victorian characters was "not fitting in all that one wanted to do, but spinning out what one did to occupy the vast colonnades of leisure available." The truth of this observation, evident in so many ways in women's embroidery and needlepoint, men's amateur fossil collecting, wing-shooting, and safari-ing, only came home to me personally when

I began studying the elaborate flies used for North American lake, brook trout, and bass fishing in the period 1860 to 1930. Old favorites like the Parmacheene Belle and Professor, still being touted in the period 1930 to 1950 as "taking" flies in the North Woods, demand far longer to tie than most of today's nymphs, dries, bucktails.

Today, large elaborate flies are still tied for salmon, steelhead, and bass. With synthetics, the sky's the limit: great streaming Day-Glo concoctions of marabou, Mylar, crystal flash, flashabou, ice chenille, ersatz, and other pop-named synthetics. Purple fuchsia hot orange "Oregon cheese" chartreuse hot pink cobalt acid yellow—big attractor flies make their appeals stridently, almost parodically. They are artificial, insistently so, and their names reflect this, too, with their comic-book action-hero insistence on crudeness and violence: Blood on the Water, Purple Peril, Silver Demon, Blue Max, Popsicle, Purple Moose Bomber, Marabou Madness, Flame, Trophy Hunter. These are flies you can hold by their substantial "wings," the great clots of marabou or synthetic FishHair that comprise their profile, and imagine them collapsed by the current into something long, narrow, pulsating. Their materials are shiny, reflective, skittery, undulant. Prevailing opinion has it that winter salmon and steelhead are drawn to the colors of salmon spawn—beige through pink through coral to deep salmon red—and to purple and black because of the bulk they seem to promise in dark waters. Flies tied for these fish are boundlessly flashy and illusorily huge. Casting them can be like casting a wet wool sock: crude, but effective.

The wets I choose to tie are another matter entirely. Like steelhead flies, they are general imitations, but whereas steelhead and Pacific salmon flies imitate baitfish or floating roe or, intriguingly, chunks of rotting salmon flesh (the Drifting Carcass, a confection of white-to-pink rabbit or deer hair strips wound around the hook and fished on a—what else?—dead drift), more traditional wet flies are meant to imitate drowned but generic insects. The Partridge and Orange that I tied first imitates, approximately, a dead spider. Hence the beauty of the great horned owl's feather, with individual barbs that flare, quiver, shiver with the slightest passage of air, and that in water hover fetchingly, deep in the surface film, dimpling but not breaking it.

These are flies of subdued colors: grays, olives, blacks, browns, beiges. Partridge and Orange may sound gaudy, but the orange involved is the deep autumnal orange of acorn squash—burnished, somehow ancient, anything but the hyped-up orange of, say, a Popsicle or Hickey's King-a-Bunny, two synthetic salmon flies. So, too, the yellow of a Partridge and Yellow, which is the subdued, sun-faded yellow of a chintz kept for years beneath a south-facing window. Wet-fly hooks, too, are small and reticent. Does it come as any surprise that the origin of wet flies is English, that they were designed for the chalk streams of the southern counties? It is not anglophilia that draws me to tying wets; it is the fact that opportunities exist for me to use them in my part of the world. In northern Minnesota, I am unlikely to encounter inland streams that call for pseudo-roe or purple and orange Egg-Sucking Leeches.

Almost every day, I encounter insects and roadkill mammals, and molting birds, and small stream minnows. These I have learned to look at more carefully than I did before. And so I pick up fallen feathers, clip roadside fur, net streamside insects, wonder with a closer attention at the iridescence of the blue summer damselfly and the opacity of his twinned black wings. The flies resulting from my observations resemble those made from patterns over 150 years old: March Brown Spider, Stewart's Dun Spider, Woodcock and Hare's Ear, Alder, Blue-winged Olive, Light and Dark Cahill and Hendrickson wets. A few edge toward a subdued colorfulness: the Royal Coachman (red floss body, peacock herl butt, white mallard quill wing), the Professor (yellow floss body, gold tinsel ribbing, red goose quill tail), and that appealing bee or yellow jacket imitation, and the McGinty (a wet with a torso of John Falstaff proportions, wound hugely with ropes of yellow and black chenille).

It is not for these bits of unexpected chromatic playfulness or theatrical presence that I prize wet flies, however: it is for their more usual drabness, their suggestive attention to the minutiae of tiny, usually unnoticed lives. Tying makes me a larger person, a more careful observer. It is a matter of further integrating the different parts of my world. An example: last fall, one of the season's many yellow jackets made it into the house and eventually died in the kitchen window. Four years ago I might have simply thrown her carcass out, all but unnoticed, but instead I picked her up by her stilled wings. *Hmmm,* I thought, *every fall these creatures appear by the millions. Surely some of them drop into streams at low water. Would the trout recognize them?*

As Thaddeus Norris wrote in 1864, "the angler becomes seized and possessed of many chattels, which he may husband for years before he finds use for them"—bits of information about and materials from the natural world to wonder at and to honor by use.

———

AFTER I TIED A FEW STREAMERS and wets last night, I turned to holiday gifts for my sister. These were fantasy flies tied on Alec Jackson spey hooks, to which I then glued small safety pins so she could wear them on her jacket. I baptized the first one Stranger from Another Shore—a streamer created entirely from feathers of that successful northwoods immigrant, the Asian ring-necked pheasant. It was a confection of subtle, indescribable colors climaxed by church windows, the short neck feathers of white, tipped with iridescent black-green, which I tied in as cheeks. The second was Clackamas Spey, made to honor my sister's home river in Oregon. It was colored much like Winter's Hope: silver tinsel body; purple and turquoise collars; yellow feather wings; black, white-spotted guinea hen hackle; topping and hackle of orange goose shoulder. I wound a neat red head onto it, danced my fingers through a whip finish, then gilded the head with drops of Cellire, which sealed and gave it the appearance of a drop of blood.

Downstairs the hall clock chimed eleven. The dogs wuffled in their sleep, chasing something. Time, as my culture measures it, flooded in: *time* to turn off the downstairs light, *time* to clean up the tying table, *time* to stow these feathered confections where dogs couldn't get at them, *time* to go to bed.

Soon enough, I crawled under the comforter, punchy with eyestrain, but thinking once again about maggot flies. After two years spent brooding about possible materials, I thought I might at last have found the right one. I lay in the dark and watched it form before my closed eyes: a liquid calcium capsule—a dead ringer for a maggot, with a toothsome texture, too. A bit over-size, true, maybe a half-inch in length and a quarter-inch in diameter, but such dimensions should make it even more appealing to a half-starved northern brookie. With a bit of dubbing for a head, a sparse winding of pale hackle for movement, it just might do . . .

18 Stuff

FISHING IS A PASSION THAT CAN BEGIN or end in *stuff*. Fly fishing is potentially one of the most stuff-heavy preoccupations a human being can fall prey to, but it's also potentially one of the most ascetic. It's quite possible not only to go fishing but to fish successfully with nothing more than a rod of some sort—a dapping pole, say, cut from green willow—a line, a hook, and something to bait that hook: a worm or a leech or a fly tied from feathers and thread. Such an outfit can be discarded after a single use and leave virtually no sign of its former identity, just a skinned branch, a scroll of twine, maybe a small hook glittering in the streamside grass.

But, of course, few people past the age of ten choose to fish that way. Most of us not only use more equipment in our quest for fish but also find considerable pleasure—and another quest—in acquiring our outfits.

I had fallen down the equipment rathole once before. In the years that I studied and wrote about photography, I became seriously enamored of cameras. Their intricacy, precision, beauty of design, function, and materials were like a powerfully addictive drug. I wanted to possess and know them intimately—to remove their lenses, peer at their mirrors and shutters, check out the world through their viewfinders, breathe their metal-and-leather must. I loved them all: 35mm Leicas and Contaxes, Nikon single-lens reflexes, Hasselblads and Bronicas, twin-lens reflex Rolleis and Mamiyaflexes, lovely old mahogany Deardorffs and state-of-the-art Leinhoffs, and all the old, outdated, but dear cameras no longer in wide use: Zeiss and Kodak folders, Graflexes, rollfilm box cameras for which paperbacked rollfilm hadn't been sold in years.

I don't know why this passion abated, exactly; as an intellectual prospect, I eventually found photography rather wispy. After a while, I didn't seem to have much to say about it. And as my passion for understanding how photographs were made and acquired meaning abated, my fascination with them as *stuff* dwindled, too. I still have a trunkful of oddities and rarities, all carefully wrapped in paper, but I doubt they will see the light of day again in my lifetime.

Unless, of course, I can trade them for some *rods.*

I developed rod fever about as badly as I ever did camera fever, and it was no less costly a passion. While there's *no* rod that doesn't interest me, at least momentarily, the ones that exerted the greatest fascination were bushrods of bamboo and fiberglass, 6.5 feet up to about 7.5 feet. Oh, and prebamboo greenheart rods, all twelve feet of them. And custom fiberglass surf rods. And fine jigging rods for ice fishing. And don't even let me get *started* on reels . . .

My first years of fishing were spent on Wisconsin and Minnesota streams, few of which are broad or fast. In fact, most of Minnesota's streams are so shallow and mild that you can get by in hip waders. Like the Catskill and Pennsylvania streams where U.S. fly fishing was born, northwoods fishing seldom calls for rods any longer or heavier than seven- to eight-foot, four- or five-weight. These are the rods you go to Eastern rodbuilders for—companies like Orvis and Green River, which grew up alongside creeks that ease their decorous way down the stubs of old mountain chains. On my favorite little Minnesota streams, both north and south, often the only thing you can do with longer, 8.5- or 9-foot rods is to rollcast them—even the shortest back cast is likely to snarl up your line in the waiting alders, and most up- and downstream casts will do the same. Alders don't occupy only the banks—like an invading army, they also push out over the stream, daring you to pass, much less to cast. Beneath them lurk the miniature fish befitting such an environment: brook trout.

Undulating across ancient, almost level peneplains, north-woods streams rarely hold a steady course for more than ten yards before veering giddily to one side or the other, like a drunk tugging at your steering wheel. On such streams and such fish, the current generation of popular graphite rods are overpower-ful, too stiff. When I successfully sneak into casting position on a creek no wider than my bathroom, I need a rod that will load fully with no more than five feet of line out, a rod that can cast my fly softly onto a section of stream no more than a car length above or below me. Happily, the most effective rods for such small places are also the cheapest: weepy fiberglass, the wonder material of the 1950s, now cast into a dolorous shade by its more glamorous fellow synthetic, graphite.

Fishing is as much an aesthetic as any other kind of experi-ence, and walking a scroll of stream five feet wide and six inches deep, clutching a nine-foot rod, seems distastefully out of pro-portion to me, like a late-Victorian sideboard squatting in a small back bedroom. The $500 tip-action rods so beloved of Western casters are almost useless on my nearby waters. The fast whop-per rods built by Loomis and Sage for Western rivers are radical overkill here. I love matching the miniaturization of northwoods creeks with miniature equipment.

If I still lived in the West, my choice of stuff would probably change. Most of the West's coldwater streams run hard and fast from young mountains, and where they reach the valleys, they rout out deep channels, becoming deeper and slower than the northwoods streams on which I learned to fish. Big water, big winds, big fish—big rods. Scott, Sage, and Loomis are represen-tative Western rodmakers; their most popular offerings are long—at least nine feet—and heavy—say, six-weight.

Northeastern Minnesota and northwestern Wisconsin have a few Western-style rivers that plunge in heart-stopping leaps from high Precambrian plateaux down to the graben of Lake Superior. Below their falls, steelhead, Kamloops, and salmon fin their way inland to spawn away from the lake in spring or fall. You can see these West Coast salmonids' fans lining the banks of northwoods rivers from November to April, equipped with long hunky rods, heavyweight neoprene waders, and stocking caps. I'm not interested in fishing for introduced species like the Kamloops and steelhead, so I'm spared musing about what a ten-foot, seven- or eight-weight rod and accompanying reel go for. Unless, that is, I decide to go back to the Olympic Peninsula to fish for steelhead where they *belong.*

———

I RECENTLY BOUGHT A USED eight-foot, five-weight fiberglass rod that is almost endearing in its homeliness. Built on a black blank half the diameter of a baseball bat, it was so overwrapped by its earnest, anonymous maker that it probably gained a full ounce from the thread used to tie down its guides and strippers. The red wraps were then drowned in so much Flex Coat that they look like boils—you just long to lance them. The builder finished off his masterpiece with yet another inspired touch: a handle and reel seat of puke green aluminum, powder-coated. Yum.

My fellow anglers avert their eyes when they see me with this rod. Nobody's had the nerve yet to ask me how much I paid for it ($40). The most positive comment I've received is "Ummm, that's interesting," followed, after a bated silence, by "You, uh, build it yourself?"

I'm craven enough to feel relieved to be able to say with unbecoming haste, "No—it came that way."

Anybody who grabs this rod and gives it a few tentative shakes says one of three things—

> *Man, that's a* real *noodle.*
> *Is this a wet-fly action then?*
> *What happened to your Winston?*

—in other words: *Anything is* (probably) *better than this.*

But then I reflect that most of my buddies are out after bigger fish than I am, preferably on bigger streams. Guys, I notice, are more likely than I am to enjoy long casts and long-distance hookups. I want to see fish *up close,* and I like the cloistered, secure feeling of fishing tiny streams.

Initially, such preferences stemmed from pure inexperience: I wouldn't have known what to do on a large, complex stream, particularly if (or when) it yielded a large, hyperactive fish. Six years into fishing, I find that my reasons, but not my preferences, have changed: I still enjoy fishing tiny streams, but now it's because I've become so fond of their inhabitants—tiny survivors making the most of the inadequate waters they've been introduced (and condemned) to.

I've noticed that women tend to be drawn to small rods. Bushrods are cute, and they seem more easily managed than the longer rods favored by their brothers and fathers and husbands and boyfriends (though they are not). Short rods are also—and this is important—more likely to have been chosen and purchased by women themselves.

In my first year of fishing, I attended a women-only fly fishing workshop where I was astonished by the rods other women brought to class with them. To a person, they arrived clutching behemoths or banties long since discarded by the men in their lives, who apparently believed that rods *they* no longer wanted to fish were good enough for their wives, daughters, girlfriends . . . Immense fourteen-foot, ten-weight surf-casting rods, seven-ounce bamboo production rods from the 1930s, telescoping stainless-steel rods from the 1940s. Figuratively, these guys had sent off the women in their lives to take their driver's test in a rusty beater whose muffler was held on by bailing wire and whose distributor cap had been clamped down with chewing gum.

Our instructors gazed out at the class with barely concealed disgust and suggested gently that we jettison these mournful castoff rods. We needed, she said, to acquire rods suited to our own height and weight and fishing preferences. This advice appeared to fall on thirteen of our fourteen pairs of novice ears with the force of revelation. One of the happier advantages to not being the recipient of well-intentioned but clueless male attentions is that I had chosen my own rods from the get-go. It was disconcerting to hear the anxiety with which some of my classmates talked about how hard it would be to rationalize spending money on rods for themselves. On the other hand, many of them were handsomely dressed. I don't know about you, but I'd rather wake up in the morning and see light scrolling down the length of a beautiful fly rod than across a $250 dress, so perhaps it's simply a matter of priorities: I prefer owning good stuff to good clothes.

There's no question that fly fishing can become a black hole. Between rods and fly reels—those small worlds made cunningly—every penny I make could easily be spoken for before it's been earned. Like many anglers who tie their own flies, I probably own enough materials to be able to tie at fever speed into at least the year 2500. True, I do not have to pay the $1.80–2.50 per fly that nontiers must shell out, but I suspect that if I amortized my flies against what I've happily shelled out for Hoffman saddles and French tinsel and pheasant skins, my flies would still average, oh, $3 apiece.

After more than five years of relatively giddy obeisance to stuff, last summer I decided to clean up my act. The proximate cause was not so much financial ruin as the sight of fellow anglers on one of my neighborhood rivers, the Lester. There, during the warmest, balmiest part of July, I witnessed folks slipping into the waters in full fly fishing mufti: neoprene waders, thirty-pocket fishing vests, hats coped with sheepskin bands in which reposed entire platoons of streamers and weighted nymphs. It was like watching people drag cannons onto front lawns to unload against song sparrows. By midsummer, the only trout in the Lester are naive, ten- to twelve-inch yearling Kamloops who are as readily caught by twelve-year-olds with $19 Zebco spinning outfits as by fully equipped fly fishers.

There was something appealing about wading into the

almost-warm Lester barelegged and sandal-shod, feeling the force of the current against the backs of my knees, the minnows nibbling tentatively on my naked toes. I decided to try a form of fly fishing as close to childhood angling as possible, wondering if it mightn't free me from the Cult of Stuff.

It worked, I think. Instead of streamside certitudes—always illusionary, and never more so than when they are tied to equipment—I started to court streamside vicissitudes. Now, instead of taking three rods on day jaunts, I took only one. Instead of bringing along a thirty-pocket fishing vest—a black hole vestment if there ever was one—I wore nothing more than a shirt with big pockets, a pair of shorts, one small fly box, clippers, a hook remover, and a roll of tippet. If this minimalist gear proved unsuitable for the fishing conditions I found, then I watched birds, seined for baitfish, pored over the stream's insects, trolled the slack water for feathers I could use for tying instead.

I still sleep within sight of my favorite rod, just as I slept at age eight with my copy of *Lassie Come-Home* beneath my pillow. Beloved tools are almost extensions of my own arms, legs, and brain, so I like to have them near. I love my fishing stuff perhaps even more for having pared it down. The pleasures of *stuff*, so long as they do not displace whatever work they were designed to perform, are one of angling's deepest sources of joy. When I turn over my favorite reel now, I see that it is scratched and losing its finish; banged, here and there, from one or another collision with riprap or midstream cobble. I believe I can see time embodied in it. At the beginning of each season, I pick up my two remaining rods and reels, my tying vise and fly boxes, and it's as if I am greeting beloved old friends whom I haven't seen or spoken to in months. Like old friends, my intimacy with them is instantly and passionately rekindled. They have been companions to, and agents of, some of my deepest experiences. Like dear old friends, the things I value most are now few in number and deep with my own use, deep as the lake outside my door.

19 Fishermen's Paths

THEY'RE AS DEPENDABLE AS STARS, as weather. Stop by any fishy-looking river or creek, and you'll find one, probably two, running alongside. Most are fairly faint because they aren't maintained by anyone or anything except the bootfall of fishermen's feet. Nevertheless, you can readily locate them, especially in winter: look for a trail of smooth, unbroken snow between heights of last season's shoreline grasses and sedges, and you've found one.

Angling has plenty of folkways, but few of them are as pleasing as fishermen's paths. Here are true folk expressions—anonymous, mute, consensual, some of them ancient by most human standards. I walk trails that turn-of-the-century anglers trod; they, in turn, probably followed paths laid down by the Ojibwe, who in turn used pathways made by the Lakota, who in turn used pathways made by the moose and caribou who once picked their way along these same northwoods streams. The key to the paths' charm lies in the unbroken reciprocity between so many beings, both two- and four-legged, all of us using and perpetuating them.

Except immediately above and below bridges, fishermen's paths are commonly the merest quash in the long grasses and herbs, no deeper than if a deer had slept there overnight. Farther into the woods, they take on the dendritic form of flowing waters, some leading to the riverbank, others wandering farther off into the woods, still others faithfully paralleling the stream.

Unlike formal paths like the Superior Hiking Trail, these are the most provisional of passages. Nobody has built steps into the steep grades, clipped sprawling branches or roots, taken a chainsaw to downed trees. If a tree falls across a fishermen's path, it stays there until time and other creatures use it up. Although most fishermen's paths in the North Woods run through DNR-owned or -leased land, the agency does not maintain these folk trails, other than to post special-regulations signs along them, official recognition of their importance as travel routes for people who go afoot and off-highway.

Fishermen's paths have plenty to offer anyone who wants to travel outside conventional time. They aren't linear routes between points A and B. They won't get you to the church on time. There's no room for passing, no diamond lane. But if you're looking for license to wander amid the loosest of structures, fishermen's paths offer that in abundance. Even if you haven't the slightest interest in angling or fish watching, you can follow trails to small wonders no map or guidebook has yet identified. For the directionally impaired, they're the safest possible backcountry routes to explore: just stay on the path closest to the stream, and you can't get lost.

A mile up- and downstream of highway crossings, most fishermen's paths almost disappear. This, however, is where the going gets most interesting, for where streams are remotest from human activity, there the likelihood of beaver dams increases. Beaver dams are the bane of low-flow coldwater streams, because they warm and slow currents to the point at which they may no longer support fish who need swift-moving, highly oxygenated, chilly waters. But except in the driest and hottest of summers, beaver dams on fast, shallow northern streams often do more good than harm, creating deep pools for beaver and trout alike.

In early spring, I walk fishermen's paths before the fishing season opens chiefly to savor the sparseness of the trees and banks with their gestural scribbles of inky black against the melting snow. I know that in only a month or so, these same places will be all but unrecognizable—crowded with the junglelike growth of angelica, water hemlock, cow parsnip, marsh marigold, and meadow rue, their waters deeply shaded by willows, cottonwoods, and alders.

After the season closes in the fall, I prolong it by returning to my favorite fishermen's paths. One of these is a well-worn trail on Hay Creek in southeastern Minnesota, a place that remains ice-free about a month longer than streams up north. At that postseason point in the year, my intentions toward fish become as pure as they are ever going to be: like a pining lover, I haunt their homes longing simply for a look at them.

In late fall, the fishermen's path to Hay Creek winds downward through a quarter-mile of woods raining acid yellow leaves. At the bottom of the bluff, the creek announces its eruption from the earth with great noisy gouts of water that flow speedily toward the main channel over mounds of wild watercress. To the northeast, beyond a stony pasture, lies a long, still glide. One still day in late October, I crossed the creek and climbed the abandoned road grade on the west side of the stream. From there, I had a remarkable view of the creek miniaturized to a scanty ribbon running beneath the treetops. I could see the fish, but the fish could not see me.

At first I saw only shadows instead of the animals themselves. They were brown trout, some of them very large; one, the biggest, wore a capelike cast of metallic blue on her head and shoulders. Another sported a big necrotic patch where he had probably been pecked by a heron. In fact, I had surprised a heron with my arrival, and he had flapped away hugely.

Downstream, the backwater pooled to a stillness, its surface etched by a light breeze. Where rise rings intersected the ruffled surface, they formed dizzying moiré patterns. Trout fed there under open sky in very shallow water, a fall pattern of theirs, as if they realized that most of their would-be predators had already moved on for the winter. Or perhaps the danger of Death from Above was less important than their need to fatten up on the spiders and other bugs they could catch in the surface film before winter set in.

The water was perfectly clear and shallow, the bottom silty. I moved on about an eighth of a mile until I came to another spot deep enough to hold trout. The tiny falls that flowed into this pool were lively and dancing but too shallow to hold fish. Below them in the semimilky pool at the base of a limestone cliff, its bottom silty and abloom with wafting green algae, fish finned quietly—small, pale torpedoes compared to the sturdy oldsters farther upstream. I could see that at least one had had its adipose fin clipped—a hatchery fish, then.

These trout hadn't the strong coloring of the big ones upstream: they were mud-hued, with markedly dark lateral lines. All of them had been clipped. The largest had a worn dorsal fin, perhaps a souvenir of time spent in a concrete hatchery run.

I sat and watched them for over an hour. They were not feeding, just fanning their tails slowly near the bottom. If they were eating anything at all, it was subsurface snacks. Then suddenly one surfaced with a neat BLIP!! and left a large, showy ring on the surface. The reflection of autumn trees on the ever-so-slightly striated surface rapidly broke up into pixels.

On my way back to the truck, I stood once again on the grade, looking down at the large upstream trout as they swam through their mysterious fish lives. I imagine that dogs must be as fascinated and puzzled when they watch us humans rushing madly about, never stopping for naps or a good scratch.

IN WINTER, I like to walk the streams that I fished in the full flush of spring and summer. Then, streamwalking reveals the form of waterways in a way impossible to detect while banks are thickly crowded with greenery and streams are full and running swift. By late November, only a narrow tongue of black water still flows; clear sheets of new ice have edged out from the banks, their margins marled by coffee-cream silt and decaying leaves. Skeletal alders and willows twitch overhead. Farther up the banks, aspen and birch lean into each other, scritching faintly with each rub. Above them stand spruces, cedars, and firs, the only emphatic colors left in this muted landscape. Here the North's overwintering birds can be found: spruce grouse pick beneath the spreading lower branches, while above them in the dense tracery of branches cling pileated woodpeckers, redpolls, pine siskins, and screeching jays. As if enfolding them all, the raven barks and coughs from the treetops, rasping out the most varied messages of any northwoods bird. Compared to the voices heard along the stream during temperate months, however, these back-woods stretches in fall and winter are notable chiefly for their near-silence: the wind, the creak of hardwoods, the glassy tinkle of the stream eroding its own ice, the deep *toc toc* of a raven.

Following a fishermen's path becomes easy after the first snows; the trail is bared like a groomed ski slope, the only area clear of undergrowth. Even at this closed-down time of the year, fishermen's paths are popular; footprints in the snow tell how often I've often been preceded by other streamwalkers. One New Year's Day, a fellow walker left his signature along the north side of the trail along the Kinnickinnic—N E D written in great looping spurts of pale yellow piss in the melting snow. I con-gratulated the absent graffitist: at least he didn't carve his initials into a tree. Another winter day, 150 miles north, on what is now my home stream, I traced the fishermen's trail, where I'd wanted to go all summer but hadn't, to a majestic beaverwork, a dam so deep and high that it looked as if an Israel-in-captivity of beavers, of pyramid-builders had built it.

The face of the dam was roughly fifty feet wide, with a gentle downstream arc that bulged in the middle, where it was most deeply reinforced. It was probably ten feet high at its apex, the wood dark with running water and edged by a frizzle of ice. The dam was three or four feet deep on most of its face, but crossing it was impossible because its builders had armed the dam with a *chevaux de frise* of upright birch, aspen, and black ash boughs wedged together tightly. It was easy to see why humans who chose to destroy such dams in less regulated times commonly did so by dynamiting them. These days, they are dismantled or breached stick-by-stick by DNR workers and Trout Unlimited volunteers. Individuals who presume to undertake such social and ecological engineering without the state's blessing are in for a woeful time.

It was here, roughly three miles upstream from the roadway, that the fishermen's path finally petered out. I couldn't identify where it ended, exactly: at some point, the last radiating channels of last summer's grasses simply scattered in every direction, leading off toward all points of the compass. No sudden barrier, just a simultaneity of possibilities.

———

THE DAYS OF FISHERMEN'S PATHS as foot trails may be numbered. Like still waters that now harbor more motorboats and Jet Skis than canoes, fishermen's paths are becoming the haunts of motorized traffic. All-terrain vehicles (ATVs) preferentially cross streams in gravelly shallows, tearing up fishes' nests and redds during spawning seasons, and they erode banks by grinding them down during wet seasons of the year. They widen fishermen's paths and crush the plantlife that otherwise prevents the erosion of streambanks. They turn what have been low-impact folkways into high-impact freeways.

In May 1998, the Minnesota DNR announced its intention to close most state forest and public lands to off-highway vehicles (OHVs), including ATVs. The response was predictable: OHV owners cried foul. Public lands, they argued, should be theirs to travel unimpeded, just as Jet Ski and recreational snowmobile owners have claimed title to public waterways and public lands. After all: they've paid for their licenses—how can the state then limit them to certain trails? The facts that automobiles cannot legally be driven on sidewalks, that hook-and-line anglers cannot fish streams during the spawn, that hunters cannot shoot deer and bear in the spring evidently do not sway the groups professing to speak for OHV, recreational snowmobile, and Jet Ski owners. Neither does the damage they do to wildlife, and fish cannot defend their own interests at the DNR's many public "stakeholder" meetings each year. A weighty battle is being enjoined throughout the North Woods between individual rights and the commonweal, and it is being fueled by internal combustion engines.

Last June, I walked a fishermen's path alongside Keene Creek, probably the best trout stream in Duluth. School was out for the summer, and I could hear children upstream, hidden by the dense screen of dogwood and cinnamon ferns, screaming in delight as they tried to catch tiny brookies and minnows in miniature pockets between boulders.

I walked from spotlit pools of sunlight into deepest shade, my way carpeted by blue mounds of forget-me-not and spires of wild phlox. In the stream, I could just make out last season's brookies—tiny fish made visible only by the white leading edges of their pelvic and anal fins, which were no more than 1/8-inch long. Only after spotting these could I construct the fish themselves, two- to three-inch-long creatures the color of the streambed, their backs matching the broken light on the water's surface. I crouched there in the deep, unbroken woods, fascinated, watching them.

At that point, I heard the unmistakable sound of a two-stroke engine, and I smelled an oily gust of exhaust. A moment later, Darth Vader himself backed down the fishermen's path astride an ATV and stopped abruptly midcreek to stare at me.

I stared back. Dressed as usual in khaki, I may have looked like a DNR conservation officer to him, a witness to his multiple offenses: he was riding on a foot trail, and his ATV was mufflerless. He hung there in midstream for what seemed a long time, the smoked Plexi windscreen of his helmet turned opaquely toward me. The water sloshed noisily around his tires, then quieted to a spreading brown cloud where it had flowed transparent moments before. I stood downstream amid the forget-me-nots and saw a noisome future before he gunned his throttle and charged on through the bright woods.

Postscript: Sometime shortly before 31 July 1997, the special-regulations (catch-and-release) section of Hay Creek that I've described here was poisoned. After receiving a phone call from an angler, DNR fisheries biologists drove to that remote two-mile stretch and found hundreds of rotting fish carcasses bobbing in the eddies and lining the streambanks. Approximately 98 to 99 percent of the fish had been killed.

Laboratory analyses failed to turn up the poison responsible. Mark Briggs of the DNR's ecological services believed the toxin was something that acted and dissipated quickly, making it impossible to detect: "Common sense tells us that it could easily be ammonia or bleach, which are easy to get a hold of."

That's how close our small waters are to the murder of their creatures. Two years later, nothing more has been discovered about the poisoning of Hay Creek.

20 Homewaters

I'VE REACHED THAT CRAZY STAGE of late winter when I'll read anything, watch any video, undertake any tackle repair, just to be in touch with fishing again. I tie flies continually, knocking out a dozen a night, a few streamers in the low light of afternoon, just so I'm immersed in the deeply pleasurable preludes to fishing.

At 48° North, fishing is a seasonal thing. Last winter, one of the mildest on record, moved my restlessness up by a month. Even in early February, when I stepped outside, the earth seemed to be exhaling deeply, belching up deep, peaty gouts of breath. The buds on the lilacs were already swollen and grass green, and the resident winter birds were singing mating songs. Ravens tumbled through the air in their annual displays of sexual exuberance.

At this time of the year, one of two things was going to happen: either I was going to find a way to fish, or I was going to displace that need into some all-American substitute like buying a new rod or reel—something, anything, that would pull me into alignment with rushing water, hatching insects, caroming swallows, rising fish.

I'm hardly alone in feeling this way. Wandering lonely as a cloud one February morning through a local sporting-goods shop, I recognized a fellow member of the Arrowhead Fly Fishers doing just the same: checking out new reels, surveying the steadily growing supplies of tying materials, the just-in (supposedly), better-than-ever rods. He fingered a Ketchum release tool lingeringly.

"I could kick myself that I haven't headed out to the Bighorn," he told me mournfully. "It's been in the fifties and sixties out there. Perfect." ·

"I think I'm heading down to the Whitewater next week," I replied. "I can't take it anymore."

He drifted out to the parking lot, trailed by his son or grandson, and climbed into a pickup plastered with I BRAKE FOR TROUT stickers. I got into the old beater I was driving for the winter and headed off to pick up some angling books at the public library.

———

IT'S BEEN SIX YEARS since I first marched into the library newly consumed by a need to know something about fish and the places they live. To say that my curiosity has changed my life barely gets at the enormity of what opening that first book entrained. Fish and fishing have taught me new ways to think about and act upon the world I live in, both the North Woods and the larger one—from planting saplings that anchor streambanks to offering commentary at public hearings on DNR and U.S. Fish & Wildlife Service policies and management plans. I've come to think instinctively about climate and weather in terms of their effects on fish and the complex streamwebs that feed them, which tells me how thoroughly my awareness has altered by going to the fishes. I have met people whose passion for wild fish and wild places equals or exceeds my own, whose considerable knowledge and work on behalf of fish and watersheds are disinterested, time consuming, and wholly voluntary. I have also met some anglers whose only interest in our waters seems to be how many hatchery-raised fish they can catch, as if Lake Superior and its tributaries are merely fast-food aquaria serving up their chosen menus. They catch fish only to hurl them, gasping for air, into the bushes, then go back to hook some more. These folks, too, have taught me something, if only how variable are human responses to our fellow creatures.

———

WE CAN'T LOVE, much less effectively protect, what we don't understand. There are people who won't fish because they see it as a form of animal torture for human pleasure. This is a reductive view of fishing that betrays ignorance of fishing, streams, and their inhabitants. It's entirely possible to angle without running the risk of harming fish: you simply cut off the hook on your fly. If you make a successful presentation in the right place, a fish will still take your fly, you'll feel the tug that tells you that you've read the water well, and the fish will spit out the fly like a stale cigarette and then go on her way unharmed. I have often fished this way—in fact, it's the method I've used to introduce some of my scrupled friends to the miracle of complexity each healthy stream holds. If I can get them to wade a bit deeper into stream life, they're likely to find—at least here in the North Woods—that the fast-flowing, high-grade headwaters of creeks and rivers are occupied by small, starving brook trout. Like deer herds on land from which the timber wolf has disappeared, the starving brookies who have been dumped into backcountry streams have become our charges—and our prey—by default. I catch a few of these troutlings each season and eat them, I hope reverently. The salmon who crowd some South Shore streams each fall, headed back to their native waters to spawn, are dying, whether caught by anglers or by the scythe of their own lifespan. Watching these lake dwellers before they head inland, eating one if possible, is about as close to religion as I get.

All life is at the expense of other life, whether it's a mountain chain destroying a river valley, a deer herd grazing its way through a stand of aspen, a beaver building his dam, or me, shopping at Miller Hill Mall at the expense of the trout swimming downstream in Miller Creek. There's simply no way around this tragic equation—no more so for vegans than for carnivores. The most we can do, it seems to me, is to be conscious of the lives sacrificed in support of our own and to take those lives with purpose and respect.

When I walk a stream today, it's in the knowledge that beneath its variously broken and laminar surfaces, teeming populations of creatures live all or parts of their lives. If I venture into summer water and pick up a cobblestone in the fastest, broken current, I know that I'm likely to find a big, shaggy-looking stonefly, dark and primeval looking. In slightly slower water, the sides and undersides of rocks hold swaying midge larvae, fine as thread, and the silky pup tents of net-spinning caddis, the gravel-backed homes of saddle-case caddis, the weird, stick-and-leaf–built sarcophagi of tube-case caddis. If I wade softly into the slowest water of all, I'll probably stir up some of the mayfly nymphs on the bottom and see water scorpions wearing their cryptic guise as flotsam that flicks out twig legs and captures small, unwary fish. Crawdads will dart across the warmer bottom sands in short sharp jerks, stop, dart again. In darker, colder spots, I'll find bottom-hugging sculpins—small, macrocephalic fish the hue of mud—plying the streambed for larvae, watchful of the larger, carnivorous trout. Way back beneath the old waterlogged roots of a fallen tree, I can find the oldest trout on this stretch of the stream. She—the biggest stream trout are often female—hovers just above the bottom in water still as air, watching the steady downstream procession of sodden leaves, vagrant algae, and struggling insects as they are swept along on the invisible current. Sometimes she darts out to nab something flowing by, but mostly what courses downstream offers too little return on her effort. What interests her most are the creatures who swim against, or at least head into, the current: smaller fish, the occasional struggling vole or drowning mouse. She eats less often than smaller fish, but each meal is larger: sculpins, schooling fish like shiners, and young trout. She defends her enviable home beneath the roots and leaves it only occasionally.

And that's only the life at *the bottom* of our local coldwater streams.

Higher up in the water column, nymphs of mayflies and caddisflies struggle toward the surface, borne toward the surface like so many tracers on a rocket thrust of oxygen bubbles, pursued, some of them, by the smaller siblings of the old fish back in the root wad. Once the insects have reached the surface, they struggle, not all of them successfully, from the constraining shucks of their pre-winged, pre–air-breathing bodies, and float or flutter downstream, breeze-buoyed motes of color and movement.

On warm evenings, adult mayflies and caddisflies hover in clouds above the alders and conifers, aswarm in their mating dance. Nearby, a plump caterpillar or inchworm plops from a streamside branch into the slow water along the inner bank and disappears into a tiny maelstrom, a quicksilver rush. From the highest branch overhead, a kingfisher rattles, then plunges into the pool below for some luckless yearling fish who has failed to learn his lessons about Death from Above. Swallows and dragonflies strafe the stream's surface, and damselflies bask in their metallic blues on the sun-heated surfaces of streamside grasses. Seeps trickle toward the stream almost invisibly, their courses marked subtly by taller, greener growth. All along the watercourse, whatever water is not taken up and used by trees, forbs, and grasses makes its way to the main channel and from there thousands of miles downstream to one of three seas: Arctic, Atlantic, or Gulf of Mexico.

This multistrata-ed awareness of the complexity of streams and their watersheds is what makes stream fishing seem so boundless, so symphonic. Michigan artist Glenn Wolff captures this in meticulous pen-and-ink drawings worth the proverbial thousand words. His work adorns the books of contemporary angling writers John Gierach and Jerry Dennis, and is the visual equivalent of the simultaneities of experience their writing evokes. In a typical drawing, this one a triptych, an angler stares down from a bridge at the Fox River on Michigan's U.P., Hemingway's Nick Adams stories tucked into the back of his pack, a rod strapped to the pack. Behind his unsuspecting neck hovers a northwoods mosquito the size of a trout. Across the drawing stretches a line of grasshoppers fished by Nick Adams in "Big Two-Hearted River." Below the angler overlooking the Fox, a brook trout stares out at the reader eye-to-eye, big as a house. Above these images floats the tiny silhouette of an angler in midstream, a tent and campfire on the bank behind him, and beyond them, fog-softened spruces on the far shore. Above this image, another horizontal frieze of grasshoppers. Humans in Wolff's drawings are no more or less important than the insects, fish, moving water, and forests of the watery world; hieratically, it is the animals and plants who dominate, just as they do my experiences onstream. Fishing has peopled watery places that used to seem empty, if beautiful, to me. They are peopled by nations other than my own.

———

LAST YEAR, MY SIXTH ON THE WATER, taught me sobering lessons about survival in marginally habitable streams. Most of our North Shore streams are fairly inhospitable places for coldwater fish in the best of years, offering few spawning spots, mostly all-or-nothing flows, and streambeds, many of which were scoured down to bedrock by late nineteenth- and early twentieth-century log drives. Low-water years tax stream life to its limits. In 1998, an El Niño year, I expected to see fewer fish, or none, in places where two years ago there were plenty. And that was the way it shook out. Fall arrived late after months of dry weather; the first certifiably autumnal day was October fourth, when a gale-force wind howled in from the northeast about 4 P.M., bringing torrential rains. That storm meant one thing to me: now the chinook who had gathered offshore, alerted by shortening days and dropping surface temperatures in Lake Superior, could run into the mouths of their native North Shore streams, spawn, and die.

So that morning, between one part-time job (I pet-sit) and another (I was selling wine then at a local shop), my Lab-shepherd giant Lunker and I set out for the French River to watch the salmon move upstream.

We'd been to the French several times in the previous two weeks, like hopeful lovers awaiting the return of fickle loved ones. But I had known that the water was still too warm and shallow, the days too long, to woo the fish in. I had gone to the river out of respect and desire but with little expectation, and the water had been empty of fish.

But on the fifth of October, I drove to the river with a calm certainty that the fish would be running on a day like this: gun metal sky; offshore winds that piled up waves against the neck of the river mouth, forcing water upstream; weather that made Polarfleece or wool shirts necessary just to stand out on the spit in comfort. Six ore and grain boats listed at anchor out in the Duluth harbor, unable to enter their slips because the pilot boats that guided them to their berths couldn't handle the high waves. I shifted into four-wheel drive as I took the turnoff to old Highway 61 so my balding tires could get more purchase on the rain-slick road. Out in the murk, combers rolled toward the shore and climaxed against the banks just feet from the truck. Perfect weather for big fish to slide out of the lake and into the stream. I wouldn't have accepted a thousand-dollar bet that the fish wouldn't be there: it was clear that they would have begun their annual run sometime in the past twelve hours.

And sure enough, as soon as I had parked and zipped up my Wintergreen parka and trod down the macadamed path to the big pool above the river's mouth, I saw them: big dusky chinook, already dark from their days of waiting offshore, most of them wearing blooms of white saprolegnia, and they were speeding around the pool like radio-controlled cars. One hit the mouth of the pool so hard that his forward inertia propelled him halfway across it, three-quarters of his body out of the water. Farther upstream, a boil of chinooks darkened the clear amber water just below a small falls. I couldn't see how many fish it contained, but they raised a maelstrom of current without ever breaking the surface. Farther still upstream near the fish trap, five chinooks quivered and splashed in less than two feet of water, spawning over the algae-slick rocks.

It was as if a switch had been thrown and fish had gone from HOLD QUIETLY AND INVISIBLY OFFSHORE to MASS EXTRAVAGANTLY. This is a spectacle that I hope I never tire of, made even more satisfying by the evidence it provides of my increasing rootedness here. For perhaps a brief moment in the predawn light of October, I knew something about those fish with a conviction approaching their own. The light was right. The water temperature. The volume of water surging out of the river's mouth, tonguing their bellies, parting around their snouts. *It was time,* and I knew it just as they knew it. More: I was one of a loose community of humans who knew it. During my rapt watch on the bank of the French, two male anglers joined me, looking hard into the water as I had just minutes earlier. Being able to see these river-darkened fish is a small skill, but one that takes time to learn; once learned, however, you don't think of it ever again—you just see them. All three of us saw them that morning, and all three of us broke into smiles as soon as we saw the dark waters gather shape and become fish. The unspoken collegiality of people who love and admire fish is a fine thing to observe and participate in; you may know nothing about this other person's relationships to his mate, his dog, his fellow workers, but you can instantly spot the ardor that drives him to use his lunch break, as these two electricians had done, to go fish watching on a gale-force, rain-spitting day.

———

TWO YEARS AGO, only 115 chinooks returned to the French River fish trap from the hundreds of thousands that had been released into the lake annually throughout the 1990s. Seven of the seventeen returning females were infected by bacterial kidney disease (BKD), an ailment strongly and positively correlated with stress; their eggs were destroyed rather than added to those from other returning fish. Lake Superior does not appear to be supporting chinooks as lavishly as it did a decade ago, when they were the salvation of sport and commercial fishermen. Now lakers are coming back strongly—immense, deep-dwelling char with gray-lavender bodies and creamy vermiculations, the big-water cousins of brook trout. In 1997, over 60 percent of the commercial- and sport-fishing catch in Lake Superior was lakers. Perhaps, as the president of the local Trout Unlimited chapter puts it, we should "listen to what the lake is saying" and concede that Superior cannot support all the predators who have been dumped into it since overfishing and sea lampreys first depressed native fish populations. Perhaps we should conclude that chinook no longer belong here, or never did.

Listening to what the lake, or any other body of water, is saying is what six years of preoccupation with fish has taught me to do. Some of what I "hear" is far from pretty: figuratively, I can hear the gasps of fish dying from midsummer hyperthermia in streams too warm to offer them the dissolved oxygen they need, the moans of bottom-dwelling creatures whose homes have become choked with salt and sand from parking lots and streets whenever runoff flows into the stream. I wonder about the toxic effects of the Superfund sites in Duluth's harbor on these creatures, about the damage being done by decades of tailings and barrels of leaking mine wastes dumped into Lake Superior just up the shore from Duluth. These are wrongs worth fighting against.

If I listen to the sounds coming from upstream, they're more hopeful, more intricate. Near the height of land, I imagine I can hear caddisfly and mayfly nymphs busily chewing and shitting leaf fall into form in which their cousins, the filter feeders, can consume it. This organic debris grows steadily smaller, steadily available to downstream consumers in that watery kingdom. Eventually it will turn it into the fish flesh I love and admire. If I listen to the stream, I can hear the steady trickle of ground seeps daylighting through upland sands, then coursing downhill toward the lake, where they gather and pool and nurse new life. Of course, I can also hear the sound of water rushing too swiftly downhill because logged-off soil and roots fail to absorb it. I can hear the unnatural silence of streambanks shorn of their cover and their animal life. I can listen to the roar of road crews widening Highway 61 from two to four lanes, and one, then two, then four little seeps feeding the Cross River cease trickling shoreward.

An environmental education, Aldo Leopold wrote, exposes you to a world of wounds. I would add that fishing has taught me that this world of wounds is no smaller or less full for being damaged. There is still the same mass of fish flesh being produced, although it is probably not arising in the shape or quality that most anglers or naturalists want. It is important, I think, to remember this. Yet something is being lost here in the North Woods: the specificity of the creatures inhabiting its waters. Not so long ago, each watershed contained beings who had evolved in rhythm with its weathers, rainfall, snowcover, soils and soil organisms, its neighboring land creatures, its rocks and trees. Discovering the animals who lived in these streams helped us humans define who and where we were. Now, when we peer into a coldwater stream, we are more likely to find fish who tell us about the preferences anglers have expressed to the DNR than about the particularities of the place itself. History and place are being lost to uniformity. This is a world of wounds from which streams are in no way exempt.

Call this realization my rationale for seeking out the smallest streams. Between the humble—some would say negligible—size of their inhabitants and the streams' inaccessibility, these wandering creeks of the North Woods are some of the most intact waters still around. Nobody's likely to stock them with chinook, probably no angler will seek them out for Opening Day or Fourth of July fishing. They flow darkly within swamp forests of tamarack and black spruce, surrounded by protective clouds of blackflies, no-see-'ems, and mosquitoes. Between their small scale, their tiny inhabitants, and their buggy surroundings, they demand more of potential explorers than casual curiosity.

When I drive past and catch sight of one of these narrow little brooks emerging from its wards of tag alder and balsam fir, I slow down, note it mentally, and add it to the growing inventory of streams to explore, fish, and, some of them, protect.

I stop now by running waters.

Acknowledgments

WHEN I BEGAN TO FISH, I knew nothing about water animals, fishing, or fly fishing. I received a tremendous amount of help from people kind enough to honor my eagerness and intent rather than show contempt for my ignorance. Much of the latter remains, of course, and they bear no responsibility for that.

It's fashionable to bash government employees these days. I have nothing but praise for the responsiveness and passion of the state and federal conservation workers who aided me so generously in my quest to learn more about fish and the streams they swim in. In particular, I thank the following: Minnesota Department of Natural Resources' John Huber, Mark Lawson, John Lindgren, Don Schliep, Duane Shodeen, and John Spurrier; Wisconsin Department of Natural Resources' Ron Bruch, Meg Galloway, Dennis Pratt, Karl Scheidegger, Steve Schramm, and Ted Smith; Michigan Department of Natural Resources' Tom Rezick; U.S. Geological Survey's Michael Hoff and William D. Swink; U.S. Fish and Wildlife Service's Lee Newman; Michigan Technological University's Nancy Auer. To Larry Schwarzkopf of the Fond du Lac Band's Conservation Department, and Rose Gurnoe of the Red Cliff Band, *miigwech*. The National Park Service (NPS) staff at Isle Royale National Park, particularly Greg Blust, answered all my questions about the island's coaster brook trout population, as well as offering me an artist's residency on the island in fall 1998. Thank you, Bonnie Fournier, for calling my attention to the opportunities the NPS offers to writers and visual artists through the NPS's artists-in-residency program.

Organizations that have helped me learn how to understand and help protect the streams I fish include the American Fisheries

Society, American Rivers, Cal Trout, Friends of the River, Gitche Gumee chapter of Trout Unlimited, North American Native Fish Association, River Alliance of Wisconsin, particularly its former executive director, Sara Johnson, and former employee Zev Ross, Rivers Council of Minnesota, and The Nature Conservancy.

———

Fellow anglers Sam Cohen and Kim Carpenter, Jeff Dahl, Cal Jorgensen, Matt Paulson, Jimbo Cothern, and Michael Tidmus have kept me primed with enthusiasm and great stories. Ron Vodian has done so via e-mail. Tying instructor Perry Rowlison gave form to what had been mere good intentions. Pat Farrell, who in turn learned the rudiments of tying from me, reminded me that I could once again enjoy teaching. My sister Jean Grover and my daughter Miranda Dooley have indulged my enthusiasm in more ways than I can enumerate.

———

One of the wonderful things about writing for a living is getting paid to learn what you wanted to know anyway. Editors at several magazines have indulged my passion for fishing and coldwater conservation by assigning and publishing my articles on them. Thank you, thank you, Linda Gardiner at *Women's Review of Books,* Tom Helgeson at *Midwest Fly Fishing,* Claude Peck at the late *Twin Cities Reader,* and Doug Stange and Steve Quinn at *In-Fisherman.*

———

And finally, thank you, Anne Czarniecki and Fiona McCrae of Graywolf Press, for believing that *Northern Waters* was worthy of a place in the press's fine company of books.

Afterword

THE WATERSCAPE OF OBSESSION looks different to each of us, but as a reader I am usually curious to know what water roads have led to other writers' books. Often the bibliographies and sources they provide have provisioned my own journeys. Here, then, are some way stations along my own trip into the world of coldwater fish and streams.

Departments of Natural Resources. These are variously called Departments of Conservation, Fish & Game, Wildlife and Game, Fisheries. No matter: what's important is that the outdoorspeople who work in them as stream managers, conservation officers, and fisheries biologists know the streams you're curious about as well as anyone else. Notice that I do not say *better* or more *intimately* than anyone else; probably anglers possess as much or more knowledge. DNR staff and anglers know different, if equally important, things about streams and their inhabitants. They can tell you about where the coolest—and warmest— stretches of a stream lie; where the waters are best for fish watching; where stream improvements have been made or installed; if and when the stream has been stocked, and with what fish; what the stream's biggest problems and strengths are. Fisheries biologists conduct surveys on designated trout streams on regular cycles, and you can obtain information from any or all of their completed inspections. The DNR's data are quantitative, but many DNR staff members' interests in the streams they monitor and work to improve are qualitative and matters of the heart. For responsiveness, these agencies beat all other public agencies cold.

Anglers. Fishermen commonly know streams in a more impressionistic way. Those whose attendance on a particular stream is regular can tell you about insect hatches, the times of year when different terrestrial insects become food for fish, if and when the stream ices over and the ice goes out, when and where fish build their spawning redds and nests, what birds fish the waters. Finding such anglers isn't difficult: check your local fly and/or bait shop and ask folks behind the counter who fishes that stream regularly. Call your local chapter—or state chapter—of Trout Unlimited (TU), the Izaak Walton League, and the Audubon Society.

———

Conservation Organizations. Trout Unlimited is a national organization founded in Michigan to protect coldwater streams and their inhabitants. Its state and local chapters constitute human libraries of experience and passion for local streams. Most TU chapters do "stream work"—that is, planting saplings along rivers and creeks to provide shade and to anchor stream banks, and installing riprap, low-head dams, and "lunker structures" (fixed objects under which large [lunker] trout can hide), so their knowledge of streams is intimate and ongoing. The *Izaak Walton League* is the U.S.'s oldest conservation organization. The "Ikes," as members are called, are hunters and anglers interested in preserving wild resources. They, too, do stream work and vigilantly watchdog local, state, and national governments' actions that could degrade fisheries and waters. The *Audubon Society* has national, state, and local presence on conservation issues. *The Nature Conservancy* (TNC) is a national conservation organization with often-powerful state and local presences. It works hard, smart, and effectively to preserve intact watersheds, buying easements along stream corridors—for example, 5,000 acres abutting Wisconsin's Brule River are now protected by TNC easements—as well as purchasing parcels of land outright when those contain significant intact flora and fauna. *The Federation of Fly Fishers* is a national conservation and fishing organization with many local chapters vigorously engaged in stream protection and rehabilitation. The national organization also works hard to bring women and children into the community of fly fishers.

Watchdog organizations for North American waters have been one of the conservation-growth industries of the 1980s to 1990s. The premier national organization is *American Rivers*, which is best known for its annual "Ten Most Threatened Rivers" dubious-achievement awards. *River Network* is an umbrella organization for building effective river and watershed organizations; it also acquires and conserves riverlands. On regional, state, and local levels, you can find many organizations that lobby state, interstate, and federal agencies (e.g., the Federal Energy Regulatory Commission, the Great Lakes Fisheries Commission) on measures to protect the waters, and that function as clearing houses for information and citizen action. American Rivers' website offers links to many of these organizations; so do some state groups like the River Alliance of Wisconsin and Friends of the River (California). (See the address book that ends this Afterword.)

Local citizen-action groups are at the heart of river restoration and preservation efforts. If you cannot find an organization working on streams that interest you, call your local DNR office—the stream manager can tell you whom to contact. Finally, if you cannot hook up with anyone else who is working to protect a local stream you care about, start a group yourself!

———

The Stacks. Island Press (Covelo, CA, and Washington, D.C.) is a not-for-profit publisher that has practically cornered the market on printing books about citizen efforts to protect and restore natural resources. Accounts of other people's successes are heartening as well as instructive; with them, you gain a vision of what your own stream-protection group can look like. *University presses* continent-wide are your best resources for deep written information on the fish that swim in your local streams as well as on such topics as stream ecology, geomorphology, and hydrology. *University extension services* and DNRs offer handbooks, pamphlets, and broadsides about each state's fish and waters, some of them in surprisingly deep detail. The *North American Native Fishes Association* has published a series of articles on must-have books about North America's native fish, coldwater and otherwise. *River Network* publishes a number of titles on organizing watershed/river conservation groups. (See bibliography.)

The Web. Not surprisingly, there's very little you can't find online these days about fish and waters. Most state DNRs have websites that tout the agencies' stream improvements and offer exotic-species alerts and information on their chief gamefishes. Most of this information, however, is definitely aimed at would-be anglers. For more broadly conservation-based online resources, check out *American* Rivers, *U.S. Environmental Protection Agency,* the *North American Native Fishes Association, Trout Unlimited, River Network, The Nature Conservancy,* and *U.S. Fish & Wildlife Service*—their links, as well as their own contents, are invaluable.

Address Book. Listed here are several national and state organizations of interest to fish and water watchers. All of those listed can help link you up to independent local groups as well as to local chapters of their own organizations.

American Rivers (nationwide)
1025 Vermont Avenue N.W., Suite 720
Washington, DC 20005
(202) 547-6900
www.amrivers.org
e-mail: amrivers@amrivers.org

Friends of the River (California)
128 J Street, 2nd Floor
Sacramento, CA 95814
(916) 441-3155; fax (916) 442-3396
www.friendsoftheriver.org
e-mail: info@friendsoftheriver.org

North American Native Fishes Association (nationwide)
Attn: David Hall
813 Williams Avenue
Madera, CA 93637
(209) 662-1922
www.nanfa.org

River Alliance of Wisconsin (Wisconsin)
122 State Street, Suite 200
Madison, WI 53703
(608) 257-2424; fax: (608) 251-1655
www.igc.org/wisrivers
e-mail: wisrivers@igc.org

River Network (nationwide)
P.O. Box 8787
Portland, OR 97207-8787
(503) 241-3506; fax (503) 241-9256
www.rivernetwork.org/~rivernet
e-mail: rivernet@igc.apc.org

Rivers Council of Minnesota (Minnesota)
1313 Fifth Street S.E.
Minneapolis, MN 55414-4504
(612) 676-1745; fax (612) 676-1750
www.riversmn.org
e-mail: info@riversmn.org

Bibliography. There's a world of titles out there, and happily more all the time. So many books have played a part in forming my understanding and appreciation of coldwater streams, their inhabitants, and human responses to them that I have chosen to list only those which are most readily available and accessible to the not-already-converted. My apologies to the writers of the many other soulful accounts I have not included here.

Fish

Moyle, Peter B. *Fish: An Enthusiast's Guide.* Berkeley: University of California Press, 1993. A superb introduction to fish anatomy, physiology, behavior, ecology, habitats, and conservation. A classic.

Quinn, John R. *Fishwatching: Your Complete Guide to the Underwater World.* Woodstock, Vt.: The Countryman Press, 1994. Emphasizes scuba-diving and snorkeling to watch fish.

Smith, C. Lavett. *Fish Watching: An Outdoor Guide to Freshwater Fishes.* Ithaca: Comstock Publishing/Cornell University Press, 1994. More of a local-streams, low-tech, ecological approach to fish watching than Quinn's book.

Wright, Leonard M., Jr. *The Ways of Trout.* New York: Lyons & Burford, 1985. The fruits of an obsessive trout angler's twenty-three years of fish watching on a single stretch of river in New York State.

Savoring the Waters

Dennis, Jerry. *A Place on the Water: An Angler's Reflections on Home.* New York: St. Martin's Press, 1996. Fine yarns, some of them haunting, about fishing Michigan's Upper and Lower Peninsulas.

_____. *The River Home: An Angler's Explorations.* New York: St. Martin's Press. More engaging fishing tales, some of these farther afield.

Montgomery, M. R. *Many Rivers to Cross: Of Good Running Water, Native Trout, and the Remains of Wilderness.* New York: Simon & Schuster, 1995. A Westerner-gone-East returns on summer rambles throughout the West to search for native trout.

_____. *The Way of the Trout: Anglers, Wild Fish and Running Water.* New York: Alfred A. Knopf, 1991. The finest recent all-around account of one person's obsession with trout, angling history, and the act of fishing.

Schullery, Paul. *Royal Coachman: The Lore and Legends of Fly-Fishing.* New York: Simon & Schuster, 1999. As Yellowstone's long-time historian, former director of the American Museum of Fly Fishing, and angling historian, Schullery probably has more to say about European-American fishing through the centuries than anyone. *Royal Coachman* is a collection of essays on topics ranging from the culture of dry-fly fishing to early American trout fishing to changing values in fisheries management. Erudite, funny, and very engaging.

Wetherall, W. D. *One River More: A Celebration of Rivers and Fly Fishing.* New York: The Lyons Press, 1998. The third and, Wetherall warns us (I hope he doesn't hold himself to it) the last of his collections of graceful essays on fly fishing, mostly in Vermont and New Hampshire.

_____. *Vermont River.* New York: Lyons & Burford, 1984. Exquisite essays on a self-taught fly angler's time on his homewaters.

_____. *Upland Stream: Notes on the Fishing Passion.* Boston: Little, Brown, 1991. More of the same: notes from the intersections between this fine novelist's fishing and personal history.

Understanding the Waters

Dennis, Jerry. *The Bird in the Waterfall: A Natural History of Oceans, Rivers, and Lakes.* New York: HarperCollins, 1996. Stream ecology 101.

Leopold, Luna B. *A View of the River.* Cambridge: Harvard University Press, 1994. Stream dynamics for the mathematically fluent.

Outwater, Alice. *Water: A Natural History.* New York: Basic Books, 1996. A highly personal interpretation of North America's waters crisis.

Pielou, E.C. *Fresh Water.* Chicago: University of Chicago Press, 1998. A less technical introduction to stream dynamics and ecology than Leopold's *A View of the River* by a noted northern ecologist.

Muddying the Waters: Politics

Bates, Sarah F., et al. *Searching out the Headwaters: Change and Rediscovery in Western Water Policy.* Covelo, CA: Island Press, 1993.

Bolling, David M. *How to Save a River: A Handbook for Citizen Action.* Covelo, Calif.: Island Press, 1994. Anecdotes, steps to take, and political blueprints for forming river-protection organizations by the founding executive director of Friends of the River.

Hart, John. *Storm over Mono: The Mono Lake Battle and the California Water Future.* Berkeley: University of California Press, 1996. A textbook case on regional water politics with a real-life fairytale ending.

Reisner, Marc. *Cadillac Desert: The American West and its Disappearing Water.* New York: Viking Press, 1986. The most influential popular account of Western water politics yet published.

Stream Improvement (Physical)

Hunt, Robert L. *Trout Stream Therapy.* Madison: University of Wisconsin Press, 1993. The fruits of over sixty years of experience in rehabilitating Wisconsin streams. Great color photographs.

Hunter, Christopher J. *Better Trout Habitat: A Guide to Stream Restoration and Management.* Covelo, CA: Island Press, 1991. Roll-your-own stream improvement guide.

Williams, J. E., et al, eds. *Watershed Restoration: Principles and Practices.* Bethesda, MD: American Fisheries Society, 1998. Sounds dry as dust, doesn't it? But this collaboration between the AFS, U. S. Forest Service, and federal Bureau of Land Management outlines some fine restoration efforts on range, farm, national forest, and city watersheds.

Stream Improvement (Political)

David M. Bolling/River Network. *How to Save a River: A Handbook for Citizen Action.* Covelo, CA.: Island Press, 1994. Anecdotes, steps to take, and political blueprints to forming river-protection organizations by the founding executive director of Friends of the River.

Palmer, Tim. *Lifelines: The Case for River Conservation.* Covelo, Calif.: Island Press, 1994. Survey of contemporary arguments for and examples of U.S. river restorations.

River Network. *Starting Up: A Handbook for New River and Watershed Organizations.* Portland, OR: River Network, 1996.

JAN ZITA GROVER is a transplanted San Franciscan now happily living in northern Minnesota. She is the author of *North Enough: AIDS and Other Clear-Cuts* (Graywolf Press, 1997), which won the 1998 Minnesota Book Award for creative nonfiction. She divides her time between writing, editing, pet-sitting, and other part-time jobs — a thoroughly northern Minnesota way of earning her livelihood.

This book was designed by Donna Burch. It is set in Minion type by Stanton Publication Services, Inc., and manufactured by Edwards Bros. on acid-free paper.

Graywolf Press is dedicated to the creation and promotion of thoughtful and imaginative contemporary literature essential to a vital and diverse culture. For further information, visit us online at: **www.graywolfpress.org.**

Other Graywolf titles you might enjoy are:

Fables and Distances: New and Selected Essays
JOHN HAINES

A Hundred White Daffodils
JANE KENYON

Diary of a Left-Handed Birdwatcher
LEONARD NATHAN

Except by Nature
SANDRA ALCOSSER

The Way It Is: New & Selected Poems
WILLIAM STAFFORD

Crossing the Expendable Landscape
BETTINA DREW

The Graywolf Silver Anthology